International Civil Society

edited by

Taco Brandsen
Gemma Donnelly-Cox
Matthias Freise
Michael Meyer
Filip Wijkström
Annette Zimmer

Volume 18

Min Ji

Chinese Foundations and Grassroots Social Organizations

Characteristics and Interactions

 Nomos

The dissertation and its publication were made possible
by the support of *Brot für die Welt*.

The Deutsche Nationalbibliothek lists this publication in the
Deutsche Nationalbibliografie; detailed bibliographic data
are available on the Internet at http://dnb.d-nb.de

a.t.: Westfälischen Wilhelms-Universität in Münster, Diss., 2020

ISBN   978-3-8487-8072-3 (Print)
        978-3-7489-2458-6 (ePDF)

British Library Cataloguing-in-Publication Data
A catalogue record for this book is available from the British Library.

ISBN   978-3-8487-8072-3 (Print)
        978-3-7489-2458-6 (ePDF)

Library of Congress Cataloging-in-Publication Data
Ji, Min
Chinese Foundations and Grassroots Social Organizations
Characteristics and Interactions
Min Ji
241 pp.
Includes bibliographic references.

ISBN   978-3-8487-8072-3 (Print)
        978-3-7489-2458-6 (ePDF)

Onlineversion
Nomos eLibrary

1st Edition 2021
© Nomos Verlagsgesellschaft, Baden-Baden, Germany 2021. Overall responsibility
for manufacturing (printing and production) lies with Nomos Verlagsgesellschaft mbH
& Co. KG.

Abstract

The 2008 Wenchuan earthquake increased the need for disaster relief and reconstruction projects in China. This disaster created an upsurge of Chinese grant-making foundations, which, in turn, gave rise to expectations. However, the majority of grassroots SOs in China face an existential crisis of survival due to a shortage of funding from such foundations. A gap still exists regarding the interaction between foundations and grassroots SOs in China. The research questions and purpose of the study seeks to explore how do Chinese foundations interact with grassroots SOs and why do Chinese foundations act the way they do.

This study employs well-documented empirical investigations conducted in China. A mixed methods approach is based on documentary analysis, face-to-face interviews and participatory observation. Coding were implemented based on the themes through the lens of two methodological approaches, evolution of cooperation and resource dependency theory. This research is conducted with anecdotal evidence accumulated over a 10-year period from 2008 to 2019 when the Chinese foundations started their interaction with other SOs.

My findings show that Chinese foundations interact with grassroots SOs in six different ways, namely special funds, joint fundraising, high-engagement grantmaking, making grants to projects, making grants to organizations and making grants to individuals. However, Chinese foundations' grant-making logic does not overlap with the needs of grassroots SOs, because they do not fully understand each other's difficulties and because their focus and path of development are not the same, resulting in less interaction. In addition, due to the fact that their needs differ greatly, possible cooperation relations would be imbalances, thus foundations are reshaping and changing organizational growth and working approaches through grantmaking. The cooperation between two organizational forms is still in its infancy. This study does not provide new and inspiring insights for scholars, but also speaks to the practitioners working in China's third sector.

Acknowledgments

Writing a dissertation, especially wring a doctoral dissertation in Germany as a single Chinese mother with a 5-year-old son, is never an easy life but a significant academic challenge to me and my little boy. It couldn't be completed without the help and support of the following people.

First and foremost, I would like to appreciate my two excellent first supervisors, Prof. Annette Zimmer and Prof. Katja Ruth Levy, who never give me up throughout my whole doctoral study even when one of them changed the university. This is also why I am very pleased to change from Free University of Berlin to Münster University and continue to be supervised by both of them. I gratefully acknowledge my supervisors for their guidance, inspiration, encouragement as well as insightful criticism from the very beginning until the end. Moreover, I am very thankful that I could experience my doctoral study at two universities, respectively at Free University of Berlin and Münster University, to get a close look at how a doctoral researcher should do.

I am also grateful to my second supervisor, Prof. Dr. Matthias Freise, for his kind and immediate help in the later stage of my doctoral study since I changed to Münster University. His support and guidance are very important for the accomplishment of the work presented in this study.

Additionally, I would like to extend my deepest gratitude to Prof. Rongping Kuang, my former boss and my advisor in all my life. He's the most humorous advisor and one of the wisest people I know. He has not only inspired my doctoral research, but also provided me a lot of very helpful contacts when doing field research. At the same time, he has been teaching me how to move forward in life.

I also own a special thank to the Bread for the World in Germany. I was very lucky to be awarded as the scholarship for consecutive 46 months, including an opportunity of Germany language learning in Bochum for 7 months. Under this great financial support, I would focus on my research and looking after my son. Furthermore, I would like to thank the great non-financial supports from its staff for their caring of my trivial life, especially Beata Schreiber, Fanny Kamptz and Carolin Rölle. I am proud of calling them my dear friends. They have been very supportive during my whole doctoral study, from my application, setting down in Bochum and

Berlin, looking for apartments and a place in the kindergarten. I also thank to Nadine Ebinghaus, Ulrike Küstner, etc.

I sincerely thank to my wonderful and generous friend, Dr. Clemens Striebing, for providing academic suggestion and friendship. I would like to think of him as a brother of ideas. He is very professional and helpful about everything related on German foundations and organizations. I appreciate his help very much.

I also thank my friends, Anja Ketels and Roman Paul Turczynski, who share the same major as me. Anja Ketels does not encourage me spiritually, but also corrects mistakes in the dissertation and academic presentations, and helps me adapt to the German academic atmosphere. Roman Paul Turczynski is a great person assisting me in university's enrollment and dissertation submission. I wish them also successfully complete their doctoral study and a bright future.

Deep appreciation also goes to my former colleagues, all of whom have provided great help and recommended peers working in Chinese foundations and grassroots social organizations during my interview. I thank Hongyan Yang (for her great help in my scholarship approval), Jing Sun (for her recommendation of a workshop on the foundations), Ming Xue (for his recommendation of other interviewees), Zhi Zuo (for his great work at Eco-Women Network while I study), Dr. Hong Dou and Chunliang Li (for their recommendation of a workshop on the foundation), Li'na Ren (for her caring of my trivial life).

My deep gratitude goes to interviewed experts, Prof. Guosheng Deng from Tsinghua University, Shuwen Wang from Guangzhou Harmony Community Foundation, Prof. Anthony Spires from the University of Melbourne. My field research could be done successfully by the support of those old and new friends who are working in the grassroots social organizations and foundations in China. They helped me to recommend other interviewees.

I would also like to thank all of my interviewees from foundations, grassroots social organizations, scholars who were involved in the interview during the field work. Without their passionate participation and input, the interview could not have been successfully conducted.

Last but most important, my gratitude goes to my little son, Yuchen Guo (Alex), who moved with me when he was 2.5 years old from China to Germany. This period of life means exactly the common growth of our two people. The mutual accompany does not only teach me how to do thinking and be a good mother, but how to keep learning and live a better life.

Finally, tremendous thanks go to my family, my father, my mother, my brother, my sister-in-law and my little nephew. My hard-working parents are always be there for me with their unconditional love and care of me and my little son. They always support my decisions and dreams. I love them so much and I would not have made it this far without them. My brother and beautiful my sister-in-law take great care of my parents when I have been from home.

Table of Contents

Acknowledgments   7

List of Acronyms   21

1 Introduction   23

1.1 Personal Context   24

1.2 Statement of the Problem   25

1.3 An Overview of previous research on the development of
     Chinese foundations   29
     1.3.1 Chinese scholarly attention on international foundations,
            primarily American foundations   30
     1.3.2 On foundations' internal governance   32
     1.3.3 Chinese foundations' administration and laws   32
     1.3.4 Foundations' roles and evaluation   33
     1.3.5 Comprehensive development of Chinese foundations   34
     1.3.6 Academics on state-society relations   36
     1.3.7 The predominant understanding of the relationship
            between Chinese foundations and grassroots SOs   38

1.4 Structure of the study   41

2 Definition and categories of foundations   43

2.1 Definitions at the international level   43
     2.1.1 An Exotic Phenomenon?   43
     2.1.2 Definitions in the United States and Europe   44

2.2 Definition in China   45

2.3 Categories of foundations in China   47

2.4 Current applied regulations and laws on Chinese foundations   51

2.5 Definitions of grassroots social organizations (grassroots SOs)   52

2.6 Discussion on definitions   55

3 Methodology 57

3.1 Polulation and sample selection 57

3.2 Documentary analysis 63

3.3 Participant observation 64

3.4 Data analysis 65

3.5 Theoretical framework 65

    3.5.1 The evolution of cooperation 66
    3.5.2 Resource interdependence theory 73
    3.5.3 Discussion 77

4 The overall development and characteristics of chinese philanthropic foundations 78

4.1 An overview of previous research 78

4.2 Two main stages of Chinese foundations from 1949 to 2017 and the analysis of different characteristics 81

    4.2.1 Before the promulgation of RMF-2004 81
        4.2.1.1 Period from the founding of PRC in 1949 until 1978: Gap 81
        4.2.1.2 From 1979 to 2003: Appearance of government-affiliated foundations 82
    4.2.2 After promulgation of RMF-2004: Appearance of NPFFs in the early periods 87

4.3 Development of Chinese foundations from 2008 to 2017: Transition and new tendency 91

    4.3.1 The increasing number of Chinese foundations, especially NPFFs 93
    4.3.2 Steady Growth of total assets of Chinese foundations 96
    4.3.3 Continuous growth of total income of Chinese foundations 98
    4.3.4 Total expenditures of Chinese foundations: PFFs' expenditures are still greater than NPFFs'. 103
    4.3.5 Uneven geographical distribution of Chinese foundations: East over West 104
    4.4.6 Working areas of Chinese foundations: Much the same as the government's working priorities 105

4.4   Discussion on the characteristics of Chinese foundations   108
    4.4.1   Characteristics of Chinese foundations from 1949 to 2007   108
    4.4.2   Characteristics of Chinese foundations from 2008 to 2017   109
        4.4.2.1   Political restrictions on foundations' registration
              and evaluation   110
        4.4.2.2   Political Restrictions on foundations' tax and
              independence   111
        4.4.2.3   The changing role of Chinese foundations in
              supporting grassroots SOs   112

5   Understanding cooperation from the perspective of both
   foundations and grassroots sos   113

5.1   Under what circumstance can cooperation begin between
    foundations and grassroots SOs?   113
    5.1.1   Why grassroots SOs need to cooperate with foundations,
        especially on funding resources   114
        5.1.1.1   Why do grassroots SOs have difficulty raising
              funds?   115
        5.1.1.2   Yet, the question worth asking is, where do
              Chinese donations go if not to grassroots SOs?   116
        5.1.1.3   Why international foundations drastically
              lowered their once abundant funding to Chinese
              grantees   118
        5.1.1.4   Government's attitude toward overseas
              organizations   119
    5.1.2   Why Chinese foundations do not make grants to
        grassroots SOs   121
5.2   How cooperation is initiated between foundations and
    grassroots SOs in China   124
    5.2.1   Successful examples of foundations and SOs working
        together   124
    5.2.2   Transition from an operating foundation to a grant-
        making foundation: A case study of one local PFF   131
    5.2.3   How many Chinese foundations are supporting
        grassroots SOs?   134
    5.2.4   Grant-making is important, but alone is far from
        sufficient   138
    5.2.5   A case study on how capital flows in grant-making
        foundations—He Foundation   141

5.3 Problems and complaints during interactions 142

5.4 Discussion 146

6 Understanding how foundations interact with grassroots SOs from the perspective of foundations 148

6.1 Grantee selection before interactions and cooperation 148

    6.1.1 Seek grantees actively 150

    6.1.2 Public tendering and a request for proposal 151

    6.1.3 Recommendation from peers, colleagues, and experts 155

    6.1.4 Connecting through workshops, networks, and competition via TV and online platforms 155

    6.1.5 Findings and problems 157

6.2 Concerning the application guidelines 160

6.3 How to finalize cooperation 164

6.4 Grant-making management and control 167

    6.4.1 Average amount of funds and duration of the project. 168

    6.4.2 Mostly multiple installments. 169

6.5 Project monitoring and evaluation by foundations 170

6.6 Sustainability of cooperation 172

6.7 Discussion 173

7 Understanding cooperation from the perspective of grassroots SOs 175

7. 1 How to seek potential foundations by grassroots SOs 177

7.2 Foundation project official's role during project application, implementation, and evaluation 179

7.3 Grant amount and period of grants 180

7.4 Project evaluation and further cooperation 183

7.5 Are programs mainly planned by foundations or grassroots SOs? 185

7.6 Discussion 186

8. Analysis of the changing views 188

8.1 Interactive categories between foundations and grassroots SOs 188

8.2 How trust affects cooperation   193
   8.2.1 Trust can also be the key to promoting cooperation   194
   8.2.2 Distrust between foundations and grassroots SOs in
       China   195

8.3 How resource interdependence affects cooperation   197

8.4 Views from experts and supporting network/platform   201
   8.4.1 Independence of foundations   204
   8.4.2 The dominance of the project   206
   8.4.3 Grant lifespan and amount   211

9 Conclusion and Discussion   214

9.1 Findings   214

9.2 Review of research questions and their connection to previous
    research   216
   9.2.1 Two main research questions   216
       9.2.1.1 Research question 1: How do Chinese
           foundations interact with other grassroots SOs?   216
       9.2.1.2 Research question 2: Why do they act the way
           they do?   217
   9.2.2 Connections to previous research   218
   9.2.3 Connection to theories   219

9.3 Limitations   221

9.4 Suggestions for the future   222

Bibliography   223

News reports & Annual reports   234

Appendix 1: Sampling population   237

Appendix 2: Guide and In-depth Interview Questions to
Foundations and grassroots SOs   239

List of Figures and Charts

Figure 4-1: Numbers and growth rate of Chinese foundations from 1979 to 2007   80

Figure 4-2: Growth of Chinese foundations 2008–2017   94

Figure 4-3: Total assets of Chinese foundations from 2008 to 2017   97

Figure 4-4: Net assets of PFFs and NPFFs by the end of 2015   98

Figure 4-5: Donations and growth rate of Chinese foundations from 2008 through 2017   99

Figure 4-6: Total income of PFFs and NPFFs by the end of 2015   100

Figure 4-7: Percentage of foundations with different incomes by the end of 2015   101

Figure 4-8: Total expenditures and growth rate from 2008 to 2017 (billion/year)   103

Figure 4-9: Number of Chinese foundations in different provinces on December 31, 2017   105

Chart 5-1: Proportion of donations received by different bodies in 2017   117

Figure 5-1: He Foundation charity plan   141

List of Tables

Table 2-1:   Major differences between PFFs and NPFFs
              according to the 2004 Regulations for the
              Management of Foundations   47

Table 2-2:   Categories of foundations by Shang (2003)   48

Table 2-3:   Eight principal forms of Chinese foundations and
              their characteristics   50

Table 2-4:   Current applied administrative regulations on
              philanthropic development promulgated by the State
              Council.   52

Table 4-1:   The number of categories of social organizations
              from 2008 to 2017   92

Table 4-2:   The number of PFFs and NPFFs from 2008 to 2017   93

Table 4-3:   Average income of PFFs and NPFFs in 2015   100

Table 4-4:   Income source percentage of PFFs and NPFFs in
              2015   102

Table 4-5:   Average expenditures of PFFs and NPFFs in 2015   103

Table 4-6:   Working area distribution of Chinese PFF and NPFF
              projects in 2014   106

Table 5-1:   A glance at several leading grant-making
              foundations/foundations which make grants to other
              organizations/individuals in China   126

Table 5-2:   Profile of Chinese Foundations with missions of
              grant-making as stated in the foundations' website 136

Table 5-3:   Numbers and amounts of Jingxing Plan from 2011 to 2016   140

Table 5-4:   What grassroots SOs expect from foundations in China   144

Table 6-1:   How the foundations interviewed sought grantees   149

Table 6-2:   RFPs by Chinese foundations in May 2019   153

Table 6-3:   Authority of approval based on the amount of grant from One Foundation   165

Table 6-4:   A study on how the Narada Foundation's Jingxing Plan selects its grantees   166

Table 7-1:   Profile of social organizations interviewed   176

Table 8-1:   Interactive categories between foundations and grassroots SOs   189

Table 8-2:   Changing views of foundations and grassroots SOs   190

Table 8-3:   Profile of interviewed experts   202

Table 8-4:   Profile of interviewed supporting platform/network   202

Table 8-5:   Profile of interviewed overseas foundations   202

             Interviewed Overseas Foundations   237

             Interviewed experienced experts and scholars   237

             Interviewed Chinese foundations   237

             Interviewed grassroots SOs   238

             Interviewed network/platform   238

List of Acronyms

ACWF	All-China Women's Federation
CCAFC	China Charities Aid Foundation for Children
CCTF	China Children and Teenagers' Fund
CCTV	China Central Television
CFDP	China Foundation for Disabled Persons
CNIs	Civil non-enterprise institutions
CSCLF	China Soong Ching Ling Foundation
CSOs	Civil society organizations
Grassroots SOs	Grassroots social organizations
NGOs	Non-governmental organizations
NPFFs	nonpublic fundraising foundations
PFFs	public fundraising foundations
RMF-1988	Regulations for the Management of Foundations in 1988
RMF-2004	Regulations for the Management of Foundations in 2004
SUF	Shanghai United Foundation

1 Introduction

From China's reform and opening-up onwards, the diversification of social structures in China improved under its rapid economic development, especially the emergence and development of non-profit organizations. Over the past 40 years, the development of the non-profit sector made tremendous achievements in promoting social welfare, and the public had already realized its importance and influence in social changes. A variety of social organizations have proliferated, for example, the great emergence of Chinese foundations and the boom of Chinese grassroots organizations. By the end of 2017 in China, there were 6,307 Chinese foundations and 755,000 other social organizations. The significance of the diversity of social organizations reaches far beyond just their increasing number and is one of the major signs in China's entire diversification process.

Although there are still many obstacles and difficulties in the survival and development of the third sector, it can be seen very clearly that China's non-profit organizations will make a difference with the progress and modernization of Chinese society. The diversity of social organizations has attracted the attention of many scholars, while its social significance has been far less studied than the economic sphere. This lack of research needs to be addressed and strengthened in terms of both dimensions and depth, like the specific function and role of each category of social organizations rather than a general analysis.

Progress has been made. For example, over the past three decades, Chinese foundations have played an active role in solving social problems and promoting social innovation in the development of the diversification process. Moreover, the 2008 Wenchuan earthquake triggered cooperation between foundations and grassroots social organizations (hereafter grassroots SOs). After more than ten years of cooperation exploration between the two, this dissertation clarifies the current status of the interactions between Chinese foundations and grassroots SOs and how they interact in the future.

1.1 *Personal Context*

My research interest stemmed from my working experiences for over ten years. After finishing my university studies, I worked in an influential environmental grassroots social organization based in Yunnan, a province in Southwest China, that had many cooperative arrangements with the United States, Europe, Australia, and Asia. I developed a particular interest in the organization's international efforts to promote women's participation in environmental protection issues and capacity building, as well as the development of social organizations in China.

Through the efforts of my team and under the guidance of Professor R. P. Kuang, I established a cooperative relationship with several distinguished foundations from several countries, including the United States, Germany, and the Netherlands, and was allowed to raise funds. I still remember, and find it hard to express, my excitement after my first successful application for a three-year grant. Because of those projects, I was able to work with rural women and children in China on environmental management and education. I was shocked by the big gap between the living conditions in rural areas and urban areas, so I decided to find more funding resources and work further with the rural women and children.

In the intervening years, my abilities have improved and my views have enlarged through participation in national and international conferences and a United National University training program. In 2013, I started my master's studies at Potsdam University in Germany, with a special focus on organizational management and policy analysis in the third sector, and ended them with an analysis of Chinese social organizations.

After my master's studies, I registered for a grassroots SO called Eco-Women Network, which was an independent project group in my former organization, Pesticide Eco-Alternatives Center, and with great support and encouragement of those organizations. I became board chair of Eco-Women Network, recruited the executive director and other staff, applied for international projects from the Netherlands and Germany, and accepted a postdoctoral fellowship from University College Cork on a science-based project. However, when the Charity Law and the Overseas NGO Management Law came into effect in 2016 and 2017, respectively, the pressure to gain funding for my organization increased due to the sudden withdrawal of overseas funding. We tried to switch to domestic funds and contacted many Chinese foundations. Unfortunately, there were few interactions between foundations and grassroots SOs in China, including the problems of grantmaking. In other words, few foundations and funders provide grants for grassroots SOs, yet most of them are still operating organizations. A more serious challenge is, the local civil affairs department notified this grassroots SO to find a supervising unit in 2016, though it successfully registered in 2014. However, no government department was willing to become the supervising units of a grassroots SO, while it was not required in 2014. Hence, the legal registration of this grassroots SO will be canceled, although we made various efforts to deal with this problem.

In light of this situation, via face-to-face interviews, my goal was to gain insight into the characteristics and development of Chinese foundations from a historic perspective and develop a deeper understanding of the degree of their interactions with grassroots SOs. Although I spent most of my time in Germany when pursuing my academic research, I stayed in close contact with my former organizations and some partner organizations and foundations to stay apprised of changes and developments over time.

1.2 Statement of the Problem

From a holistic perspective of the development and structure of Chinese foundations, it is difficult to find their interactions with grassroots SOs. Due to the government's dominating role in Chinese philanthropic foundations (Lai 2017, 64), those foundations have not interacted with grassroots SOs since the appearance of these foundations in the 1980s. At that time, most foundations were founded as project-oriented foundations or with a specific mission in mind, for example, Project Hope (Xi Wang Gong Cheng) and Water Cellar for Mothers (Mu Qin Shui Jiao), two of the best-known projects. Project Hope was organized by the China Youth Development Foundation and the Communist Youth League Central Committee in 1989, providing public services for education in rural areas. Water Cellar for Mothers was jointly launched by the All-China Women's Federation (ACWF), the Beijing Municipal People's Government, and China Central Television (CCTV) in 2001, aiming to resolve rural women and their families' difficulties in procuring drinking water in western China. Both projects are designed by the foundations and then are implemented by administrative and organizational networks connected to these foundations' work supervising units,[1] which is a top-down administrative order of authoritarianism within the government's system.

---

1 According to the Notice on the Reconfirmation of the Supervisory Agencies for SOs (2000) issued by the Ministry of Civil Affairs, the supervisory agency refers to

From the 1980s until the late 2000s, little collaboration took place between the foundations and grassroots SOs (Shieh 2017, 1791), which is also the top-down model with the assistance of government as a contracted-out service to a few grassroots SOs (Xu 2010). Xu's research suggested that public foundations prefer to collaborate with official systems, such as government agencies and public institutions. During this period, the Chinese philanthropy has continued to be dominated by the official governmental mechanism.

This was the case in 2004, when the Regulations on Management of Foundations was established (RMF-2004), which regulates two categories of foundations: public fundraising foundations (hereafter PFFs) and non-public fundraising foundations (hereafter NPFFs). The former is allowed to raise funds from the public, while the latter cannot. Scholars have argued that NPFFs are supposed to and are encouraged to play a bigger role in making grants to grassroots SOs (Fulda 2017, 73; Lai 2017, 14). During my interview with Mr. Haoming Huang, who participated in drafting RMF-2004, he noted that this regulation aimed to encourage more private foundations to make grants to grassroots SOs. Unfortunately, the interactions between foundations and grassroots SOs have not been satisfactory, although Chinese NPFFs have since achieved rapid growth. Most new NPFFs can be seen as complementary to the state with a rather weak link to grassroots SOs, although more and more private foundations are increasing their business influence in the third sector (Chan and Lai 2018, 15; Lai 2017, 14).

The year 2008 was a turning point for interactions between foundations and grassroots SOs when the Wenchuan earthquake accelerated their work with each other. When many grassroots SOs, foundations, and volunteer groups took widespread part in the rescue and reconstruction of the disaster area, academics and practitioners became more attentive to their interactions (Shieh 2017, 1791–1792; Chan et al. 2018, 10; Woqi Foundation

---

the following types of government agencies: ministries and commissions under the State Council and relevant departments above county level; functional departments under the Central Committee of the CPC and relevant departments above county level; administrative offices of the NPC & CPPCC, Supreme People's Court, Supreme People's Procuratorate, and relevant departments above county level; and supervisory organizations empowered by the CPC office, State Council, and CPC Commissions, and the People's governments above county level. The supervisory agencies within the military system are determined by the General Political Department under the Central Military Commission, https://www.globethics.n et/documents/4289936/17452664/GE_China_Ethics_7_isbn9782889311781.pdf.

2018, 1). Scholars have attempted to view the interactions in various forms. Concerning the emergence of joint action to earthquake relief, which is subjectively selected under external institutional and internal organizational limitations, Zhu and Lai (2014, 187) defined the strategy of NGO alliance in 2008 as being incomplete collaboration without sustainability. Yang (2015, 66) claimed that cooperation among SOs in a cooperative network is spontaneously and voluntarily self-organized cooperation to achieve integration of organizational resources.

From the perspective of foundations' financial support, the Narada Foundation, the You Cheng Social Entrepreneur Foundation, the Red Cross Society of China, and the One Foundation provided funding to grassroots SOs that participated in the relief of the earthquake (Woqi Foundation 2018, 1). Yongguang Xu, a former Communist Youth League official and current director-general of the Narada Foundation, declared that "foundations and grassroots SOs enter the era of cooperation" (Xu 2009).

Overall, scholars and observers have perceived the interactions as spontaneous forces of society and the first large-scale collective appearance of Chinese SOs (Yang 2015, 67; Zhu and Lai 2014, 189). Shieh and Deng (2011) noted that the Wenchuan earthquake triggered "an unprecedented display of public-spiritedness, charitable giving, volunteering, and networking in Chinese society" (194). Within this context, both the public and the government recognized the value of grassroots SOs and volunteer groups, which caught the attention of domestic foundations. Thus, foundations started discussing how to interact with grassroots SOs and embarked on the road of transferring from an operating model to a grant-making model. However, afterward, mutual criticism between foundations and grassroots SOs caused cooperation between them to plunge.

After 2010, a series of news reports on the criticisms and lack of cooperation increased scholarly concerns and led to a few discussions on this state of affairs. For example, Feng (2015, 139) noted two reasons why Chinese foundations do not like to support grassroots SOs: first, most Chinese foundations still cannot fund themselves fully; second, most of them lack confidence in grassroots SOs, so the foundations prefer to operate projects by themselves rather than support grassroots SOs. Besides, Shieh (2017) noted that communication between foundations and grassroots organizations in China is poor, and it is very difficult for foundations to find grassroots SOs capable of implementing projects and achieving mutual goals.

Additionally, a study by Xu (2010) pointed out two different pathways regarding how foundations emerged in China: (1) foundations were under government promotion resulting in the emergence of government-background or government-rooted PFFs, and (2) since the promulgation of the RMF-2004, NPFFs developed organically. In 2103, Yongguang Xu, a leading philanthropist, mentioned the two divergent pathways of PFFs in China and added accordingly that grassroots SOs have no natural relationship with the government's "family." As a result of the different pathways, Xu (2012, 129-130) explained various difficulties related to cooperation between PFFs and grassroots SOs. However, in practice, grassroots SOs have difficulty and limited cooperation with PFFs. Subsequently, Shieh (2017, 1793) also adopted this argument and then applied it to both PFFs and NPFFs and, at the same time, to grassroots SOs, with the conclusion that the different developmental pathways taken by foundations and grassroots SOs are obstacles to working with each other.

Thus, this research begins with the exploration of the historic development of Chinese foundations since the founding of the People's Republic of China (PRC) in 1949. Foundations and grassroots SOs should be "natural allies and strategic partners" (Shieh 2017, 1787). Because cooperation between foundations and grassroots SOs is under constant discussion in practice, my dissertation examines the path of foundations' development from a historical perspective and analyze the characteristics of cooperation between the two entities.

Prior research on interactions between foundations and grassroots SOs indicates that Chinese foundations were established originally to operate projects by themselves but under government departments. The "closed way" (Xu 2010, 177) in China (i.e., fund disruption under the administrative system without involving grassroots SOs) is closely related to its historic development and background, which is why I chose to analyze the developmental characteristics of foundations as a prerequisite for the analysis of the cooperation between foundations and grassroots SOs.

Specifically, I start by analyzing the developmental characteristics of Chinese foundations and exploring the interactions between foundations and grassroots SOs. By introducing the cooperation theory and the resource interdependency theory, I examine how cooperation between foundations and grassroots SOs commences, how it proceeds, and what exactly happens during cooperation, as well as the existing resources that affect their cooperation. The combination of these two theories can provide a better understanding of the current status of the interactions between Chinese foundations and grassroots SOs, including an analysis of the problems and challenges they face. Besides, with the decline and even disappearance of overseas foundations in China, grassroots SOs must obtain essential funds and abundant resources from domestic foundations, especially after the Law on Administration of Activities of Overseas Nongovernmental Organizations in mainland China (hereafter Overseas NGO Law), which went into effect on January 1, 2017.

Given the development and challenges to foundations, there is a striking knowledge gap when it comes to the interaction between foundations and grassroots SOs. This dissertation addresses the two research questions which are not yet answered fully in the existing literature:

a) How do Chinese foundations interact with grassroots SOs?
b) Why do Chinese foundations act the way they do?

1.3 An Overview of previous research on the development of Chinese foundations

Here I first examine the overall academic research conducted on foundations in China. Then I discuss recent studies concerning interactions between Chinese foundations and grassroots SOs. As the research of foundations is still a nascent field in China (Fulda 2017, 63; Chan 2018, 14; Shieh 2017, 1790), the previous research and practical experiences are based in part on those in Western countries. However, Anheier (2001) explains the lack of international academic research on foundations as follows: "Even efforts that explored the role of nonprofit organizations more generally, most prominently the Johns Hopkins Comparative Nonprofit Sector Project did not focus on foundations explicitly" (1).

Although Chinese foundations emerged in the mid-1980s, few scholars were concerned with foundations at that time. Moreover, after the Fourth World Conference on Women was held in Beijing in 1995, scholars focused on the third sector and the development of NGOs or civil society instead of Chinese foundations. Most of the studies broadly explore the foundation-related literature and related topics, rather than specifically focusing on the foundation.

This literature review seeks to provide an overview, particularly on the studies of Chinese foundations, rather a wide-ranging discussion on the development of the third sector, civil society, or SOs in China. Therefore, this summary offers a selected number of studies and a brief analysis of certain key points made in the literature. I present a discussion on Chinese foundations for three reasons. First, some PFFs with close ties to the government—for example, their leaders are assigned by government agencies or the foundation works as a subsector under government agencies—do not categorize themselves as NGOs or CSOs (civil society organizations). Second, based on the assumption that the emergence of foundations and grassroots SOs was different (Shieh 2017, 1799–1802), this study explains the development of Chinese foundations, especially how their early development influences their interactions with grassroots SOs. Third, this study focuses on the interactions between foundations and grassroots SOs from the perspective of foundations in China. Thus, the goal of this literature review is to summarize the existing literature precisely by focusing on foundations in China instead of the role and development of nonprofit organizations, NGOs, or the third sector.

According to Wang (2018a), "The first article in the core Chinese academic journals dealing with Chinese foundations did not appear until 1995, and before 2004 the number remained as low as 11" (298). Also, he claimed that the details of earlier observations were not correct. This was especially true because the foundation landscape had changed dramatically (Wang and Yao 2016, 5). Interestingly, at almost the same time Chinese scholars began studying foundations, many Western scholars were studying Chinese foundations while transplanting the concept to China in the 1990s. Thus, for this study, I first look at Chinese scholars' work on international and domestic foundations in China, followed by an examination of foundations' internal governance, their administration and law, their role and evaluation, government–foundation relationships, and the relationships between foundations and grassroots SOs.

1.3.1 Chinese scholarly attention on international foundations, primarily American foundations

As foundations were still a new sector in China in the 1990s, Chinese scholars began their research on foundations by studying several well-known American foundations, such as the Rockefeller Foundation, the Ford Foundation, and the Carnegie Foundation, all of which had made a great impact on grassroots SOs in China. Because of the lack of experience with philanthropies in China, the research on American foundations was greatly helpful to Chinese foundations, both in theory and in reality.

As early as 1996, Zi (1996) analyzed the Rockefeller Foundation's work in China, presenting an overarching work on the role of social change. Research related to American foundations continues even now. A similar development can be found in a book by Ma (2013) that is regarded as the first academic monograph to discuss the cultural experience of Chinese and Western cultures through a comprehensive discussion of the Rockefeller Foundation's century-long experience in China.

Besides, a series of books on translation and compiling caused widespread concern and had a great impact on domestic foundations and scholars with insufficient international experience. For example, Zi (2003) wrote a book that is considered to be the first comprehensive introduction and analysis book on American foundations in China. Besides, Li Tao (2008) studied the origins and history, culture, religion, society, and institutions of American foundations; and analyzed the characteristics of different types of foundations and the relationships between American foundations and their government.

Moreover, in addressing the relationship between China and the United States, many political science scholars have contributed greatly to their analyzes of international foundations, mostly on the origins and categories of American foundations, as well as their relationship with politics and society. More specifically, in 2005, Li presented a reference on the origin of American foundations, including their definition and categories. He noted that American charitable foundations flourished in the early twentieth century under a unique historical, cultural, religious, and technological development, which gave birth to modern American foundations. Likewise, Wang and Cao (2006) explained foundations' definitions and categories from the perspective of their origins and tax status in the United States. Besides, a study by Qian (2003) emphasized international relations between the United States and China, as well as American private foundations' impact on China. The academic observations during the early 2000s played an important role in helping Chinese scholars focus on foundations and gain a better understanding of them. Perhaps more importantly, that scholarship provided a perspective on the relationship between the United States and China.

Likewise, Fulda (2017, 65) thinks that civil society researchers have so far primarily concerned themselves with theory-building but lack scholarly interest in practical work in China. Currently, effective theory and methodology on foundations built by Chinese scholars are extremely limited. Therefore, most of the studies still apply the experiences of the United States and other Western countries to explain the origin of Chinese foundations.

Chinese scholars predominantly focus on studying the historical development and the institutional framework and mechanisms of foundations, generally beginning with the basic situation at their genesis and then following with their relationship with the government, the comparative studies between China and Western countries, project management and internal mechanisms, and human resource management.

1.3.2 On foundations' internal governance

The independence of Chinese foundations is discussed to explain the characteristics of Chinese foundations since their early stage of development. Estes (1998) wrote the most influential and earliest academic paper on emerging Chinese foundations, in which he pointed out that, at the early stage, Chinese foundations are in reality government-organized SOs that operate their programs with their financial resources, instead of supporting other organizations in their day-to-day activities. Moreover, the author noted that Chinese foundations function as quasi-private/quasi-public institutions that work together and have strong political and financial ties to the government. Many scholars have recognized Estes's conclusions and conducted similar studies.

To advance the importance of public interest and property rights during the governance of foundations, Wang and Jia (2003) wrote an article in which they examined the monitoring, management, and mechanism of Chinese foundations. Song and Hu (2009) proposed that the analysis of foundations' property rights is supposed to be the premise for the foundation governance mechanism in China. To explore this mechanism, other researchers have focused on the internal governance of staffing and decision-making procedures and the external management of monitoring and evaluation (e.g., Wang et al. 2010; Xu and Ye 2009). A work based on case studies conducted by Zhu et al. (2015) analyzed different kinds of foundations in an attempt to understand the operation and management of Chinese foundations. The work, which was contingent on the concept of governmental choice and social choice, compared the traditional operation of PFFs to the grant-making approach of NPFFs.

1.3.3 Chinese foundations' administration and laws

Previous reports on Chinese foundations are restricted mostly to fundraising and operation of foundations. However, a significant amount of existing research analyzes SOs or the third sector regarding the study of foundation laws and regulations in China, rather than focusing on Chinese foundations. Hence, the literature on Chinese foundations is still limited.

Laws and related regulations: Before and after the Regulations on the Management of Foundations in 2004, few studies focused on the interpretation and comments of the new law as well as related foundation laws and regulations and future influences. A book by Guang Xu (2007) is regarded as the first comprehensive introduction of the legal system of Chinese foundations, which was drawn from similar experiences in other countries.

Researchers have also explored the lack of a legal system for foundations, which limits their development in part. There is an urgent need to emphasize the importance of the current reforms of the legal system as they relate to foundations in China. Tax law is very important for the development and survival of foundations, but foundations' tax privileges remain a challenge in legislation. Wang and Zheng's (2004) study discussed the tax rules for foundations based on their characteristic practices and then proposed that a tax advantage should be given to the foundations in China. Feng (2015) clarified that the influence of the government-dominant management model still restricts the development and growth of all foundations and suggests that registration procedures and dual management should be simplified, there should be a clear division among the government, enterprises and civil society, and the induction of tax incentive system should be induced.

The China Charity Law was introduced in 2016 and the Overseas NGO Law in 2017, and the following study of the two laws is offered as a way to examine the changing landscape of foundations shortly.

1.3.4 Foundations' roles and evaluation

Early scholars preferred to analyze a certain aspect or a certain point or problem of foundations, or they preferred to describe a special case, which led to further findings on the role of Chinese foundations. Kang (1997) adopted one case study to analyze a foundation and a philanthropic project of the China Youth Development Foundation that attracted widespread academic attention on empirical research of Chinese philanthropy. One particularly appealing example is the China Youth Development Foundation and its Hope Project. The project has been used frequently as a case-study approach to explore foundations' influence and how they operate in China at a given time, including their functions and roles in societies and communities. An article by Zhuang (2004) proposed countermeasures to improve foundations' abilities for decision-making, resource mobilization, project implementation, social interaction, and institutional innovation to cope with the challenges.

Those studies fit existing situations when the public or even a foundation's staff did not clarify the general purpose of the foundation. However, such studies offered only one-sided accounts of the overall landscape of Chinese foundations and their development and transformation. Xu (2010, 10) pointed out that the vast majority of studies are based on the China Youth Development Foundation (CYDF) in the late 1990s and early 2000s due to the leading role it played in Chinese foundations. However, it is not representative of Chinese foundations or even a special case of Chinese foundations.

The evaluation of Chinese foundations is based on the Regulations on the Administration of Foundations in 2004 (RMF-2004 hereafter) and a series of evaluation indicators issued by the Civil Affairs Department, mainly registration management, internal governance, and external social impact. The earliest academic research was Deng et al.'s 2007 analysis of the foundation evaluation system as part of an evaluation of social organizations, with a focus on the purpose of the government's management and transparency to the public, as well as how to set evaluation criteria and how to rate foundations. Lu (2012) sorted out the historical process for evaluating foundations and the main evaluation indicators. Later, Lu et al. (2014) conducted a systematic and comprehensive monograph on foundation evaluation in China, based on an evaluation of 139 foundations. From these data, a set of theoretical frameworks were formed for innovative social organization evaluations that reflected the essential attributes of the foundation, and a systematic, scientific, and practical foundation evaluation index was constructed accordingly.

Overall, these evaluations and assessments of foundations are applied by the government mainly for rating a foundation and for management by the Ministry of Civil Affairs. Chinese foundations' interactions with other grassroots SOs remain unidentified.

1.3.5 Comprehensive development of Chinese foundations

Reviewing the existing literature, one finds that only a few studies are concerned with the general development of Chinese foundations, and those are from one or more specific viewpoints. Or they are based on one or more case studies such as Project Hope or Project Happiness, which do not represent the comprehensive progress of Chinese foundations. As foundations in China have increased in number and importance, a major challenge of studying them is the lack of data and documentation, which is not new in China. Foundations appear in a wide range of sizes and activities, which makes it hard to collect data, especially for grant-making foundations, all of which adds to the confusion. Nevertheless, both academic and non-academic studies have greatly improved our knowledge about the general development of Chinese foundations.

Among the previous academic research, Xu (2010) conducted a comprehensive literature review on Chinese foundations that demonstrated the developmental history and transformation of characteristics and discussed foundations' governance and structure, property rights, and legislation. This study underlined the unique facets related to how Chinese foundations raise funds, under the promotion of the government to the market. The study also highlighted how funds are distributed in the name of public interest, from a closed way to an open way, referring to the fact that Chinese foundations are transitioning from operating their projects to supporting the third sector. Likewise, a comprehensive introduction on Chinese foundations by Tao and Liu (2014) explained foundations' operating systems in detail and then clarified that the external environment of foundations has been transformed from government choice to social choice. Government choice means that the survival and development of a foundation are completely determined by the government, including the establishment and legal identity of a foundation and the acquisition of resources.

Interestingly, nonacademic reports, which were not available until the early 2010s, provided a comprehensive introduction and paid special attention to the statistics and changes in Chinese foundations. The most popular examples are the *Development of Chinese Foundations: An Independent Research Report* (for the years 2011, 2012, 2013, 2014, 2015, 2017), *Blue Book of Philanthropy: Annual Report on China's Philanthropy Development* (for the years 2011, 2012, 2013, 2017, 2018, 2019) and *Blue Book of Foundation: Annual Report on China's Foundation Development* (for the years 2012, 2013, 2014, 2016). The Blue Book of Philanthropy and Blue Book of Foundation by the Chinese Academy of Social Sciences reviews and summarizes the development of China's philanthropy in the previous year, including major events in the philanthropic field, while the Foundation Green Book is the data analysis and research report written by the China Foundation

Center.[2] Both are published by the Social Sciences Academic Press of China and provide a dynamic picture for academic research and practices.

In summary, the studies on Chinese foundations are still limited and lack in-depth analysis, and most of them automatically apply overseas' concepts (Yang 2010, 58). Xu (2010, 8) noted that studies on Chinese foundations are presented in two extremes. One concentrates on an overall descriptive introduction, lacks logical analysis and argumentation, and does not easily reveal the internal developmental mechanism of foundations; whereas the other focuses particularly on a case study of a specific foundation or even a project because the operating model of the foundation or project and its impact were fresh at the time. Given the ongoing social transformation and the complex political influences, scholarly research that advances with the times is needed.

As described, academic researchers in the 2010s—for example, Liu (2011), Xu (2010), Feng (2015), and Zhu et al. (2015)—were examining cooperation between foundations and grassroots SOs, but under the influence of previous thinking on foundations operating in China. The focus is still on foundations' inherent operating model and influence, for example, the relationship between foundations and the country, but with little mention of the impact of grant-making on the third sector. Hence, insights as to the new perspective of foundations' interaction with grassroots SOs are far from sufficient.

1.3.6 Academics on state-society relations

Apart from addressing the relationship between China and the United States, some scholars have predominately observed the development of Chinese foundations from the perspective of state-society relations, with American experience as a reference. This knowledge is essential for understanding the survival and management of foundations as a new creation. For instance, Xie (2003) examines foundations' dependence on the government, government controls on foundations, as well as the limitations and problems involved in foundations' development.

Several similar analyses include those of Xu (2008) and Lai &Tao& Spires (2015). Xu argues that unsymmetrical dependence is the manifested pattern of the relationship between foundations and the Chinese govern-

---

2 China Foundation Center is a private information platform that collects and publicizes data and research reports on foundations in China.

ment because foundations are much more dependent on the government than vice versa. Lai and colleagues found that the government is still influencing the development of Chinese philanthropy in important and consequential ways, regardless of the increase of private foundations created by a great amount of private wealth.

One recent study (Wang and Yao 2016) used the resource dependency theory to discuss the foundations' dependent relationship with the Chinese government. Empirically, they used four groups of variables: organizations' characteristics, boards of directors, attitude and value, and external environment. A study by Johnson and Ni (2015) did not necessarily show that political connections between the state and foundations influenced the number of private donations but did show a benefit toward the legitimacy of NGOs and a positive relationship to what foundations received. Another related study by Ni and Zhan (2017) examined the financial benefits of state–foundation relations and explored the idea that embedded government control can enable foundations to acquire various resources and then increase foundations' revenues, for example, government subsidies, donations, and market fundraising.

Zheng et al. (2016) noted, "Surprisingly, many Chinese scholars are outspoken about their views toward the government, particularly about the need for greater autonomy to strengthen the third sector" (4). Nie, Liu, and Cheng (2016) also investigated voluntary disclosure by foundations and found that it was negatively influenced by government intervention through government funding and placement of its people in leadership positions in foundations or by direct control over individual foundations. This study suggested that the government should increase the autonomy of foundations to meet public and social needs, which is at the heart of what matters most for foundations as an independent sector.

Above all, the relationship between the state and the third sector, including foundations and grassroots SOs, is a central theme in contemporary China, thus much of the academic attention is still paid to state-society relations (Wang 2016, 3). Generally, but not exclusively, those studies attach great importance to the government's role and control over Chinese foundations' development and management. The government's control of foundations, on the other hand, limits the development of Chinese foundations in the context of being a unique partner with or having a dependency on different levels of government.

1.3.7 The predominant understanding of the relationship between Chinese foundations and grassroots SOs

Based on the previous thinking that Chinese foundations are primarily operating social organizations, researchers have predominantly perceived foundations as operating social organizations with a dependency on the state, while overlooking their relationship with grassroots SOs.

Seeing the effect that foundations had on society by funding grassroots SOs during the 2008 earthquake, more researchers and practitioners started to show a great interest in the interactions between Chinese foundations and grassroots SOs, especially those independent organizations with few ties with the government, although the reality was that Chinese foundations provided little support to grassroots SOs. However, Liu (2011) defined NPFFs as public interest suppliers to support grassroots SOs, through an analysis of five supply methods: direct supply of funding, direct supply of services, an indirect supply of funding, an indirect supply of services, and supply through foundation agents.

Another study saw the collaboration among different SOs as an action strategy under organizational limitations internally and institutional restrictions externally, which is referred to as informal collaboration or incomplete collaboration (Zhu and Lai 2014, 191–192). Because this incomplete collaboration is based on a temporary agreement, it is fragile and weak. Note that, in this dissertation, collaboration refers to cooperation among all SOs, not only to foundations and grassroots SOs.

Moreover, lack of knowledge about Chinese foundations as part of the third sector is in marked contrast to their increasing income and expenditures (see chapter 4) as well as their contributions from a social and economic perspective, along with China's growing role in international organizations.

In recent years, we have witnessed an increase in and transformation of foundations in China, especially NPFFs, which are regarded as the main financial resource for grassroots SOs, although disappointing so in reality. The aim of the research in this dissertation is to explore the interactions between foundations and grassroots SOs by examining the characteristics and the scant evidence of the connection between them. I also examine why foundations do not like to work with grassroots SOs, especially why direct grant-making from foundations to SOs is still limited. Although research on their interactions is still rare (e.g., Fulda 2017, 65), they do point toward a new trend.

The literature on why Chinese foundations do not make grants to grassroots SOs
The study from Lai & Tao & Spires (2015) pointed out that there is still little evidence of widespread formal linkages between grassroots SOs and new philanthropic institutions, given that government priorities are still structuring the field of Chinese foundations in key and consequential ways. This continues to be the case even though the number of private foundations in China has grown rapidly.

In 2017, Fulda examined "how foreign and domestic foundations, public and private Chinese foundations, operating and grantmaking Chinese foundations, are interacting with Chinese SOs" (64) in the context of mainland China. He argued that, by operating their projects, Chinese foundations excluded grassroots SOs from their activities. In other words, Chinese foundations are normally unwilling to provide funds to other SOs, while foreign foundations prefer to provide grants directly to grassroots SOs from a pragmatic perspective.

In a 2017 article, Shawn Shieh addressed the divergent pathways taken by PFFs, NPFFs, and grassroots SOs (1789). He explained that foundations tend to be consistent with the government and enterprises, emphasizing the importance of professional, innovative, and result-driven assessments; whereas grassroots SOs are more independent, meet beneficiary needs effectively, and make comprehensive assessments. Lai and Spires' (2020) article explicitly observed the appearance of grant-making foundations and the shaping behavior of marketization logic, which affects the development of grassroots SOs by investigating the conflicts between them. Using a practical and theoretical combination, he noticed that foundations always try to implant their grantees the concepts of marketization and commercialization. This "marketization logic" is applied to enhance the grantees' capacities and efficiency, which in turn satisfies the foundations' expectations despite the reluctance of grassroots SOs. What is clear from the abovementioned literature is that both studies investigated the conflicts between foundations and grassroots SOs, explaining that, even though they are conceptually two forms of civil society organizations, Chinese foundations do not want to support grassroots SOs because of their divergent pathways and particular viewpoints.

Concerning why Chinese foundations fund grassroots SOs, a study by the Woqi Foundation (2018) is considered the seminal research on Chinese grant-making foundations.[3] The study lists eleven influential founda-

---

3 See the preface in *"Preliminary Study on the Value of Grantmaking—Review of Case-studies on Grantmaking Foundation"* (2018).

tions in a state of transition toward supporting grassroots SOs via various pathways. This research does not provide exhaustive documentation for why and how these foundations started funding grassroots SOs, but it is a good reference for future studies on grant-making foundations in China.

Based on an analysis of why Chinese foundations do not make grants, Shieh (2017, 1799–1802) presented the following factors:

1. Foundation's orientation as an operating foundation

   Foundations do not make grants to others because their orientation is to operate projects

   a) by their staff;

   b) by the party and government as well as their subordinate groups under the government, institute, or state-owned enterprises; and

   c) as additional administrative or "reputation projects" (mian zi gong cheng 面子工程) that work with government agencies.

2. Political reasons:

   Some foundations are built with a certain political task, e.g. raising money from its members or local rich people to help the poor or disadvantaged.

   For political security reasons, some foundations do not make grants to politically sensitive groups or projects.

3. Influenced by decision-makers or main funders:

   The foundations do not make grants because their strategic direction is made by the funders, who

   a) want to operate projects by themselves;

   b) do not trust the government and grassroots SOs, so they prefer to conduct their charitable activities;

   c) feel confident in spending the money themselves;

   d) do not have any experience in making grants to grassroots SOs;

   e) do not know how foundations make grants to others; and

   f) establish foundations for individual interests or vanity.

4. Foundations do not make grants to grassroots SOs because of the mind-set of the foundations' decision-makers, who

   a) do not believe grassroots SOs can carry out impactful projects;

   b) do not want to take the risk for the grantees; and

   c) do not want to take the risk of cooperating with grassroots SOs.

Just as laws and regulations followed practices in foundations, so did academic research. Previous scholars' lack of practical experience is also an important reason for the dearth of in-depth research. In general, academic research and practical development are separated in the research of foundations. People conducting academic research think that practitioners do not understand academics, while practitioners believe that scholars are just building theories rather than practical applications.

The 2018 article by Chan and Lai (1–17) clarified that Chinese foundations had already changed from a statist model to a corporatist model, though most foundations still did not cooperate with grassroots SOs, and only a few foundations had started making small grants to grassroots SOs. The most recent study by Yi Kang (2019) indicated that private foundations' connections with Chinese grassroots SOs still "remain underexplored" (500), which is exactly the significance of this dissertation's research on Chinese foundations and their interactions with grassroots SOs.

Overall, the literature review in this section is based on extensive research of the existing literature on civil society, NGOs, and SOs in China, in addition to foundations in general. Even more importantly, individual studies on Chinese foundations were chosen for further in-depth reviews. I intend to present this review in such a way that it can clarify the current research progress and address the major research points related to foundations from a pragmatic perspective.

1.4 Structure of the study

This study is comprised of nine Chapters. Chapter One provides an introduction, background of the problems and significance of the study. This introductory chapter begins with the socio-economic developments of the People's Republic of China that led to the development of social organizations in China with foundations and grassroots SOs in particular.

Chapter Two examines the definitions and categories of foundations in China, and outlines the characteristics of grassroots SOs in China, which are the scope of this study. The literature review is also included in this chapter, with a special eye on the scholarly attention on the interactions between foundations and grassroots SOs.

Chapter Three outlines the research design of the empirical study, description and collection of data, ensuring the reliability of the data. The study is based on a mixed method design of documentary analysis, face-to-face in-depth interviews and participatory observation. This chapter present a theoretical framework that emerged from two methodological approaches, evolution of cooperation and resource dependency theory.

Chapter Four presents the overall development characteristics of Chinese foundations at different stages from 1949 to 2017, with a focus on its emergency, past historic development and present growth pattern. The finding reveals that government-affiliated foundations formulated their own approaches to fundraising and their own operating model, and Chinese foundations excluded grassroots NGOs in their operating mechanism since the very beginning.

Then, the main analysis of the study takes place in the Chapter Five, Six and Seven. Chapter Five presents an overview of the funding distribution of foundations in China. Specifically, I examine the number of existing Chinese grant-making foundations and whether they make grants to grassroots SOs. I argue that Chinese grant-making foundations not only are limited in number but also do not include grassroots SOs in their funding scheme. Chapter Six and Chapter Seven take separate perspectives on the issue of cooperation through a day-to-day routine. How and to what extent the two parties, grant-making foundations and grassroots SOs, interact with each other at different steps. Chapter Six takes the perspective of the foundations. Based on the interview, I describe how the foundations select, engage, manage and control the funding that they offer to grassroots SOs. Chapter Seven moves to the perspective of the grassroots SOs, which are all legally registered and have different organizational forms. My argument is that grassroots SOs are in a subordinate position in their relation to the potential funding with foundations.

Chapter Eight conducts a systematic comparison of the two perspectives based on the interpretation of the empirical data including the interviews from both foundations and grassroots SOs, as well as experts and practitioners.

Chapter Nine presents and discusses the research findings in three parts. Firstly, I sum up the insights on the foundations' development in China. Secondly, I summarize the relationship between foundations and grassroots SOs. Thirdly, I discuss the future of the relationship between these two types of organizations.

2 Definition and categories of foundations

In this chapter, I examine the definition of foundations in China by ana-lyzing the legal regulations and practices and refer to definitions in other countries such as the United States and Germany. I analyze the unclear and somewhat indeterminate definition of foundations in the Chinese le-gal system in terms of its relationship with grassroots SOs. Additionally, I discuss the categories of foundations to explain how various foundations work and how they relate to grassroots SOs. Furthermore, the political en-vironment plays an important role in the development of foundations, thus a series of policies undertaken during the past three decades are listed and discussed.

2.1 Definitions at the international level

2.1.1 An Exotic Phenomenon?

In the Chinese context, both foundations and grassroots SOs are still re-cent creations. Many scholars think that foundations were a kind of exotic phenomenon that started in Western countries and then were introduced into China in the 1980s (Estes 1998, 169–70) with a new era under China's reform and opening-up policy (Shang 2001). Chinese foundations have been influenced by overseas foundations for both legislation and practices.

The appearance of Chinese foundations was initiated by the government in the 1980s. As previously explained, the people and agencies that estab-lished foundations did not understand the meaning of international foun-dations, including the people who drafted the first regulation of 1988 on foundations in China, and for this, they are criticized by scholars (Yang 2010, 58). However, when RMF-2004 was drafted, many experiences were adopted from Europe and the United States. In subsequent practices, many foundations also borrowed or referred to the practices of overseas founda-tions, for example, the Narada Foundation from the Ford Foundation and the Guangdong Harmony Foundation from the Rockefeller Brothers Fund.

Studies on the development of philanthropic foundations from an inter-national perspective seldom include Chinese foundations because of their small numbers as compared with other countries, as well as their dependence on the state. As discussed in the previous chapter, foundations are not construed as an independent sector in earlier studies. Moreover, the lack of even the most basic data and information on Chinese foundations and the conceptual issues from a comparative perspective further complicate the involvement of Chinese foundations internationally.

2.1.2 Definitions in the United States and Europe

To date, there is no commonly accepted worldwide definition of foundations due to "substantial differences in the history and traditions of foundations across countries and significant variations in the shapes foundation sectors take" (Toepler 1999, 215) in different cultural and political contexts. The term "modern philanthropic foundation" arose early in the twentieth century when the millionaires in the United States, such as John D. Rockefeller and Andrew Carnegie, sought a new approach to distributing their wealth aimed at bringing about social changes and processes (Roelofs 1987, 31; Toepler 1999, 25–26). Thus, these two influential philanthropic donors founded the Rockefeller Foundation and the Carnegie Corporation of New York, respectively, which are considered as the models for modern philanthropic foundations. They made grants to other non-profit organizations even before the United States promulgated the legal definition and regulations for foundations (Toepler 1999, 25–26).

Helmut Anheier and Stephan Toepler reviewed the definitions of philanthropic foundations in the United States and Europe. Toepler (1999, 26) concluded that the term "foundation" is legally and essentially a creation from tax laws. More specially, the Foundation Center defines a foundation in the United States as

> *a non-governmental entity that is established as a non-profit corporation or a charitable trust, with a principal purpose of making grants to unrelated organizations, institutions, or individuals for scientific, educational, cultural, religious, or other charitable purposes.*[4]

Toepler (1999) discussed the rich tapestry of foundations in Europe. For example, in Germany, the law does not distinguish between grantmaking and operating foundations (similar to the Chinese definition), which can

---

4 From the American Foundation Center website, https://grantspace.org/resources/k nowledge-base/what-is-a-foundation, accessed February 7, 2019.

be established with a variety of nonfinancial assets (Toepler 1999, 218), which is different from Chinese foundations because the initial capital is required at different levels (see table 2-1).

Besides, as explained by Heydemann and Toepler (2006), basic differences exist between foundations and associations as the main legal forms of nonprofit institutions in traditional civil law in continental Europe.

> *Associations are member-based, whereas foundations are asset-based organizations. Members may contribute assets to an association, but the foundation does not have members. Accordingly, the founding act and the donor's intention to transfer assets to an independent organization are integral parts of what constitutes a foundation in the European understanding.* (9)

Interestingly, Toepler also noted that some types of foundations in the United States are not counted as part of the foundation sector but as "supporting organizations" (Toepler 1999, 222) that are used as fundraising arms of other organizations. These so-called "supporting organizations" also include single donor endowed foundations but lack independence.

Finally, Anheier and Toepler (1999) noted that the basic form of a foundation is that "the foundation idea is based on the transfer of property from a donor to an independent institution whose obligation it is to use such property and any proceed derived from it, for a specified purpose or purposed over an often undermined period" (11).

2.2 *Definition in China*

In China, according to the Regulations for the Management of Foundations, the definition of a foundation has experienced two different phases, one in 1988 and one in 2004 (RMF-1988 and RMF-2004, respectively).

As the first legislation on foundations in China, RMF-1988 noted that foundations

> *refer[red] to in these Regulations are corporate bodies limited to domestic and foreign associations, other organizations, and non-governmental nonprofit institutions which are operated through willing donations by individuals* (RMF-1988, Article 2).
> 本办法所称的基金会，是指对国内外社会团体和其他组织以及个人自愿捐赠资金进行管理的民间非营利性组织（是社会团体法人）。

This definition cannot differentiate between foundations and other corporate bodies (or associations), which is unlikely to be a basic difference between foundations and social associations. Strangely, even though RMF-1988 specifically pointed out the "non-governmental" nature of foundations, by that time, foundations were all government-organized as discussed.

In 1989, the Regulation on Registration and Administration of SOs came into effect, which reconfirmed foundations' legal status as SOs. Shang (2003) clarified that, because RMF-1988 defines a foundation as a corporate body, foundations are the only social organization supervised by the two preceding regulations from the State Council. After careful preparation and learning from foreign experience, the State Council issued a new regulation that went into effect in 2004 that defined a foundation as follows:

> *A non-profit legal entity established following these regulations that employs assets donated by actual persons, legal entities, or other organizations to engage in some public benefit enterprise.* (RMF-2004, Article 2)
> (基金会是指利用自然人、法人或者其他组织捐赠的财产，以从事公益事业为目的，按照本条例的规定成立的非营利性法人)

Chan and Lai (2018) explained that the definition of "foundation" in RMF-2004 is not much different from the one in RMF-1988 from a legal perspective, which has been defined as a nonprofit entity based on donations of natural persons, juridical persons, and other organizations. However, Xu (2010, 28–29) clarified that RMF-2004 was a significant improvement over RMF-1988, which defined a foundation as a social association, although RMF-2004 did not specify the characteristics of "financial group legal person" (cai tuan fa ren 财团法人) under the restrictions of legal classifications in the General Rules of Civil Law. She pointed out three differences in her study: first, RMF-1988 called a foundation a corporate body, while RMF-2004 defined it as a nonprofit legal entity; second, RMF-2004 emphasized that the purpose of a foundation is to engage in public welfare; and, third, RMF-2004 did not emphasize the "nongovernment" characteristics of a foundation. Xu deemed that this change was related to the history and situation at that time, and RMF-2004 expands the scope of the regulations. With private foundations being encouraged in the 2000s, RMF-2004 was able to embrace foundations that are not completely nongovernmental, especially when compared to the emphasis on "nongovernment" in Europe and the United States.

It is worth noting that both definitions focus specifically on the source of funds, while not highlighting foundations' activities how the funds are spent.

In this context, the widely used definition of RMF-2004 is adopted when referring to foundations in China and is the definition applied to this study. All Chinese foundations mentioned and interviewed in this study are formally registered according to the regulations and laws.

2.3 Categories of foundations in China

In China, RMF-2004 legalized two classifications of foundations according to their source of funding: public fundraising foundations (PFFs) and non-public fundraising foundations (NPFFs). The basic difference between the two is that public fundraising foundations can raise funds from the public, while NPFFs are not allowed to raise funds from the public.

Table 2-1: Major differences between PFFs and NPFFs according to the 2004 Regulations for the Management of Foundations

Articles	PFFs	NPFFs
Article 6	The Ministry of Civil Affairs under the State Council is responsible for the registration and management of the following types of foundations and bodies representing foundations: national-level PFFs.	The Ministry of Civil Affairs under the State Council is responsible for the registration and management of the following types of foundations and bodies representing foundations: NPFFs whose original funds are more than 20 million RMB and whose founder applies to establish as a foundation to the Ministry of Civil Affairs under the State Council.
Article 8	The original funds of national PFFs should be more than 8 million RMB; the original funds of local PFFs should be more than 4 million RMB.	The original funds of NPFFs should be more than 2 million RMB.
Article 20		For NPFFs established using the assets of a private individual, no more than a third of board members may be close family relations of that individual.
Article 29	The amount of money spent annually by PFFs on the public benefit activities stipulated in their charter must not be less than 70% of the previous year's income.	NPFFs annual expenditure on the public benefit activities stipulated in their charter must not be less than 8% of the surplus from the previous year.

Source: Congressional-Executive Commission on China, https://www.cecc.gov/reso urces/legal-provisions/regulations-on-the-management-of-foundations-chinese-text, accessed October 14, 2019.

Another common division of foundations that Chinese scholars follow is construed from the perspective of government-based foundations and private foundations (nongovernment-based), that is, according to the relationship between foundations and the state. As discussed in the development of Chinese foundations, the fundamental distinction for foundations in China is whether they are created and governed by the government or not, to know how foundations work. Although this division is quite old, it helps to understand the approximate landscape of the foundation by the time.

Table 2-2: Categories of foundations by Shang (2003)

	Categories	Characteristics	
1	State-run with non-state support	State-run: established by the government and run like a government agency; with non-state support: fundraising from the public and overseas organizations	China Soong Ching Ling Foundation (CSCLF); China Agricultural Science and Education Foundation
2	Non-state-run with state support	Non-state-run: created and managed by the foundation itself with non-governmental bureaucracy; State support: mostly, part or all of the initial capitals are from the government agency	China Environment Foundation
3	(completely) private foundation	It is called a private foundation, referring to its establishment, funding, leadership, and management are rarely intervened by the government.	China Children and Teenagers' Fund (CCTF), Amity Foundation
4	Enterprises foundation	Created, run, and managed by the enterprise.	Beijing International Meedoo Art Foundation
5	Celebrity Foundation	In the name of a celebrity or with the use of celebrity effects.	China Soong Ching Ling Foundation (CSCLF)

Source: Shang (2003), compiled and adapted by the author.

The most notable classifications mentioned by Shang (2001) were the state-run foundations and the non-state-run foundations (private foundations), which depended on their funding, management mechanism, and operating system, which in turn created their different roles and social status. Also, he noted that both state-run foundations and private foundations were under the management and supervision of the government. Therefore, no private foundations existed at that time.

Likewise, Xie (2003a, 64) divided Chinese foundations into three categories: completely state-run foundations (similar to non-state-run foundations with state support), government-affiliated foundations with a private background (具有民办色彩的官办基金会, 亦被称为官办民助型基金会, similar to Shang's category 1 in Table 3-2), and private foundations with a government background (具有官办色彩的民办基金会, similar to Shang's category 2 in Table 3-2).

Xie and Shang's preceding classifications are confusing, take, for example, CSCLF, which can be classified into two categories. However, this example shows that, in the 1990s and 2000s, a completely private foundation had only limited ability to exist. Consequently, no foundation was able to be independent of the government before RMF-2004 was instated. I list these methods of classification in this study because they still have a strong influence on the thinking of foundations in terms of state mechanisms. Whether foundations are government-organized still greatly affects the development of the foundation sector in China. In addition, government-organized foundations have always been more important and influential than other types of foundations.

According to foundations' funding and activities, Liu (2017, 6–10) distinguished eight principal forms of foundations, which is somewhat similar to Toepler's classification of European and American foundations. Examples include American classifications of private independent foundations, community foundations, corporate or company-sponsored foundations, and operating foundations. Even though these classifications are not stable and are sometimes confusing, they help to describe foundations more clearly. Accordingly, here are eight principal forms of foundations in China:

- Independent foundations, which are generally endowed by individuals, enterprises, or single families
- Family foundations, which are generally established by family assets and are mostly run by family members
- Corporate or company-sponsored foundations, which are similar to independent foundations but are established by companies
- Church-related foundations, which generally pursue charitable and religious purposes
- Government-affiliated foundations, which are generally initiated by the government or quasi-government agencies that engage in public welfare for which the government is responsible
- Community foundations, which receive donations from multiple donors and are governed by local communities they serve

- Operating foundations, mainly refers to foundations that primarily operate their programs or projects but may also provide funds to other organizations
- University foundations, which raise funds and then focus only on university-related affairs

Table 2-3: Eight principal forms of Chinese foundations and their characteristics

		Value & Position	Characteristics	Examples
1	Independent foundations	The vehicle for social innovation	Abundant funds and resources, focusing on social innovation	One foundation, Narada Foundation
2	Family foundations	The vehicle for the family spirit and wealth innovation	Set up by family assets and run by family members for charitable giving	Laoniu Foundation, Heren Charitable Foundation
3	Corporate or company-sponsored foundations	Public welfare aligned with corporate strategies	Closely related to corporate strategy and corporate social responsibility	Tencent Foundation, Vantone Foundation
4	Church-related foundations	Charity and faith-based supporters	Set up and supported by religious organizations and faith-based believers	Amity Foundation
5	Government-affiliated foundations	The connection between government and civil society	Government-organized or otherwise government-based for achieving government's functions	
6	Community foundations	Builders of sustainable communities	Trustee management service for charity assets, resource integration, and resource providers for grassroots SOs	Guangdong Harmony Foundation
7	Professional operating foundations	Solving social problems directly	An SO of being good at mobilizing resources	A Dream Foundation
8	University foundations	Attend to scientific exploration and cultural issues	Raise funds and then focus only on a university-related affair.	Qinghua University Foundation

Source: Liu's study (2017, 6–10) and Xu (2015, 16-17). Adapted by the author.

Scholarly studies on foundations often divide them into grant-making and operating foundations according to their type of activity. There is no clear-cut connotation of either one in China, thus mixed foundations include the activities of both. Anheier (2001, 5) proposed these three categories

- Grant-making foundations: Endowed foundations that primarily engage in grantmaking to other organizations with specific purposes

- Operating foundations: Foundations that primarily operate their pro-grams and projects
- Mixed foundations: Foundations that operate their programs and projects, and engage in grantmaking to grassroots SOs

If grant-making foundations refer to those that primarily engage in grant-making to other organizations with specific purposes but do not operate their programs and projects, then there are no purely grant-making foundations in China. However, some Chinese foundations that run a large percentage of their projects are oriented as grant-making foundations, as discussed in the previous section. This is not to say there are no grant-making foundations to speak of in China but to question whether grant-making foundations in China favor operating than grant-making projects.

In conclusion, this study makes use of the classification by RMF-2004 of PFFs and NPFFs by rule of the law, which is frequently adopted in the Chinese foundation sector. The division of grant-making foundations and operating foundations is adopted to explore their relationship with grass-roots SOs according to the foundations' activities.

2.4 Current applied regulations and laws on Chinese foundations

Regardless of the definitions of foundations, three legally registered forms of SOs in China are derived from the General Rule of Civil Law and are directly governed under three administrative regulations, as follows:
- Social associations (shen hui tuan ti, 社会团体) under the Regulations on the Registration and Administration of SOs (1998)
- Civil non-enterprise institutions (CNIs) (min ban fei qi ye, 民办非企业) under the Interim Regulations on the Registration and Administra-tion of Private Non-Enterprise Units (1998)[5]
- Foundations （ji jin hui, 基金会） under the Regulations on the Ad-ministration of Foundations (2004)

Additionally, these three categories of social organization cannot cover all social organizations in China because there are still many other grassroots SOs that are registered as for-profit businesses, or are unregistered but still function as SOs in China, or are "claimed sponsorship under another orga-

---

5   This type social organization is allowed to provide social services and welfare to the private sector.

nization"[6] (*gua kao zai bie de ji gou de xia mian,* 挂靠在别的机构的下面) (Spires, Tao, and Chan 2014, 76). Organizations registered as for-profit businesses do not need the approval of a governmental "supervisory agency" (*ye wu zhu guan danwei* 业务主管单位), which is necessary to be registered as CNIs. I did not add the unregistered category in this study, even though those organizations still work or function as SOs, but are not recognized by law and are difficult to take into account. Some of those organizations cannot be registered if they work in sensitive fields or on sensitive issues in the eyes of the government, for example, labor rights, religious, and advocacy organizations; some of them prefer to keep an unregistered status, if they still can operate under other organizations, especially under government agencies.

The development of Chinese foundations has been influenced by policies since the appearance of the Regulations on the Administration of Foundations (RMF) in 1988 (as explained in chapter 4). Here is the list of related regulations and laws from 1988 to 2017, to understand further the current regulations on foundations and grassroots SOs.

Table 2-4: Current applied administrative regulations on philanthropic development promulgated by the State Council.

Promulgation Date	Title
1998.10.25	Regulations on the Registration and Administration of SOs
1998.10.25	Interim Regulations on the Registration and Administration of Private Non-Enterprise Units
2004.3.8	Regulations on the Administration of Foundations
2007.12.6	Regulations on the Implementation of the Enterprise Income Tax Law
2011.7.19	Regulations on the Implementation of the Individual Income Tax Law
2014.11.24	Opinions on Promoting the Sound Development of Philanthropy
2016.03.16	The Charity Law

2.5 Definitions of grassroots social organizations (grassroots SOs)

The concept of "grassroots social organization" has always been ambiguous in China's system. It is difficult to have a precise definition for various reasons. The most important reason is that "grassroots social organization" or

---

6 In Spires et al.' study, this category has no legal from, "but which is sometimes invoked to indicate political patronage by a government agency, university or GONGO" (Spires, Tao, and Chan 2014, 76).

"grassroots organization" is not an official term but is seen as the general meaning of "social organizations" by Chinese law. Moreover, an understanding of what a grassroots SO refers to in the context of China differs among academics. Moreover, the international understanding of NGOs is not suitable in China, nor is it a popular term or a legally recognized one. Grassroots SOs embrace many kinds of unregistered social organizations that are understandably illegal.

In the following analysis, I explain the definition of grassroots SOs that I adopted for current purposes. For the most part, my analysis is based on research and long-term observations of many social organizations in China.

Although getting an accurate definition of "social organization" is difficult, it is more easily recognized in practice according to four characteristics. The most critical characteristic relates to the registration authority of formal laws and regulations. Thus, a social organization should be registered in civil affairs departments. The second characteristic is its non-governmental nature. Social organizations are not run by the government. The exception is that many social organizations registered in civil affairs departments are operated by various government departments or as a supplementary agency, which cannot be identified as social organizations. The third is that SOs are not-for-profit organizations. Private kindergartens, schools, and hospitals, for example, are exceptions that claim not-for-profit status but in practice are regarded as profitable organizations by the public. Public kindergartens, schools, and hospitals are not run for profit but not registered in civil affairs departments. Besides, there is also a discriminatory understanding of the society that a social organization is an organization that is neither organized and nor managed by the government. The fourth characteristic is that a social organization should be independent of the state, including any pattern of government agencies, and enjoy some degree of autonomy.

For this study, I use the term "grassroots social organizations" (grassroots SOs) to refer to organizations that are independent of civil society organizations and that are also separate from the government and foundations. Thus, mass organizations and government-organized non-governmental organizations (GONGOs) do not qualify as a research subject in my analysis, and the organizations that are registered as business groups and unregistered grassroots organizations do not qualify for this research.

I begin using the term by considering grassroots SOs or "folk organizations" (known as cao gen zu zhi in China, 草根组织), which refer to organizations that are independent of the government or are not directly part of government agencies, "neither created by nor officially incorporated into the Party-state" (Spires, Tao, and Chan 2014, 67). In an earlier study, Spires also defined grassroots organizations:

They are not government creations or spin-offs of some government agency looking to push cadres into early retirement or to create an NGO "hat" for officials to wear when traveling overseas. By and large, they receive neither funding nor tangible assets (like free office space) from government agencies. They are run by local Chinese people and do not answer to headquarters in some other country. They may receive funding from foreign governments or foundations or locally from their founders, volunteers, or members. They may be organized by social elites or by people without a high-school education. They may operate under top-down power structures and clear hierarchies, or they may show a higher degree of internal democracy. They may be composed of staff, of volunteers, of members, or some combination of the three. Finally, they may be registered with the government as legal NGOs (min jian zu zhi) or as businesses, or they may not register with the government at all, in any form. (Spires 2011a, 10–11)

However, folk organizations and grassroots organizations are not recognized as legal terms. Thus, I next turn to the term "grassroots NGOs," which is a sensitive word in China. Prior researchers have also pointed out that NGOs and nonprofit organizations in China are different from those in Western countries. In the interviews, one organization's representative explained why he likes to be referred to as a grassroots organization or NGO:

In the past, we called our organization as an NGO, but later we found that local government officials do not like the name of NGO, because it means antigovernment.[7] Well, the grassroots organization might be better, but there are still lots of disadvantages. For example, when we go to the villages and tell the villagers that we are a grassroots organization, the villagers normally think that my organization is unconvincing unformal or unprofessional, or not recognized by the government. Until the year 2008, the word of social organization was widely accepted by the local government. So far, we are very happy to be called as a social organization, which sound[s] also very close to society and the public.

---

7   The English phrase "nongovernment" is translated into Chinese as "Fei Zheng Fu," and "Zheng Fu" means government. "Fei" is synonym of "Fan" and also sounds like "Fan," while "Fan" means "against" or "anti". In the Chinese context, "*against* government" or "*anti*-government" is considered insensitive. Hence, to avoid misunderstanding, it is not commonly used by some Chinese people.

Officially, SOs are regarded as the Chinese term for NGOs and NPOs (Shieh 2017, 1797), while there are three legally registered forms of SOs within the current regulations, even including foundations.[8] Moreover, similar to Chinese foundations, one big challenge is to distinguish between government-organized SOs and nongovernment-organized SOs. Based on the objective of this research, I do not intend to conduct a specific analysis or make a distinction between the above concepts, but instead, use the generally accepted term "SOs."

Hence, I adopt the term grassroots SOs, mainly to differ them from SOs that have ties with particular government agencies and other public enterprises or from institutes that normally enjoy a certain privileged status. Broadly speaking, grassroots SOs refers to formally registered nongovernmental organizations, grassroots organizations, or folk organizations, which are defined as those organizations that primarily engage in nonprofit activities and are characterized by not-for-profit and voluntary associations apart from non-government agencies. Nonetheless, grassroots SOs usually enjoy more autonomy than other SOs, e.g. government-affiliated organizations and associations, and are especially warranted as being independent organizations.

2.6 Discussion on definitions

Just as not all organizations called foundations are foundations (Anheier 2001, 2), not all SOs labeled as SOs are SOs. In reality, some small foundations operate like SOs. For example, foundations receive funds only at their inception or through a single donor and then operate one or two projects by themselves; whereas some government-organized SOs are eligible to raise funds from the public to operate projects as foundations do.

Because of the vague definition and development of foundations in China and, most foundations operate funds by themselves through various forms, like through local governments or donating to hospitals or individuals directly, instead of making grants to grassroots SOs. And foundations'

---

8 China's "social organization" as a term with a specific meaning was first proposed in the report of the 17th National Congress of the Communist Party of China in October 2007; it mainly referred to organizations other than the market and the government. At the National Social Organization Construction and Management Work Experience Exchange Conference held in November 2007, the Ministry of Civil Affairs decided to replace the concept of "civil organization" with the concept of "social organization".

abilities in fundraising and investment are generally low, which makes no difference between foundations and grassroots SOs.

The question becomes, what kind of problems arise when foundations work as SOs or SOs raise funds and operate projects as foundations do?

As a result of vague definitions in the legislation, the line between grant-making and operating foundations is blurred. It is therefore common to find that some foundations are oriented as both grant-making and operating foundations. Often, a foundation will not make grants to grassroots SOs but still be oriented as a grant-making foundation or, at certain times, will change its orientation from grantmaking to operating.

Foundations can replace SOs to conduct projects, although grassroots SOs will have less and less opportunity to survive. As mentioned, the main purpose of large foundations is to raise funds from the public and accept overseas funding (Xu 2010, 101). Moreover, foundations are created in part to serve as administrative arms of government agencies basically to provide jobs for retired governmental officials or to work as fundraising arms or supporting organizations for certain organizations or individuals. Some foundations are registered as foundations to work easily under the name of charity and philanthropy, rather than functioning as a true foundation, so they do not follow the rules for foundations. The reason some entrepreneurs set up foundations is straightforward, that is, only to gain a good reputation, and after their establishment seldom work or have a staff, which can explain why some foundations have not functioned. Some NPFFs set up by private enterprises or individuals are strongly influenced by corporate (or their bosses) values and culture. Accordingly, philanthropic activities are regarded as a way to promote enterprises or an individual's public image and to strengthen relations with the government (Zhang et al., 2010).

3 Methodology

This chapter outlines the mixed-methods design of this study. The research design is based on documentary analysis, face-to-face interviews and participatory observation. Under the premise of understanding Chinese foundations and grassroots organizations, the choice of methods is ultilized to answer the research questions. The advantage of this methodology draws heavily on an in-depth empirical analysis of interaction between foundations and grassroots SOs throughout China.

3.1 Polulation and sample selection

The purpose of this study is the interaction between foundations and grassroots social organizations, thus interviewees are targeted on foundations that have interacted with grassroots SOs and grassroots SOs that have interacted with foundations. Considering which research objects are most able to provide complete and sufficient research data, this study chooses non-probability sampling. The sampling concludes sixteen foundations, thirteen grassroots SOs, five scholars and experts who have been working on foundations and grassroots SOs for a long time, the representatives from four well-known and influential supporting platforms for foundations in China, two representatives of overseas foundations that have worked in China for more than ten years, a series of workshops by foundations and grassroots SOs. Thus, this section explains how and why to explore new findings and problems arising from fieldwork, including how and why certain organizations were selected as samples for my in-depth interviews.

These samples include organizations that can provide as much information as possible. Because of my previous working experience with foundations and grassroots SOs, I was already familiar with some of the interviewees, which enhanced my ability to acquire information and materials during the in-depth interviews. Based on their work with both overseas and domestic foundations, I also selected certain experienced grassroots SOs to gain more information regarding the problems of Chinese foundations and grassroots organizations and to use overseas foundations as a reference. With the recommendation of scholars and grassroots SOs, I selected the interviewees according to their ability to provide as much information as possible.

Location and selection of interviewees for field research
The locations for the field research were not randomly selected; instead, they were selected due to their different roles in and perspective of the development of Chinese foundations and grassroots SOs, and also because they attempted to work with each other or because of foundations' success in supporting grassroots SOs. Based on anecdotal evidence and the geographical distribution of Chinese foundations, the top five places (Guangdong, Beijing, Jiangsu, Zhengjiang, and Shanghai) have more than half the total number of Chinese foundations. Beijing, Guangzhou, and Yunnan have a collection of active grassroots SOs (Spires, Tao, and Chan 2014, 68), Xi'an has several long-established foundations and grassroots SOs that I know well.

Likewise, sampling is not selected randomly but because of the diverse features to gather as great a diversity of opinions and materials as possible. Whether from foundations, grassroots SOs, scholars, or experts, each voice is significant in a relatively small sample. More specifically, to maximize understanding of their roles and perspectives, foundations were chosen for interviews primarily because of their orientation and positioning as grant-making foundations or operating foundations, as national foundations or local foundations, or as NPFFs or PFFs. Besides, due to other foundations' recommendations, I was able to contact the founders or leaders of certain foundations. Interviewed grassroots SOs were chosen based on their locations and brief descriptions on their websites. A number of grassroots SOs were chosen because of my familiarity with their experiences in applying or conducting domestic foundations and overseas foundations.

Also, three representatives from German and American foundations, three representatives from four well-known platforms for grant-making foundations in China, and five experienced scholars and experts were interviewed. To further enhance understanding of the existing overseas organizations in China, three representatives from overseas foundations were interviewed, based on the fact that many grassroots SOs were supported by overseas funding before the 2010s and that Chinese grassroots SOs gave overseas foundations higher ratings than domestic foundations according to the China Foundation Rankings in 2013 and 2015. Three representatives from well-known platforms for grant-making foundations in China and five experienced scholars and experts were interviewed to explore their attitudes and comments regarding interactions between foundations and grassroots SOs in China. Five experienced scholars and experts were interviewed due to their many years' experiences and contributions in academic research or their practices in evaluating or operating foundations or grassroots SOs.

Finally, I selected Kunming, Hangzhou, Guangzhou, Beijing, and Xi'an, in which I interviewed the organizations' representatives from eleven cities. The first interview was conducted in Kunming. And the first interview representative was my former colleague, who was working as secretary-general in an influential local environmental foundation and was able to provide me with valuable information and suggest other potential foundations for interviews. She has worked in that grassroots organization many years; therefore, she has a deep understanding of how foundations cooperate with grassroots SOs and the kind of cooperation the two sides need.

The second field location was Hangzhou, where I was invited to take part in the Chinese Philanthropic Foundations Grantmaking Development Forum. Through this workshop, I had the chance to get to know more foundations. Besides, in recent years, the total number of foundations in Zhejiang has increased along with the number of wealthy people. Unfortunately, because of the organizers' requirements and workshop confidentiality, I could not use the information and materials of this workshop in my research.

The third location was Guangzhou, the capital city of Guangdong province, and this province has the largest number of foundations of any other province in China. Furthermore, the Guangdong Harmony Community Foundation is a well-known grant-making foundation in China and was named one of the five best Chinese foundations in a China Foundation Ranking award in 2018.

The fourth location was Beijing, the capital city of China, which has the second-largest number of large-scale foundations. The final location was Xi'an, which has a few SOs that were supported by overseas foundations in the past and are now applying for domestic grants; this site was chosen because the interviewees could provide relatively comprehensive thoughts on the situation and development of both overseas and domestic foundations.

Semi-structured, in-depth interviews

To gain a thorough insight into the cooperation between foundations and grassroots SOs, I adopted semi-structured, in-depth interviews for three reasons. First, abundant and valuable information could be accessed through the organizations' official websites and reports before the interviews. Thus, semi-structured interviews offered structured themes and provided focus, which kept them from being too lengthy. Second, because of the different, numerous responses and the ability to explore new issues in-depth, such interviews, as qualitative research, are used to attain deep and detailed information. Third, through conducting intensive individual interviews in a natural setting, they consisted of more than just verbal responses; they also provided nonverbal cues that added context to the answers to the questions.

The interview questions (see Appendix 1) were formulated based on the hypothesis of the cooperation theory and the resource interdependency theory.

In accordance with the cooperation theory, I offer the following hypotheses:

- H1-a: Foundations and grassroots SOs are competitive with each other on overseas funding and domestic, private, and public funding.
- H1-b: Trust is a problem when foundations make grants to grassroots SOs.
- H1-c: Trust is a problem in maintaining and sustaining a cooperative relationship between foundations and grassroots SOs.
- H1-d: The dilemma between foundations and grassroots SOs is that they complain about each other, which means that foundations complain that they cannot find grassroots SOs capable enough to receive grants, whereas grassroots SOs complain that foundations prefer to carry out projects by themselves rather than fund grassroots SOs (Shieh 2017, 1787).
- According to resource interdependency theory, I offer the following hypotheses:
- H2-a: Foundations have more funding resources than grassroots SOs, and funding is a crucial resource for grassroots SOs.
- H2-b: Foundations can achieve their missions and extend organizational influence through grantmaking to grassroots SOs.
- H2-c: Foundations' dependence on grassroots SOs is lower than grassroots SOs' dependence on foundations, which creates asymmetrical dependence.
- H2-d: Grassroots SOs acquire resources, like funding, information, and so on, from foundations.

With an in-depth interview, the thinking of multiple focus groups and people is captured from different perspectives and experiences. The first and most important perspective is from the foundations, whereas the views of grassroots SOs, networks and platforms, experts and scholars, and overseas foundations still working in China are also considered to achieve a greater depth of understanding of the subject of this research. The interviews included a total of forty interviewees from forty-one organizations (one interviewee worked in two networks) and universities from eleven cities: Kunming, Beijing, Guangzhou, Hangzhou, Shenzhen, Nanjing, Haikou, Xi'an, Lanzhou, Hefei, and Meishan. However, interviews were conducted in only seven places: Kunming, Hangzhou, Guangzhou, Shenzhen, Beijing, Dali, and Xi'an. In detail, from March 1, 2019, until May 15, 2019, I interviewed sixteen representatives from sixteen Chinese foundations, thirteen from thirteen grassroots SOs, three from four networks or platforms, five experts and scholars, and three representatives from overseas foundations from Germany and the U.S..

During the face-to-face interviews, I used a standardized written questionnaire, which was performed mostly with grassroots SOs and foundations leaders but also with project officers. On average, each interview took approximately forty minutes. Thirty-eight interviews were face-to-face interviews, two were performed via WeChat,[9] and one via a questionnaire.

The interviews were recorded on tape and transcribed. After the eleventh interview with foundations and the eighth interview with grassroots SOs, I decided that the saturation point had been reached, as interviewees' responses to the questions were similar.

Additional thoughts about interviewees
During the field research, because it was a big challenge to choose and then contact interviewees, I got great help (e.g., to introduce interviewees, because it takes time to get to know them and then do a successful interview) from partners or former colleagues, especially leaders or influential people who knew the operation and history of organizations.

Interviewees from the foundation sector: The interviewees from this sector normally did not want to be interviewed. Here are two examples. The first case involves a project officer from a foundation who was polite and pleased to talk with me about the general development of Chinese foundations and wanted to introduce me to other foundations when I got in touch with him via WeChat. However, when I said I would like to interview him about his foundation, he tried to refuse using excuses like he was not in Beijing, or doing so was inconvenient. Another case involved a representative from a foundation in Beijing who tried to pass the interview to

---

9   WeChat is a mobile text and voice app developed by Tencent in China, and is also the most popular messaging platform with Chinese people.

another colleague who said that she was too busy or that it was not convenient to do so. Both of them were polite and professional but were not willing to be interviewed.

Interviewees from grassroots SOs: In comparison with interviewees from the foundation sector, those from grassroots SOs agreed to interviews more easily. However, when the interview involved unpleasantness regarding foundations, they are less willing to talk in any detail. The primary fear was the risk of offending foundations. From such behavior, a preliminary impression of grassroots SOs' dependence on foundations in China can also be surmised.

Interviews with experts and scholars : The interviews with experts and scholars were relatively easy. I had met these experts before or they had been recommended by other experts. The interviews were done without a guiding question but with a focus on the interactions between foundations and grassroots SOs. These experts and scholars provided a great benefit because of their unique and rich insights.

Attendance at workshops: During the field research, I took part in three workshops, two by foundations and one by grassroots SOs. During one foundation's workshop and after the organizers learned that I doing doctoral research, one organizer informed me that the workshop's content, including documents, discussions, and speeches, could not be used in my research. Nevertheless, I was grateful to be invited to participate in the conference. One advantage I gained from the workshop was the ability to get in contact with people from the foundation sector and then make appointments to interview them.

Another point worth noting is the negative influence the term civil society had on my interviews because it has increasingly become a sensitive and controversial topic in China. For example, when the development of foundations was mentioned, some interviewees tried to avoid talking about anything that might be related to the development of civil society or NGOs, both of which were sensitive words in China. It also happened that the interviewees did not want to be taped for self-protection, even when there was no sensitive topic.

Negative effects of tape during the interview: During the interview process, nonverbal cues are a valuable source of gaining information, but the process might be influenced by social interaction between the interviewer and interviewee.

3.2 Documentary analysis

During my research, I attempted to gather a large amount of secondary data such as academic literature and newspapers, and other reliable social media, as well as organizations' reports and websites. Compared with primary data, I found that secondary data for my research of foundations and grassroots SOs was not only less expensive but also could be quickly and easily accessed and understood and also aided me in analyzing the material.

However, there was one drawback. It was difficult to determine whether data from secondary materials were accurate. For one thing, no statistical data existed for certain topics. Take, for example, the number of grant-making foundations in China. As discussed earlier, different sources have declared different numbers of grant-making foundations in China. Also, secondary materials have different statistical standards and different interpretations of numbers. Thus, I spent a great deal of time ensuring the accuracy of the data I collected.

Other main sources were annual reports of individual organizations, especially those involved in grant-making activities and foundations. The biggest challenge was that there was no single comprehensive source. The numbers of foundations differed between the official data from government departments and some research reports, such as the Foundation Green Book series and the Foundation Blue Book series; in such cases, I gave the official data priority.

Besides, to date, scholarly papers on cooperative interactions between Chinese foundations and grassroots SOs are still quite rare, which made it difficult to find research articles on certain topics, such as complaints between them. Therefore, articles accessed on websites were important sources for deciphering topics on foundations and grassroots SOs. Three online public media are provided as references: China Development Brief, created in 1996 and registered as an enterprise in 2017, is known as China's first independent information platform for civil society both in English and in Chinese; China Philanthropy Times, founded in 2001 and supervised by the Ministry of Civil Affairs and compiled by the China Association of Social Workers, is known as China's first national comprehensive newspaper in the field of philanthropy; and China Philanthropist Magazine, created in 2010, has numerous articles on foundations and philanthropy.

Moreover, WeChat, now one of the most visited and used social platforms, enables users to exchange and communicate news and articles and to publicize requests for proposals so that colleagues can forward them to other people and organizations.

The data and documents presented in this study deal not only with Chinese foundations but also with those from certain Western countries for reference purposes. The latter enabled me to use successful experiences from other countries to assess the disadvantages of Chinese philanthropic organizations and make relevant policy recommendations. Because they did, and still do, play a leading role in the origin of philanthropic organizations, from both theory and practice perspectives, targeted foreign countries included both Germany and the United States, or only one of them.

3.3 Participant observation

I attended several workshops focused on interactions between Chinese foundations and grassroots SOs, one workshop organized by grassroots SOs, two foundations' meetings regarding how to work with grassroots SOs, and one national Chinese foundation's wrap-up meeting on the selection process for making grants to grassroots SOs. In this way, I had opportunities to observe, learn about, and participate in foundations' activities in a natural setting.

Besides, I participated in a workshop organized by a local NPFF with the goal of developing a project with four grassroots SOs. This foundation's efforts to cooperate with the grassroots SOs helped me understand the cooperative process from the perspective of a foundation. I also had an intensive discussion with one local grant-making foundation when its project officer was conducting project monitoring, collecting information on how and why the foundation monitors its projects, such as the process, tools, difficulties, and other related issues. Interestingly, I also observed the final selection round of one influential Chinese foundation together with a grassroots organization, which gave me a detailed look at the whole application and selection process from the perspective of a grassroots SOs.

With their consent, I had informal, but valuable talks with colleagues who were experts and practitioners in the field of Chinese grassroots SOs and foundations. Also, I have worked in grassroots SOs for more than ten years. Thus, many informal conversations that provided additional information occurred before and after the interviews.

3.4 Data analysis

For the first phrase of data analysis, all guiding interview questions derived from hypothesis were divived into different themes which were centered on research questions. Labeling and storing transcripts was conduced during and immdiatefly after data collection.

For the second phrase, coding in-depth semi-structured interview and observation transcripts was an important procedure of this study. Two cycles were implemented to read the transcripts and indentify themes. The first cycle was to develop a coding scheme based on each interview questions and to code the transcripts. The second stage was to describe and summarize the codes, the links between the themes.

For the third phrase, interpretation was implemented according to different themes, which were generated from theoretical framework. Throughout the study, I use pseudonyms for participants (and also for locations) to provide anonymity, maintain confidentiality, and protect them from unnecessary trouble or controversy. Therefore, the interview participants were assigned sequential alphabetic characters or numbers. Because only a few foundations are active and the number of grant-making foundations is very limited, and thus easily recognized, I did not disclose the location of the foundations interviewed. On the contrary, the very fact that grassroots SOs are hardly recognizable, their locations are disclosed.

3.5 Theoretical framework

The theories of civil society (Han 2017), corporatism (Spires, Tao, and Chan 2014), institutional theory (Lai 2017), and resource dependence theory (Xu 2010; Ma, Wang, Dong, and Li 2017; Lai 2017) are well-accepted in previous research on Chinese foundations. Much of the discussion on the theoretical framework of civil society and corporatism in the context of China, has been challenged recently. For example, in a recent study, Wang (2016) noted the following:

Civil society is gradually reduced to an optimistic expectation to use the Western experience to speculate China's democratic transformation. Corpo-

> *ratism was questioned by the facts that the corporative NGOs do not exhibit*
> *uniformity in their interaction with the government. (3).*

Regardless of whether these two theories have been criticized, they are mainly concerned with the relationship between the state and social organizations. However, the intention in this study is to underlay the cooperation between foundations and grassroots SOs, thus two theories are applied in the hope of providing a new perspective, namely the evolution of the cooperation theory by Robert Axelrod and the resource dependence theory by Jeffrey Pfeffer and Gerald R. Salancik. The first theory is used to contend with the current dilemma between foundations and grassroots SOs and then how they can cooperate under existing circumstances; the second theory is used to contend with both parties' abilities to acquire and maintain resources for survival and future development.

The dilemma between foundations and grassroots SOs, take their complains about each other for an example, while the dilemma is also exactly the question that the cooperation theory originally explored. Besides, When talking about the cooperation, resources, especially funding resources, are an unavoidable topic. As such, both theories are applied to explain the interactions between foundations and grassroots SOs in China.

3.5.1 The evolution of cooperation

In this part, I first present an overview of Robert Axelrod's cooperation theory, as proposed in his 1984 book, *Evolution of Cooperation*. This theory originally emerged from the prisoner's dilemma, an example of game theory, which has long been used to help explain how cooperation might be promoted and persist. Based on the cooperation theory, I further analyze the existing problems between Chinese foundations and grassroots SOs, to explain this theory's connection to their interactions.

Robert Axelrod's development of the cooperation theory
In 1981, political scientist Robert Axelrod and evolutionary biologist William D. Hamilton (1981) co-published an influential paper entitled, "The Evolution of Cooperation." It was written from two perspectives: biological and social context. Central to this work was the conclusion that cooperation can evolve under the condition of reciprocity, with the application of Darwin's emphasis on individual advantage and the prisoner's dilemma game theory.

> *To account for the manifest existence of cooperation and related group be-*
> *havior, such as altruism and restraint in competition, evolutionary theory*
> *has acquired two kinds of extensions, broadly speaking, genetically kinship*
> *theory and reciprocation theory.* (Axelrod and Hamilton 1981, 1390)

Subsequently, Robert Axelrod (1984) expanded and popularized the cooperation theory in his book, *The Evolution of Cooperation*, in which he proposed that the cooperation theory could be employed among individuals,
organizations, and nations. From this perspective, Axelrod studied individual interests and then drew upon organizational behaviors as a whole.
Based on a review by Paul Milgrom (1984, 308), Axelrod's cooperation theory made an important contribution to the topic of game theory and is
highly recommended for researchers from the perspective of evolution.

An overview of Axelrod's cooperation theory
Axelrod's cooperation theory addresses the following questions: to cooperate or not to cooperate and how to cooperate. To begin, the prisoner's
dilemma is considered as the standard strategy for analyzing the cooperation theory, and one that illustrates the study of selfish behavior. The cooperation theory is developed from this elementary game theory and then is
tested in a given strategic context.

The prisoner's dilemma: Two suspects are arrested and imprisoned after a
crime. They are placed by the prosecutors in separate rooms with no
means of communicating with each other. The prosecutors lack sufficient
evidence to convict them, so they offer the two suspects a bargain. They
have the opportunity to defect or cooperate with one another without
knowing the other's choice. Each is asked separately whether he wants to
confess the crime or remain silent. In other words, each suspect two choices that will lead to four possible outcomes:
1. If both confess, each serves two years in prison.
2. If prisoner A confesses and prisoner B remains silent, prisoner B serves
   three years in prison, and prisoner A is set free (and vice versa).
3. If both remain silent, both serve only one year in prison.
What would you do under these circumstances? The study showed that it is
better to defect regardless of whether you think the other one will cooperate or defect. So, no matter what the other player does, it pays for you to
defect. However, the paradox in prisoner's dilemma is that both receive a
worse result if both defect than if both cooperate (Axelrod 1984), even if
the defection is the best choice from an individual perspective.

Iterated prisoner's dilemma: Different from the prisoner's dilemma, during the iterated prisoner's dilemma, the players perform prisoner's dilemma repeatedly in succession and thus can choose their strategies according to the available information and what they learn about each other's behavioral tendencies. Axelrod (1984) used a computer tournament to investigate people's choices that would effectively meet their needs. In this model, professional game theorists and scholars were invited to write a program that embodied a rule requiring that, on each move, two players decided whether to cooperate or defect. It was played iteratively through a number of rounds in order to establish a stable estimate. The outstanding characteristic of this computer tournament was that people from different disciplines with rich experiences and achievements in the game theory, particularly on the prisoner's dilemma, were allowed to participate in and interact with each other in a common form and language. The tit for tat strategy, offered by Professor Anatol Rapoport from the University of Toronto, won the competition.

Tit for tat, on the other hand, starts by offering a player a cooperation option and thereafter reacts to what the other player did on the previous move. It is the most well-known and most discussed strategy of the prisoner's dilemma, and although it is a simple strategy, it has proved to be the best strategy. Axelrod (1984) pointed out that what makes tit for tat successful is the combination of the accord as opposed to trouble, retaliation against defection, forgiveness for restoring cooperation, and the benefit of long-term cooperation.

Starting from a simple problem on how to pursue individual interests in a short time, the cooperation theory advanced to address what works for an entire system's organizational behavior from a long-term perspective (Axelrod 2000). The Game theory explained both individual and organizational benefits with theoretical stringency.

Axelrod (1984) took a theoretical approach to explore how to apply the results from the computer tournament mentioned above. Various cooperation choices were set up to demonstrate the need for urgent cooperation, as well as to promote the evolution of cooperation in three phases: first, the urgency for cooperation; second, the development of cooperation; third, cooperation based on the best strategy. Following Axelrod's logic, "egoism" (for example, egoism of foundations and grassroots SOs which look after their interest and desires first) implies a wide range of unknowns between having a sense of urgency and making a decision to cooperate. Put another way, why choose cooperation strategy in the first move? As Axelrod (1984) noted, the purpose of tit for tat is not to defeat the opponent, but to lead to a reward of mutual cooperation.

Based on this theoretical approach, the cooperation theory also addressed the empirical analysis and historical cases, such as the accuracy of the predictions derived from the theory. For example, the case of the live-and-let-live system in World War I, in which British soldiers and opposing German soldiers avoided shooting at each other seriously in trench warfare. This case shows how cooperation can be started and sustained in major battles.

> *Many other institutions have developed stable patterns of cooperation based upon similar norms. Diamond markets, for example, are famous for the way their members exchange millions of dollars' worth of goods with only a verbal pledge and a handshake. The key factor is that the participants know they will be dealing with each other again and again. Therefore, any attempt to exploit the situation will simply not pay.* (Axelrod 1984, 177–178)

Axelrod also not only attached great importance to the evolution of cooperation but also its stability. To simplify, he addressed how to start and develop cooperation, as well as how to persist the mutual cooperation. In the conclusion to his book, Axelrod (1984) explained that the basis of cooperation is not trust but the durability of the relationship. Particularly, in the long run, the conditions of building a stable mutual cooperation pattern are more important than whether the parties trust each other or not.

How cooperation relates to interactions between foundations and grassroots SOs in China

Promoting cooperation between foundations and grassroots SOs in China is not just a matter of lecturing two institutions on what they can gain from mutual cooperation as opposed to mutual defection. It is also a way to clarify their characteristics and roles in their interrelationship so that mutual cooperation can evolve and be maintained in the future.

Below I paraphrase Axelrod's (2000) three principal theoretical questions regarding the evolutionary process of cooperation:

1. Under what circumstance can cooperation start and be sustained among foundations or grassroots SOs?
2. What best practices are currently used and can be suggested to foundations or grassroots SOs under the given circumstances or the current noncooperative situation?

3. What advice can be offered to reformers or practitioners who want to change interactions to promote the emergence of cooperation?

Foundations and grassroots SOs are defined as organizations that pursue public interests. Their definitions, therefore, do not differentiate them (Tao and Liu 2014, 12), because both are conceptually part of the same civil society sector (Shieh 2017, 1787) with the pursuit of welfare undertakings. Thus, in my study, I regard them as two similar institutions. Accordingly, foundations play an important role in the social funding and public sectors, and my research focuses on how they make full use of their social characteristics and how they cooperate with grassroots SOs.

Once cooperative behavior is initiated, the question is, how can it be sustained in the future? To enhance opportunities for cooperation, foundations and grassroots SOs must interact with each other more frequently. If foundations are built so that they do not cooperate with grassroots SOs, how can cooperation ever emerge? Shieh (2017) listed various reasons (as mentioned in the literature review section) why the two have such difficulty cooperating in terms of trust and foundations' missions and roles. In this regard, consideration of the prisoner's dilemma strategy would be highly useful. The dilemma is that foundations and grassroots SOs blame each other for the lack of cooperation; that is, foundations claim they cannot find grassroots SOs capable enough to receive, whereas grassroots SOs claim that foundations prefer to carry out projects by themselves rather than fund grassroots SOs (Shieh 2017, 1787).

When Chinese foundations are asked why they prefer to operate projects themselves instead of funding others and do not cooperate with grassroots SOs, the foundations note that SOs lack clear missions. Whether Chinese foundations have a clear short-term goal and long-term mission also needs to be considered to understand their cooperation strategy.

Currently, one of the biggest problems between foundations and grassroots SOs is the matter of trust, above all, the trust of the foundations for grassroots SOs, which many scholars have noted. For example, in Shieh's (2017, 1800–1803) comments on a questionnaire he conducted, he noted that, when asked why there are so few grant-making foundations in China, most foundations' interviewees referred to trust as the major barrier.

An encouraging finding is Axelrod's 2000 study is that the evolution of cooperation can be speeded up via the foresight of players. Without consideration of the future, it becomes difficult to maintain and sustain cooperation. From the perspective of Chinese foundations, grassroots SOs are too new, have relatively less experience, and thus are weak. Whether Chinese foundations have enough time and patience to wait for grassroots SOs to mature is very important. Perhaps if they come to understand this process, they can use their foresight to promote cooperation, or even speed up the process.

Cooperation is needed for Chinese foundations to move to a new level of cooperating with other organizations from unnecessary connection to partnerships that achieve mutual goals. Based on a theoretical game perspective and analysis of the evolution of the cooperation theory, I explore the following four issues in this dissertation.

1. First, I analyze the current relationship between Chinese foundations and grassroots SOs. Notwithstanding the rapid rise of foundations and grassroots SOs in China, rarely do they cooperate, particularly from the 1980s to the late 2000s, regarding their different developmental pathways (Shieh 2017); no trust is given to grassroots SOs (Shieh 2017; Feng 2014; Chan and Lai 2018); and foundations follow a "closed ways" means of distributing funds (Xu 2010). However, the Wenchuan earthquake in 2008 became an important turning point toward cooperation among SOs in China, which led to a period of mutual trust, resource interdependency, common goals and institutionalization, and a flexible working mechanism (Yang 2015). At the same time, because most foundations are still founded and operated with the backing of the government, cooperation with and funding to grassroots SOs are still limited.

2. Second, I look at the problems that exist between Chinese foundations and grassroots SOs. On the one hand, the early foundations operated under the closed connection model with government agencies and public institutions (shi ye dan wei, 事业单位) within the official system (Shieh 2017). On the other hand, foundations have no trust in grassroots SOs and believe they cannot find organizations capable enough to receive support or to strategize. At times, foundations have not even provided opportunities for implementation of tit for tat strategies, nor applied the principle of reciprocity to their advantage. Once foundations find or hear about problems with grassroots SOs, they immediately cease cooperation or never again trust SOs. The studies of Shieh (2017) and Chan and Lai (2018) concluded that there was a strong statist philanthropic culture in Chinese foundations because of the dominance of the government-organized mechanism before 2004. However, Chan also pointed that the Chinese foundation regime has already changed from statist philanthropy to a corporatist model because of more emergence of NPFFs and the relationship between foun-

dations and the state after 2004, both of whom are working on social welfare and education.

3. Third, congeniality, retaliation, forgiveness, clarity are four factors that make tit for tat successful. It is noteworthy that the Wenchuan earthquake in 2008 caused conditions to explore and create cooperation, subsequently through the NGO Cooperation Forum for 512 Post-Disaster Reconstruction on May 21, 2009, organized by the Narada Foundation to discuss the mutual cooperation. Afterward, one important initiative was the establishment of the China Foundation Forum (CFF), which brought together and enhanced cooperation between foundations and grassroots SOs. At the same time, practitioners such as Yongguang Xu, Jiangang Zhu, and Xiaogang Liu encouraged cooperation. Although only a small number of Chinese foundations provided funds to grassroots SOs at the time, cooperative behavior was in progress, which provided an opportunity to see whether foundations and grassroots SOs could work together based on the principle of reciprocity.

4. Fourth, concerning the cooperation theory, a question arises about how cooperation can be maintained and sustained because stability is very important in the long run. Illuminating the "shadow of the future" (as expressed in Axelrod 1984, 182) becomes necessary because mutual cooperation will be stable if two players think the future is as important as the present. Making interactions more durable and frequent are two ways to do so. Effective payoff can be altered to ensure that both players perform good works in society. Teaching people to care about each other promotes cooperation and altruism among different people and organizations. Teaching the principle of reciprocity helps to control the whole sector by punishing those who are exploitive so that all parties are rewarded. The ability to recognize past interactions and their relevant features is necessary to encourage and sustain cooperation. By recognizing capable and qualified SOs, foundations can cooperate with them. Those skills can be offered to policymakers and practitioners who will then encourage interactions between foundations and grassroots SOs to aid in the emergence of the new cooperation, as well as to sustain current cooperation.

In light of the cooperation theory, on the one hand, foundations and grassroots SOs can choose the proper cooperative strategy to increase influence in the future; on the other hand, both sides need to be aware of the potential risks. Sound recommendations need to be made about appropriate approaches to intervention and effective risk management during the process of cooperation. As Axelrod (1984) wrote, "The core of the problem of how to achieve rewards from cooperation is that trial and error in learning is slow and painful" (191). It involves the comprehensive analysis of the current situation, as well as the reason entities, acts as they do. The study of the implications of the cooperation theory allows further exploration of the conditions of cooperation, as well as its future stability.

By pursuing the most effective and collective reward, both foundations and grassroots SOs can anticipate long-term cooperation. The biggest challenge for grassroots SOs, especially small grassroots SOs, is the shortage of funding. Because they did not have fundraising qualifications before the Charity Law went into effect in 2016, grassroots SOs had difficulty obtaining donations from the public. Take the statistics of the China Charity Information Donor Center in 2011, for example, only one percent of the charity donations went to grassroots SOs and the rest went to the government or GONGOs (Deng 2013, 28). On the other hand, foundations are functional organizations meant to raise funds from the public and the government, while they lack the professional staff to implement the projects.

3.5.2 Resource interdependence theory

This section covers the resource interdependence of Chinese foundations and grassroots SOs within a resource dependence theory framework, predominantly based on a book by Jeffrey Pfeffer and Gerald R. Salancik (2003), which is the seminal work in this field of research. First, I discuss the resource interdependence of Chinese foundations and grassroots SOs and analyze how resource interdependence theory relates to my study about interactions between foundations and grassroots SOs in China.

The resource dependence theory originated in the 1970s and was central to Pfeffer and Salancik's 2003 book. Starting with the question of how organizations survive and manage themselves, the authors were concerned with three main themes: first, the environment or social context is very important for an organization's survival, regardless of whether the organization owns the resources or the resources are controlled by other organizations; second, problems arising could be solved through resource interdependencies when the organization is obviously affected and constrained by the environment; and third, social power is crucial to the organization's dependencies and interdependencies.

Pfeffer and Salancik (2003) saw the resource dependence theory as being characterized by networks of independencies and the social environment. Concerning the scope of resource dependence theory, they analyzed how the social environment affects organizations and how organizations manage to survive, that is, their ability to acquire and maintain resources. They proposed in the book that interdependence exists in social systems and organizational interactions whenever an organization does not control all the conditions and necessary resources to achieve its goal (40). Besides, the authors chose social service agencies to illustrate that those SOs are regulatory bodies with the function of possessing and controlling certain resources that other organizations need, which creates the chances for interactions.

Resource dependence theory has been widely used to analyze the development of SOs, typically regarding collaboration and non-collaboration between the state and SOs. For example, Wang and Yao (2016) studied the government-NGO relationship empirically in China; Xu (2010) explained raising and distributing funds by Chinese foundations, based on resource dependence theory from an open-system perspective; and Lefroy and Tsarenko (2014) explained the relationship between dependence and alliance for NPOs, grounded in resource dependence theory. Scholars generally agree that resource dependence theory is well-documented with empirical evidence and theoretical research, as well as being highly compatible and applicable in the study of SOs (Saidel 1991; Xu 2010; Wang and Yao 2016).

Additionally, during Xu's (2008) analysis of the relationship between the government and SOs in China, she concluded that Chinese foundations are much more dependent on the government than the other way around, thus their powers are unequal. Accordingly, unsymmetrical dependence is the pattern manifested in the relationship between foundations and the government in China. Some scholars have argued that the degree of an organization's dependency is determined by its importance, concentration, and alternatives for resources (Pfeffer and Salancik 2003; Froelich 1999). In terms of resources between foundations and grassroots SOs in China, foundations are an important funding resource for grassroots SOs, while most Chinese foundations operate their own projects. This situation makes SOs more dependent on foundations. Take the Yunnan Youth Development Foundation as an example. It operates projects through subdivisions of the Communist Youth League. Those kinds of foundations do not need resources from grassroots SOs.

Resource interdependence is curial to organizations because they can achieve desired outcomes through the use of the available resources (Pfeffer and Salancik 2003, 41). During the process of acquiring and maintaining resources, problems of uncertainty, or unpredictability arise for organizations due to a lack of coordination among them. Pfeffer and Salancik suggested in the book that the evaluation of interdependence among organizations depends on the importance and amount of the resources as well as the owner of resources power to control the resources. They also emphasized that increasing behavioral interdependence among organizations can solve the problem of uncertainty through mutual control of each other (Pfeffer and Salancik 2003, 43).

The concept of resource interdependence is useful in describing the survival and management of an organization, as well as how to increase specialization and division among organizations. Pfeffer and Salancik (2003) noted that it is important to organize and coordinate social service organizations, such as foundations and grassroots SOs, in a given environment to avoid competition for funding resources and excessive overlapping of activities (180). As concerns professionalism, the authors also proposed that interdependence between foundations and grassroots SOs increases along with the increase of specialization and division of labor among organizations (43). Under the conditions of limited staff and funding, foundations are expected to achieve their goals through exchange with grassroots SOs. The acquisition and maintenance of critical resources require an organization to interact with individuals or groups that control and provide resources (Froelich 1999, 247).

Accordingly, this theory is applied in my research to explain the relationship between foundations and grassroots SOs. Neither foundations nor grassroots SOs are self-sufficient but rely on their environment and others. They must rely on a variety of activities and obtain resources from others to achieve their missions. By applying resource interdependence theory to the relations between foundations and grassroots SOs, foundations could achieve their missions through making grants to others within restricted purposes and priorities, while grassroots SOs could obtain financial resources for survival, to achieve their goals, and, in return, complete the required and supporting programs.

By understanding resource interdependence, it is possible to find out how foundations and grassroots SOs interact with each other. Their resources are normally controlled by other organizations; therefore, interactions between organizations and the social environment can be considered as the interactions between foundations and grassroots SOs. Various resources are the common connection between them, which helps them accomplish their individual goals.

What would foundations get in return if they were to decrease their operation costs and allocate the funds saved to grassroots SOs? And what would social organizations offer in exchange if they were to receive funding from foundations? Resource interdependence between foundations and grassroots SOs was explained clearly by Froelich (1999). She noted that some experienced foundations, such as the Ford Foundation and Carnegie Foundation, on the one hand, achieve their own missions and extend their influence when they select and support grassroots SOs through a grant-making approach under certain requirements and program priorities. She wrote that, on the other hand, they can also exert greater influence on SOs through matching funds cosponsorships. She also noted that simultaneously, the grantee organizations receive the funding which is the scarcest resource, a typical phenomenon among Chinese grassroots SOs (Froelich 1999, 253).

Therefore, the professionalization of grassroots SOs can be reinforced during this process through opportunities of fundraising, exchange, training, and project implementation, which in turn can solve major problems that Chinese grassroots SOs face, such as the stigma of marginalization, shortage of resources, incapacity, and unprofessionalism (Shieh 2017). Both foundations and grassroots SOs grow in pace with each other accordingly.

Of course, funding is not the only resource that grassroots SOs require from foundations. Foundations also provide platforms for information, capacity building, and organizational development in cooperation with grassroots SOs. At the same time, foundations can help grassroots SOs achieve their organizational and social objectives, which is important for their financial stability and competitive appeal. In return, the recipients adapt to the foundations' quality standards through competitive proposals based on the requirement from foundations, and in this way helps them to achieve their goals, keep up their good reputation, and extend their influence.

Regarding the competitive relationship in interdependence, Shieh (2017) viewed the situation between foundations and grassroots SOs as paradoxical; that is, they are similar but share no common vision. In past decades, both foundations and grassroots SOs received funding from overseas organizations, which played an important role in Chinese SOs' survival and development. It also happened that overseas funding went to government-based foundations because it was much easier to cooperate with them, while it was much riskier to work with grassroots SOs. A reliance of Chinese SOs on foreign funds was described by scholars (Shieh 2017; Spires, Tao, and Chan 2014), until the introduction of several laws, including the Charity Law in 2016 and the Law of the People's Republic of

China on the Administration of Activities of Overseas Non-Governmental Organizations within the Territory of China in 2017. As overseas financial funding was decreasing, domestic funding was becoming more important for grassroots SOs in China. Those grassroots SOs' dependence became more obvious and urgent on the domestic funding from foundations. Organizations will look to enhance their abilities through collaboration rather than running away (Lefroy and Tsarenko 2014).

3.5.3 Discussion

This chapter contributes to explain the interactions between foundations and grassroots SOs, through a combination of two theories, cooperation theory and resource interdependence. Their interactions are considered very important to the development of foundations and the survival of grassroots SOs. Although this topic is often discussed in practice, there is still a large academic gap in the existing literature on the development of grant-making foundations in China. Thus, to cooperate, not to cooperate and how to cooperate between the two, as well as their cooperation centered on resource dependence will be explored in the following chapters.

4 The overall development and characteristics of chinese philanthropic foundations

To understand the influences on foundations' interactions with grassroots SOs, and using previous literature as a guide, I first explored the overall historical development of Chinese foundations and their different characteristics at different stages. This section, therefore, begins with an overview of the development of Chinese foundations from 1949 to 2007, which shows how foundations emerged and then developed in China. Then I examine Chinese foundations tendencies from 2008 to 2017 and point out the corresponding characteristics exhibited in the different periods.

4.1 An overview of previous research

Here, the overarching question is, what stages have Chinese philanthropic foundations experienced since the founding of the People's Republic of China (PRC)? Scholars have focused on studies of philanthropic foundations in China since their appearance in the 1980s (Ma et al. 2017), with only a few references to them before that time, likely due to a lack of space for them under the political and economic context in China.

Both Estes (1998) and Yang (2010) concluded that the development of Chinese foundations occurred in two movements; they also analyzed the foundations' funding resources. The first movement arose from the government's establishment of the China Children and Teenagers' Fund (CCTF) in 1981 and the China Soong Ching Ling Foundation (SCLF) in 1982. Estes (1998) also pointed out that neither foundation was financed by endowment funds but by private, government, and international NGOs. Estes (1998) and Yang (2010) noted that the second movement began in 1988 during the second year of the Regulations on the Administration of Foundations (RMF) when most Chinese foundations originated as social associations and thus could be registered as charitable foundations. Foundations during this period ranged from small to large and had mixed funding sources (Estes 1998, 170–173). The foundations' changes kept pace with the related regulations and laws.

Along with the similar arguments of Xu (2010) and Shieh (2017), I now introduce two pathways to the emergence of foundations, as well as their developmental characteristics, one occurring from 1979 to 2003, the other from 2004 to 2007.

Two pathways to the emergence of foundations in China, as proposed by Xu (2010) and Shieh (2017): At the appearance of Chinese foundations in the 1980s, their main goal was to accumulate money from the public and receive funds from foreign organizations. In their studies, Xu (2010, 99-108) and Shieh (2017, 1972-1804) proposed that foundations in China followed two developmental pathways.

Here are the two pathways, as proposed by Xu (2010):

The first pathway for the emergence of the foundation: under government push

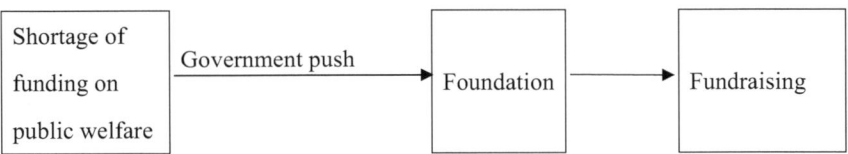

Source: Xu (2010,103); adapted by the author.

In the above pathway, Xu offers two reasons for the Chinese government's urgent promotion of foundations, that is, to meet the needs of certain social groups and to solve social problems. More specifically, as a result of the government's constraints on access to social charitable resources and lack of funding, the government needed to (1) raise funds through foundations and (2) accept financial resources, including domestic and overseas funding at a time when many international organizations expressed their willingness to support China.

The second pathway for the emergence of foundations: market endogenous

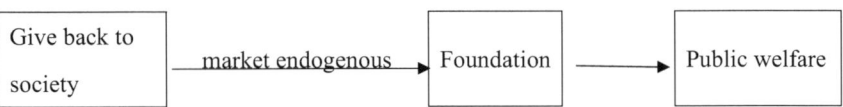

Source: Xu (2010, 108); adapted by the author.

Concerning the second pathway, the appearance of NPFFs occurred after the enactment of RMF-2004. It was intended that foundations play a vital role in the progress of society by providing essential funds and abundant resources for social interests, as well as make great contributions to society over time (Hammack and Anheier 2010). By the late 2000s in China, there was an increasing acceptance of philanthropic foundations and the development of SOs, as the government realized its limited capacity regarding the economy and social services.

Likewise, Chan (2018) suggested two foundation regimes in China before and after "the 2004 landmark reform in the regulation of foundations" (1). In his study, he referred to the first stage as the "statist model," in which, before 2004, most foundations were established by government agencies and served them as executive helpers; the second stage was referred to as the "corporatist model," because most Chinese foundations were expected to supplement the government's provisions. Additionally, due to the Wenchuan earthquake, 2008 is regarded as the turning point for activating cooperation between foundations and grassroots SOs. Therefore, it is important to explore changes in the development and characteristics of Chinese foundations from 2008 to 2017 as they relate to mutual cooperation.

Figure 4-1: Numbers and growth rate of Chinese foundations from 1979 to 2007

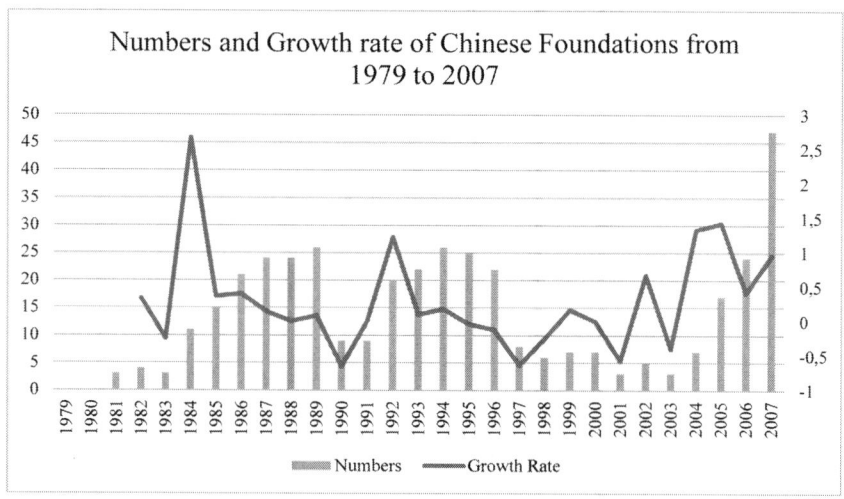

Source: Xu (2010, 48) adapted by the author.

Figure 4-1 shows the ups and downs of the development of Chinese foundations from 1979 to 2007. One might ask why the foundations emerged in China after 1979 and what factors contributed to their ups and downs during this period. According to the historical development of foundations, I discuss the two main stages as being before and after RMF-2004, because the appearance of NPFFs in 2004 divided Chinese foundations into PFFs and NPFFs.

I subdivided the first stage into two periods, according to their different characteristics, gap (1949 to 1978), and the appearance of government-affiliated foundations (1979 to 2003).

The second stage is subdivided into two periods, the appearance of NPFFs in the early periods (2004-2007) and the rapid growth of NPFFs (2008-2017). Moreover, the first foundations that can be traced back and positioned as grant-making foundations were established in 2007 and 2008, namely the Narada Foundation and SEE Foundation. Additionally, due to the Wenchuan earthquake, 2008 is regarded as the turning point for activating cooperation between foundations and grassroots SOs. Therefore, it is important to explore changes in the development and characteristics of Chinese foundations from 2008 to 2017 as they relate to cooperation with grassroots SOs.

4.2 Two main stages of Chinese foundations from 1949 to 2017 and the analysis of different characteristics

4.2.1 Before the promulgation of RMF-2004

Before the promulgation of RMF-2004, the development of Chinese foundations had two completely different stages. The following will clarify the causes and trajectories of the foundation based on the two stages.

4.2.1.1 Period from the founding of PRC in 1949 until 1978: Gap

From 1949 to 1978, social welfare was still the responsibility of the government. Scholars think that, at that time, there was no role or space for foundations and grassroots SOs (Yang 2010, 57; Deng 2001, 36), let alone cooperation. Moreover, Xu (2010, 46) believed that long-term egalitarianism and lack of supplies led to the loss of an economic base for philanthropy. Also, another study showed that philanthropy was denied by labeling it as a tool of imperialist spies and using outdated feudal rules to win the public's support (Zhou 2014, 83).

4.2.1.2 From 1979 to 2003: Appearance of government-affiliated foundations

In the early period of 1978, due to China's reform and opening-up policy, the Chinese economy was still underdeveloped; for this reason, government agencies sought private financial resources to fill in the resource gap for public welfare. Initiated by government agencies, a few foundations were established to raise funds from the public and absorb financial resources from overseas Chinese and international organizations (Chan 2018, 3), as overseas organizations tended to donate funds and cooperate with SOs instead of the government. It is noteworthy that the China Children and Teenagers' Foundation (CCTF) is perceived as the first foundation to emerge in China. Specifically, it was founded by twenty-two government departments in 1981 as the first nonprofit philanthropic organization in China; these organizations are referred to as "governmental foundations" or "government-led foundations." The government's main goal was to raise funds from the public and then work on social services, such as poverty alleviation and development of education, from the perspective of and under the administration of related government agencies (Chan and Lai 2018, 3).

In May 1982, the China Soong Ching Ling Foundation (CSCLF) was founded, and in March 1984, the China Foundation for Disabled Persons (CFDP) was established. The mission of CSCLF is to promote friendly international relations and safeguard worldwide peace, to strengthen exchanges across the Taiwan Straits and advance reunification of China, and to show concern for the future of the nation and develop children's works. CFDP works on promoting humanity and love while serving disabled persons with the initial purpose of accepting overseas funding (Xu 2010, 101). Those three foundations were the prelude to China's development of foundations.

Thus, Chinese foundations began from a need for such government-based foundations. However, at that time, regulations for foundations did not exist and the foundations lacked experience, nor did the government have requirements for legal registration. Nevertheless, foundations were quickly established throughout the country to the public's great interest. However, the absence of legal and regulatory mechanisms led to chaos, with the most obvious chaos occurring in the southern coastal areas. Due to the rapid development of the economy under the reform and opening-up policy, Chinese people originally from those southern coastal areas but living overseas began to gain wealth and wanted to reward society or their hometown. Since then, various SOs called foundations have emerged in quick succession. A group of SOs called foundations have also spread across many rural areas and, in the process, presented a range of financial and management risks (Yang 2010, 56; Xu 2010, 47–48). The government gradually removed these foundations through a cleanup and reorganization based on subsequent laws and regulations.

A glance at the political environment and policies

In 1988, the Regulations for the Management of Foundations (hereafter 1988-RMF) was adopted at the 21st executive meeting of the State Council, which was the first time the legal nature and status of Chinese foundations were clarified in legislation. In 1989, the Regulations on Social Group Registration and Administration (hereafter 1989 Regulations) reaffirmed the legal nature and status of foundations, as well as the dual registration of foundations, as both foundations and social associations. Accordingly, foundations were defined as "social associations." Although they have functions similar to those of other social associations, the two forms are ambiguous. Based on the two preceding regulations, the government's registration of foundations is under triple supervision; that is, it is managed by supervising units, approved by the People's Bank of China, and administrated by civil affairs departments. In practice, foundations were treated as quasi-financial institutions or financial institutions by that time, which is why the People's Bank of China is responsible for approving registrations.

Yang (2010, 56–58) commented that the people who drafted those regulations and who established foundations did not understand the meaning of foundations internationally and had no idea of the difference between public fundraising organizations and foundations. Therefore, the common understanding of a foundation's function was to raise funds; however, from their inception, many foundations did not raise funds or conduct any activities (Xu 2010, 110).

In 1989, Chinese foundations entered a period of slow development. The relevant policies of the country were more cautious due to the political unrest that year. Also, the public had little concern and enthusiasm for foundations at that time; thus only a few foundations were established nationwide. Foundations were mainly initiated by the government or its affiliates and were not motivated by individuals and enterprises during this period. The existing foundations generally had a strong administrative function and a quasi-government management mechanism. They also were not robust in their fundraising efforts and the operation of their own projects.

During this period, foundations developed under a specific historical context with close ties to the government or quasi-government agencies. The first drop in the growth rate of Chinese foundations happened in 1990 and 1991, again, because of the political unrest in 1989. The second drop happened in 1995 when the Ministry of Agriculture and the People's Bank of China issued the Notice Concerning Strengthening Administration of Rural Cooperative Foundation to manage and approve the registration of foundations.

In 1998, the Regulations for Registration and Management of Social Organizations were promulgated and are still used; these regulations reclarified the roles and responsibilities of registration and administration offices and supervisory units, which also strengthened the dual administration management system. In 1999, the rural cooperative foundations established spontaneously from bottom-up were completely shut down by the government. Afterward, the total number of Chinese foundations did not change much until 2004 (Xu 2010, 11).

In short, from 1979 to 2003, foundations were restricted and constrained gradually while developing steadily and growing year by year. On the one hand, the appearance of a series of policies began to regulate the registration and management of foundations. On the other hand, the increase in the threshold for initial funds and the restrictions imposed by the regulatory authorities slowed the development of foundations (Yang 2010, 56; Xu 2010, 47–48; Kang et al. 2011, 25).

How did foundations operate during the period from 1979 to 2003?
Certainly, foundations grew out of the government during this period, which was helped foundations obtain legal status for public fundraising (Xu 2010, 101). Moreover, as described by Chan and Lai (2018):

> *Some government-funded foundations even solicited donations from individuals and corporations through administrative power. Under this circumstance, donations became an obligation "allotted" (tan pai) to these individuals and corporations. Besides, many foundations were also involved in commercial activities by directly operating for-profit companies, which obviously violated their nonprofit attribute. Although the ROF-1988 specified several provisions on these related issues, they were ignored by these foundations. The prevailing irregularities finally led to the Announcement of Tightening Regulation on Foundations released by The People's Bank of China*

(PBOC)3 in 1995, and the development of philanthropic foundations in China stagnated for several years since then. (3)

Likewise, the most distinct characteristics of those foundations were mostly initiated by the party and the government as well as their subordinate groups under the supervision of government agencies and institutes or state-owned enterprises. Even when foundations were still new to the public, they could gain support and raise funds from the public under the influence of this mechanism. They were similar or even the same as the three initial foundations, which made use of private resources to make up for the lack of public financial investments. At the beginning of China's reform and opening-up, this type of social resource mobilization was logical in light of the government's insufficient financial resources.

Since its inception in the 1980s, most Chinese foundations have been founded with a project-oriented or specific mission, such as the two best-known projects, Project Hope (Xi Wang Gong Cheng) and Water Cellar for Mothers (Mu Qin Shui Jiao). Project Hope was organized by CYDF and the Communist Youth League Central Committee in 1989 to provide public service for education in rural areas. Water Cellar for Mothers was jointly launched by the All-China Women's Federation (ACWF), the Beijing Municipal People's Government, and China Central Television (CCTV) in 2001 with the intention of resolving rural women and their families' difficulties finding drinking water in western China. Each of these examples is top-down, brand-created models that, to a large extent, have continued to influence Chinese philanthropy.

Concentrating on brand-building projects
Since the time of the previous examples, PFFs have made great progress using a top-down approach to create a series of nonprofit brands and to improve foundations' influence and impact. In addition to Project Hope for building schools (Xi Wang Gong Cheng) and Water Cellar for Mothers (Mu Qin Shui Jiao), numerous other well-known nonprofit brands have emerged nationwide, for example, Spring Bud Plan (Chun Lei Ji Hua) to help girls living in poor areas return to school; Happiness Project (Xing Fu Gong Cheng) to help poor mothers, Lifeline Express (Jian Kang Kuai Che) for medical care, Lovely Hearth Package (Ai Xin Bao Guo) for rural pupils. Building a foundation's brand was an important task by the 1980s and 1990s, which in turn generated certain social effects to raise more funds from the public (China foundation center 2014, 124).

Projects usually were given nice and meaningful names before and during their lifetime, in the hope of creating brands and stimulate favorable reactions. However, the point was not only to advertise a foundation and gain more popularity but also to influence future fundraising. From a certain point of view, whether a foundation survives is more important to others than to the foundation itself.

In two evaluation programs separately conducted by Tsinghua University and conducted by the National Research Center for Science & Technology for Development, more than half the recipients thought that the previously mentioned brand project, Happiness Project, was organized and supported by the government, rather than by financial resources from the public, which means that foundations are largely regarded as a subsector of government agencies.

> *A survey performed by Tsinghua University's evaluation group collected information from 410 participating poor mothers at 6 Project Happiness program sites. Of these, 17.3% were unclear about which organization provided the assistance. Among the 339 who responded that they knew, 45.1% believed that the assistance was provided by Project Happiness. 24.2% responded that it was provided by family planning departments. 14.5% responded that it was the village government. 16.2% responded that the assistance was provided by Guangmei Wang. Still less was known of the "China Population Welfare Foundation," the unit behind Project Happiness.*
>
> *Thus, the majority were unaware of the name of the project from which the assistance came, let alone the name and nature of the foundation. This embarrassing example of the Population Welfare Foundation's Project Happiness is by no means an isolated example. Project Hope, China's most influential program of this type, has faced the same problem. Results of an evaluation of Project Hope, conducted by the National Research Center for Science & Technology for Development in 1997, revealed that most of society was unaware of the names and nature of the Project Hope's organizers and implementers. 58.6% of the public believed Project Hope to be organized by government departments. Even among donors to the project, over 50% believed that Project Hope was organized by government departments. 51% of parents of children receiving assistance through the program did not know the organizers or nature of Project Hope. 36.8% of those parents believed that Project Hope was the name of a government education department. Only 12.1% of parents of recipient children knew that Project Hope was the work of a civil organization (Xu 2010, 172-173).*

Conversely, under the influence of the brand-building operating model, foundations have been concentrating on how to operate their own projects in their own way, which to some extent competes with grassroots SOs. In the late 1990s, scholars complained that China did not have a mature or "true" civil society because all social organizations, especially foundations, could not exist and implement projects independently under the current top-down, government-organized political system (Wakeman 1993; Shieh 2017, 1793).

Another distinct function of foundations during this period was to raise funds in various ways and then fill the government's gaps for providing public welfare and social services. Under a relatively relaxed political context and economic growth resulting from China's reform and opening-up policy in 1978, foundations blossomed in the 1980s.

The state and society were in desperate need of resources, which led to the boundaries between foundations and the state being blurred. Foundations' staff were filled by governmental officials, and even today management remains within the government's system or quasi-government agencies, the civil services, and public institutions. Some foundations are set up to accept a great number of foreign funds. The establishment of is China Disabled Persons Foundation is a case in point. Earlier studies showed that the original purpose was to raise foreign funds. "The purpose of the foundation was to raise funds from foreign countries and to obtain foreign aid. Although the foundation [China Disabled Persons Foundation] did not receive funding from the United States, Northwest Europe after its establishment, accepting overseas donations was the direct motivation of establishing one foundation by the government agency" (Xu 2010, 101). Despite this, the development of the foundation has been driven according to this path. However, this developmental path does not pay attention to where the funding goes but attaches great importance only to where the fund is.

In the following, I will draw upon different data to outline the development of Chinese foundations from 2008 to 2017.

4.2.2 After promulgation of RMF-2004: Appearance of NPFFs in the early periods

Before the promulgation of RMF-2004, only the government was allowed to initiate the establishment of foundations, and there were no private foundations. In 2004, RMF was adopted (and is still in use), which marked a new era for Chinese foundations compared with the previous regulation in 1988. After RMF was enacted in 2004, it provided an ideal space for private foundations and non-governmental-linked foundations to register, especially those funded and founded by corporations or individuals (Chan and Lai 2018, 12). Nearly all foundations established before 2004 were closely linked with the government or served as executive arms of government agencies, while the foundations founded after 2004 were more diverse (Chan and Lai 2018, 6). The most significant change for foundations in 2004 was the induction of nonpublic foundations as receptacles of private funds and those from elite philanthropies, for example, Ai You Foundation and One Foundation. The government's original purpose for establishing this dichotomous regulatory system was to encourage the development of NPFFs, particularly those established by corporations and wealthy individuals, which were expected to be a linkage to grassroots SOs, but that quickly turned out not to be the case.

The intention and promulgation of the 2004 regulations in a favorable political environment

The people who drafted Regulation 1988 did so without clarity concerning foundations; that is, it did not regulate many aspects of foundations' organizational form, nor its internal decision-making procedures, financial accounting systems, asset management, and social supervision, which resulted in foundations having no rules in many aspects of its specific operations (Kang et al. 2011, 026). Also, with government-dominant foundations reaching a bottleneck point and having limitations, Regulation 1988 was not able to meet the development and management needs of foundations due to the deepening economic reforms and opening-up policies of China, the gradual improvement of the market economic system and the reform of government Institutions after 1992 (Kang et al. 2011, 026). After many private enterprises and individuals who had accumulated wealth showed their interest in this sector, the government realized its potential to mobilize supplemental resources and promote the participation of social forces in social welfare. Under such circumstances, to encourage all sectors to supplement public welfare and undertakings, the central government made several years' worth of efforts to amend the foundation regulations based on China's practices and international experiences since 2000.

RMF-2004 was regarded as an accelerator to the rapid growth of Chinese foundations, especially NPFFs, after 2004. It emphasized protecting the legitimate rights and interests of foundations, donors, and beneficiaries, as well as tax benefits and financial documentations. Article 26 noted, "Foundations, their donors and beneficiaries enjoy tax benefits as stipulated by law and administrative regulations." As to the specific measures for tax reduction and exemption in Article 26, the relevant departments still study and formulate relevant regulations, which would create space for individuals and entrepreneurs to engage in philanthropy. Likewise, Ai You Foundation and Heungkong Charitable Foundation could not wait to be registered as the first NPFFs in Beijing at the local level in 2004 and the first nationwide nonpublic fundraising foundations in 2005. Surprisingly, it also happened that seventeen foundations were established in one day in Zhejiang province (*Development of Chinese Foundations: An Independent Research Report* 2011, 26–27). Nevertheless, the enactment of RMF-2004 stimulated the prosperity of NPFFs created by enterprises and individuals.

From 2004 to 2007, the total number of Chinese foundations rapidly increased from 7 to 47. Two factors explain this phenomenon. The first one is the rapid growth of the Chinese economy in the 2000s. This period was also regarded as the impetus to NPFFs, especially after the implementation of RMF-2004. The second factor was encouragement based on the political environment and the implementation of positive policies, like the first national conference on philanthropy and issued the Guidelines for the Development of Chinese Philanthropy (2006–2010) in 2005 and The Enterprise Income Tax Law in 2007.

New NPFFs operating similar to PFFs, and PFFs enjoying more advantages
One of the earliest recorded instances of collaboration between a Chinese foundation and grassroots SOs was a village-level poverty-relief project in which the Jiangxi provincial government contracted out services to SOs to implement the project (Xu 2009; Shieh 2017, 1791). However, it did not arouse the foundations' interest and was not sustainable in a top-down form. A look at the foundations that were founded from 2004 to 2007 shows that the regulation did not have the expected effect. Here I discuss four aspects related to the matter:

First, NPFFs did not play a role in making grants to grassroots SOs. As specified by RMF-2004:

> *Article 29: The amount of money spent annually by PFFs on the public benefit activities stipulated in their charter must not be less than 70% of the previous year's income; NPFFs' annual expenditure on the public benefit activities stipulated in their charter must not be less than 8% of the surplus from the previous year.*
> *A foundation may not allocate more than 10% of its total expenditure to cover staff wages and benefits and overheads.*

Why did RMF-2004 set a different but low administrative fee for foundations and an item of high expenditure on activities? Tao and Liu (2014, 114) explained that, based on the legislative intent, the 70 percent and 8 percent public welfare ratio was to ensure foundations' continuous expenditure to meet the public's expectations of their public welfare undertakings. It also avoided limiting capacity-building and long-term development of the foundation. Similarly, a low administrative fee meant that foundations are a funding agency for public welfare, instead of operating projects by themselves (Chan and Lai 2018, 3). Hence, these stipulations indicated that domestic foundations will be the key funding resource for grassroots SOs.

Second, dual administrative management requires a supervisory unit under government agencies or institutions. The Civil Society Administration of the Ministry of Civil Affairs of China is responsible for the registration of social groups or SOs, including foundations. However, before they can register, organizations must find a supervisory unit within a government department that is in charge of supervision and is accountable to its superior and the Ministry of Civil Affairs. In this way, any social organization, including foundations, are ultimately under the supervision of certain government agencies. This kind of supervision is usually very loose and even invisible, but the supervisory unit has the right to decide the fate of foundations at any time when needed.

Third, a study by Chan and Lai (2018) claimed, "Theoretically, nongovernmental foundations could apply for public fundraising status, but it turned out that only a handful of cases were successful as the authorities seemingly wanted to protect the major governmental foundations in the fundraising market" (4). Both the second and third points show that PFFs are still enjoying more advantages in charitable fundraising and supervision of the government.

Fourth, what do those early-established NPFFs mainly work for? The Heung Kong Charitable Foundation's website noted,

> *In past years the Heung Kong Group contributed more than 1 billion RMB to various public welfare causes, such as education, poverty alleviation, and rescue and disaster relief. As a private enterprise, it has fulfilled its solemn commitment of "giving back to society through business excellence."*[10]

At the Ai You Foundation's website, we also find,

> *Ai You Foundation, with its inception in 2004, is the first private foundation registered in China. Initiated, managed and operated by entrepreneurs,*

---

10 From Heung Kong Charitable Foundation's website, http://www.hkf.org.cn/en, accessed August 12, 2019, adapted by the author.

it delivers programs nationwide. After over a decade of exploration and development, it is now engaged in three charity areas, including child health care, child welfare and venture philanthropy.[11]

Except for venture philanthropy starting in 2014, other working areas, such as education, poverty alleviation, rescue and disaster relief, child health care, and child welfare, are still the traditional fields, similar to those of PFFs. Those foundations are not established for making grants to grassroots SOs, and their working areas are similar to those of PFFs. The traditional charitable working areas are still the choice of NPFFs under the great influence of public fundraising foundations and strict management of the government. In other words, the appearance of NPFFs did not bring foundation and grassroots SOs together.

Notably, PFFs enjoy great advantages in charitable fundraising. In summary, as pointed out clearly in one study (Kang et al. 2011, 28), when comparing the power of the state and the power of society in China, the state is in a dominant position; hence, the government's attitudes and behaviors play a decisive role in changes in the numbers of Chinese foundations.

4.3 Development of Chinese foundations from 2008 to 2017: Transition and new tendency

The year 2008 is called the "starting year of charity" (Deng 2013) due to the stimulation of the Wenchuan earthquake. Some influential non-governmental foundations subsequently emerged during this period, such as the Lao Niu Foundation in 2004 (family foundation), the Narada Foundation and the You Cheng Foundation in 2007 (corporate foundation), the One Foundation (OF) in 2010, and so on. Those foundations started to actively and frequently interact with grassroots SOs. It was a turning point for interactions between foundations and grassroots SOs. More detailed explanations of the interactions are provided in section 5.

This section presents an overview of the growth pattern, funding scale, resources, and fields of working of foundations by way of statistical analysis to demonstrate their developmental characteristics from 2008 to 2017. Additionally, to better explain the interactions between foundations and grassroots SOs, PFFs and NPFFs are analyzed separately due to their differ-

---

11   From Ai You Foundation's website, http://www.ayfoundation.org/en/who-we-ar
    e, accessed August 12, 2019, adapted by the author.

ent pathways and views on cooperating with grassroots SOs. The basic approach was to gather the data and resources at the most convincing level, mainly from books and a series of reports from the *Annual Report on China's Foundation Development, Annual Report on China's Philanthropy Development* and the *Development of Chinese Foundations: An Independent Research Report*, as well as the *Statistical Communiqué* issued by the Ministry of Civil Affairs of the People's Republic of China. There is also information from individual studies, which are remarked on separately. The major findings in this section can be adapted to further explain the modest cooperation between foundations and grassroots SOs from 2008 to 2017.

More specifically, the data in this section are mainly from the following three reports: Statistical Communiqué issued by the Ministry of Civil Affairs of the People's Republic of China (*min jian zu zhi li nian tong ji shu ju*), *Development of Chinese Foundations: An Independent Research Report* (for the years 2011, 2012, 2013, 2014, 2015, 2017), *Annual Report on China's Philanthropy Development* (for the years 2011, 2012, 2013, 2017, 2018, 2019) and *Blue Book of Foundation: Annual Report on China's Foundation Development* (for the years 2012, 2013, 2014, 2016). Regarding the different descriptions among the different reports and studies, the available data from the Statistical Communiqué issued by the Ministry of Civil Affairs of the People's Republic of China is given preference in this study.

Table 4-1: The number of categories of social organizations from 2008 to 2017

Year	Foundations	Private Non- Enterprise Units	Social associations	SOs
2008	1,586	182,000	230,000	414,000
2009	1,829	190,000	239,000	431,000
2010	2,143	198,000	245,000	445,000
2011	2,411	204,000	255,000	463,000
2012	2,794	225,000	271,000	499,000
2013	3,226	255,000	289,000	548,000
2014	4,175	292,000	310,000	606,000
2015	4746	329,000	329,000	663,000
2016	5,521	361,000	336,000	703,000
2017	6,307	400,000	355,000	762,000

Note: These data exclude overseas foundations and their representative offices in China.

As shown in the Statistical Communiqué of Social Service 2016, there were 702,000 SOs at the end of 2016,[12] among which were 5,559 foundations (including PFFs and NPFFs). In 2016, the total number of social fund donations was 78.67 billion RMB to all types of SOs, of which 62.55 billion RMB flowed to foundations, accounting for 80 percent of donations. From this ratio, we can conclude that most of the funding resources were still in the hands of foundations, especially compared with each social organization and each foundation.

However, the total number of foundations was comparatively small, which nevertheless turned out to be the key resource owners, especially for funding resources among the entire sector of SOs. In other words, a great number of grassroots SOs had access to very little funding resources, especially with the withdrawal of foreign funds after 2010.

4.3.1 The increasing number of Chinese foundations, especially NPFFs

Table 4-2: The number of PFFs and NPFFs from 2008 to 2017

Year	PFF	NPFF	Total
2008	943	643	1,586
2009	1,029	800	1,829
2010	1,078	1,065	2,143
2011	1,115	1,296	2,411
2012	1,228	1,566	2,794
2013	1,319	1,907	3,226
2014	1,582	2,593	4,175
2015	1,548	3,198	4,746
2016	1,730	3,791	5,521
2017	1,678	4,629	6,307

Note: The data from 2008 to 2014 were collected from the *Annual Report on China's Foundation Development* (2015–2016) (Research Group of China Foundation Development Report 2016, 006), while the data from 2015 to 2017 were collected from

---

12 The most complete and up-to-date information is for the year 2016 throughout the Statistical Communiqué issued by the Ministry of Civil Affairs of the People's Republic of China, *Minjian zuzhi linian tongji shuju (2016)*, http://www.mca.gov.c n/article/sj/tjgb/201708/20170815005382.shtml, accessed September 24, 2019.

the official website of the Ministry of Civil Affairs of China,[13] excluding the registered overseas foundations in China.

Figure 4-2: Growth of Chinese foundations 2008–2017

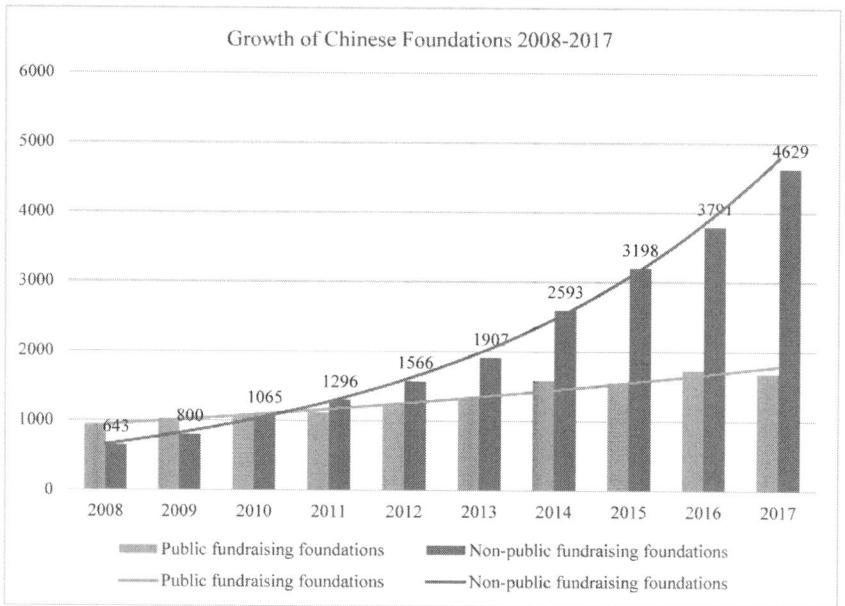

As shown in figure 4-2, the total number of Chinese foundations increased steadily from 1,586 to 6,307 in ten years. Among the 6,307 foundations by the end of 2017, there were 1,678 PFFs and 4,629 NPFFs. The number of NPPFFs increased from 40.54 percent by the end of 2008 to 73.39 percent of the total number by the end of 2017.

Notably, the number of NPFFs surpassed PFFs after 2011. Additionally, the number of NPFFs increased dramatically, while the number of PFFs did not change. After 2011, the number of NPFFs began to exceed the number of PFFs.

Conversely, the development of PFFs was stagnated, especially after 2014. This fact can be explained as follows. First, the political environment due to RMF-2004 encouraged the establishment of NPFFs instead of PFFs (*Development of Chinese Foundations: An Independent Research Report* 2011,

---

13 Found at http://www.mca.gov.cn/article/sj/tjgb/2017/201708021607.pdf, accessed September 24, 2019.

21), and gradually "non-administration" and "non-monopoly." If government officials could not hold the main positions in newly created foundations directly, government agencies would not risk approving the establishment of PFFs or being their supervising unit; registration, therefore, was becoming more difficult for PFFs. Second, the Chinese economy was growing quickly; hence more and more enterprisers were inspired to create private foundations.

The influences of new laws on Chinese foundations: Every change in policies and political circumstances affected the number of foundations. In 2016, the promulgation and implementation of the Charity Law of the People's Republic of China marked the entry of philanthropy into the rule of law in China. In the same year, the total number of national foundations increased from 928 to 5,799, the highest growth rate since the appearance of foundations in China. The Charity Law lessened the differences between PFFs and NPFFs, both of which could raise funds from the public if they were accredited as being charitable organizations by the Civil Affairs Department. Even NPFFs and SOs established before the Charity Law qualified for pretax deductions for public welfare donations. If they had been registered for two years and were accredited charitable organizations, they could apply for the right to raise public funds. That is to say, all SOs that were accredited by the Civil Affairs Department as charity organizations were able to raise funds from the public.

However, the newly born Charity Law was controversial because it gave the Civil Affairs Department more flexibility in regulating foundations and grassroots SOs, although the related text was vague. See, for example, this excerpt from Article 23:

> *Where the charitable organization fundraises from the public through the Internet, it shall release the fundraising information on the uniform charity information platform or the charity information platform designated by the civil affairs department of the State Council (Source:* Charity Law, 2016, adapted by the author).

According to this passage in Article 60, expenditures for all charitable organizations were limited: "The annual management expenses shall not exceed 10% of its total expenditure in the current year." However, some NPFFs found that the 10 percent limit was too low and did not cover the cost of employing professional staff or renting appropriate offices. This law meant that, besides serving as a supervisory unit and registration department, the Civil Affairs Department had gained stricter control. Only organizations that were evaluated by the Civil Affairs Department and defined as a certain level 3A or 4A could apply to become an accredited charity organization. Note that if a foundation made grants to sensitive grassroots SOs or projects, it might have difficulty gaining recognition from the government.

The General Provisions of the Civil Law of the PRC, which was established by the National People's Congress of the PRC in 2017, confirmed the legal position of "a non-profit legal person," which included but was not limited to public institutions, social groups, foundations, and social service organizations. Moreover, it showed that the Chinese government was gradually and systematically promoting its regulation of nonprofit entities at the legislative level.

4.3.2 Steady Growth of total assets of Chinese foundations

> *Until the end of 2013, the total amount of 3610 Chinese foundations is 101.7 billion RMB, which is the only ½ of the Bill & Melinda Foundation in the US and is also 1/40 of American Foundations.*
> (*Source:* China Foundation Center 2014, 14, adapted by the author).

According to the Annual Report on China's Philanthropy Development 2019 (Yang eds. 2019, 112), the total assets of 6,307 Chinese foundations were 156.3 billion RMB by the end of 2017, which was USD 21.95 billion.[14] When compared to the USD 51.85 billions of total assets of the Bill & Melinda Gates Foundation in the same year, we can see that the total assets of Chinese foundations were still only one-half the assets of the Gates Foundation in a single year; this is even though total assets have increased greatly over the past ten years. In other words, the total assets of all Chinese foundations are still low.

A recent study noted that PFFs' assets were greater than NPFFs' assets by the end of 2016.

> *Moreover, the average net asset of the PFFs (with 40.10 million RMB) is much higher than the NPFFs (with 25.9 million RMB). Specifically, more than half of the PFFs have a net asset of more than 10 million RMB, while more than 70% of the NPFFs have a net asset of less than 10 million RMB.*
> (Deng 2017, 053).

---

14 One US dollar was equal to 7.12 Chinese Yuan (Ren Min Bi, RMB) as of September 27, 2019.

Figure 4-3: Total assets of Chinese foundations from 2008 to 2017

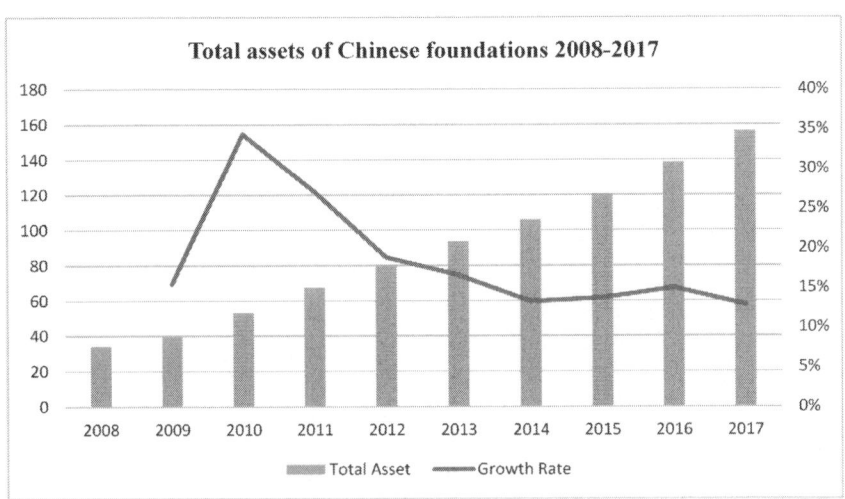

Source: Yang ed. (2018, 113; 2017, 110); adapted by the author.

Generally speaking, the total assets of Chinese foundations increased steadily from 2008 to 2017. By the end of 2017, the total assets of Chinese foundations were 156.3 billion RMB. The primary reason is that the number of foundations increased between 2008 and 2017, and the total assets of Chinese foundations increased accordingly.

Figure 4-4: Net assets of PFFs and NPFFs by the end of 2015

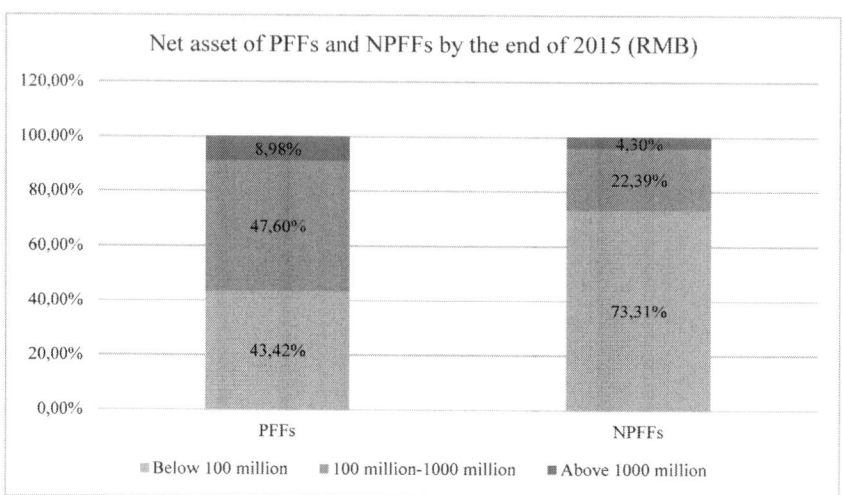

Source. (Yang ed. 2017, 55).

Note: These data were collected until December 31, 2015. A total of 3,779 foundations in China had disclosed fundraising qualification types and net assets.

Specifically, more than half of all PFFs had net assets of more than 100 million yuan. Of the NPFFs, more than 70 percent of the foundations had a net asset of fewer than 10 million yuan. Deng (2017, 053) suggested that one reason was likely related to the RMF-2004 requirements on original funds and the fundraising scale for different types of foundations. Article 2 of the RMF-2004 stated, "The original funds of national PFFs should be not less than 8 million RMB; the original funds of local PFFs should be not less than 4 million RMB; the original funds of NPFFs should be not less than 2 million RMB." The original funds of national PFFs were greater than those of local PFFs, which were greater than those of NPFFs. On the other hand, compared with NPFFs, PFFs were more likely to receive multiple incomes each year because they could raise funds from the public and also acquire funds from the government.

4.3.3 Continuous growth of total income of Chinese foundations

In recent years, the total income of the foundation has increased annually. A statistical study of 2014 and 2015 showed that

Compared with the total income in 2014, the total income of Chinese foundations has increased in 2015, but this was mainly due to the establishment of 685 new foundations in 2015. The increase in the total number of foundations led to the continuous growth of the foundations' total income. (Blue Book of Foundation: Annual Report on China's Foundation Development 2017, 58)

Figure 4-5:   Donations and growth rate of Chinese foundations from 2008 through 2017

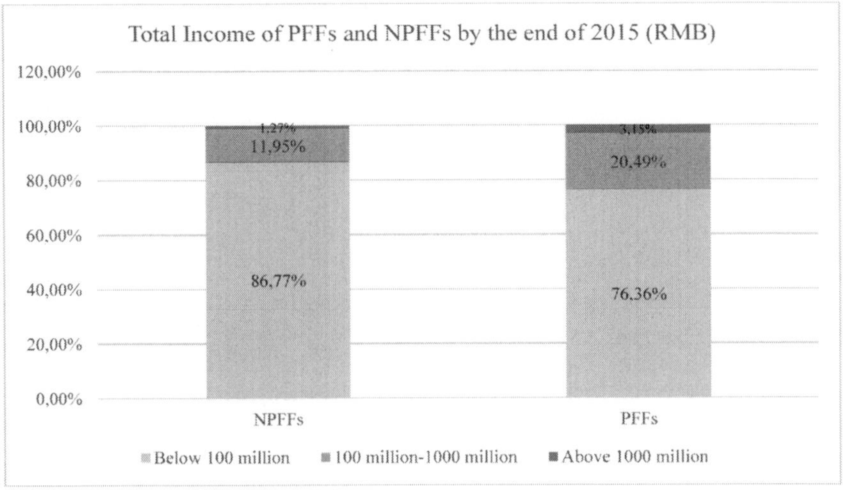

Source: Development of Chinese Foundations: An Independent Research Report 2018, 113; Development of Chinese Foundations: An Independent Research Report 2017, 110).

The preceding figure shows that overall income increased from 2008 through 2017, but with two slowdowns in 2009 and 2012. One possible explanation for the drop in 2009 is that growth in 2009 was normal, although with a slight slowdown, compared with the growth in 2008, which to the earthquake resulted in a dramatic increase in donations. The slowdown in 2012 was probably due to the Meimei Guo scandal in 2011, which decreased the public's donations to most nonprofits, but especially foundations (Ni and Zhan 2017, 731).

Table 4-3: Average income of PFFs and NPFFs in 2015

	Numbers of Foundations	Average Income (million RMB)
NPFFs	2,510	8.35
PFFs	1,269	19.8

Source. (Yang ed. 2017, 55).

Note: These data were collected until December 31, 2015. A total of 3,779 foundations in China disclosed fundraising qualification types and net assets.

By the end of 2015, the average income of PFFs, which was 19.8 million RMB, was much more than the average income of NPFFs, which was 8.35 million RMB, although the total number of NPFFs exceeded the number of PFFs.

Figure 4-6: Total income of PFFs and NPFFs by the end of 2015

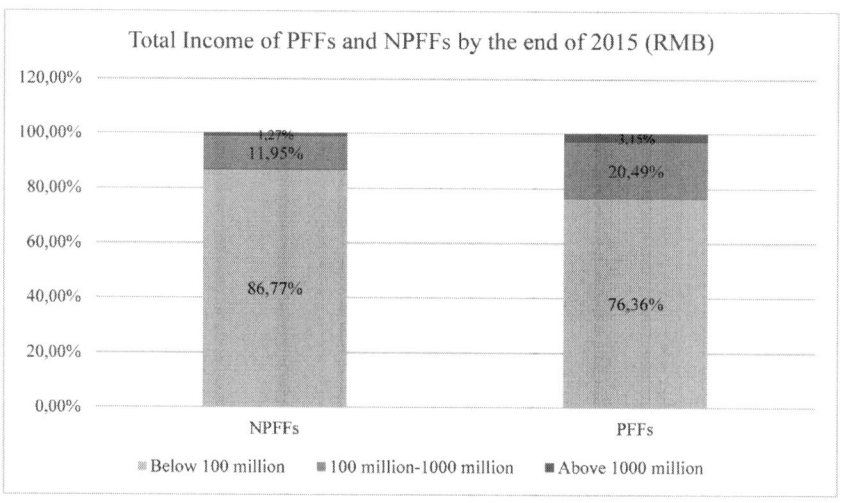

Source: (Deng & Tao 2017, 64).

Figure 4-6 shows that 86.77 percent of NPFFs had a total income of less than 10 million RMB, whereas PFFs had 76.36 percent; and 1.27 percent of NPFFs had a total income of more than 100 million, whereas PFFs had 3.55 percent. In brief, PFFs' overall income exceeded the income of NPFFs by the end of 2015. Given that the total number of NPFFs was much higher than that of PFFs by the end of 2015, the total number of NPFFs with less than 10 million RMB was much higher than PFFs at the same level.

Also, the total number of PFFs with more than 100 million RMB was higher than that of NPFFs. Specifically, PFFs had more than NPFFs in total and average income, even though the total number of PFFs was lower than that of NPFFs.

Figure 4-7: Percentage of foundations with different incomes by the end of 2015

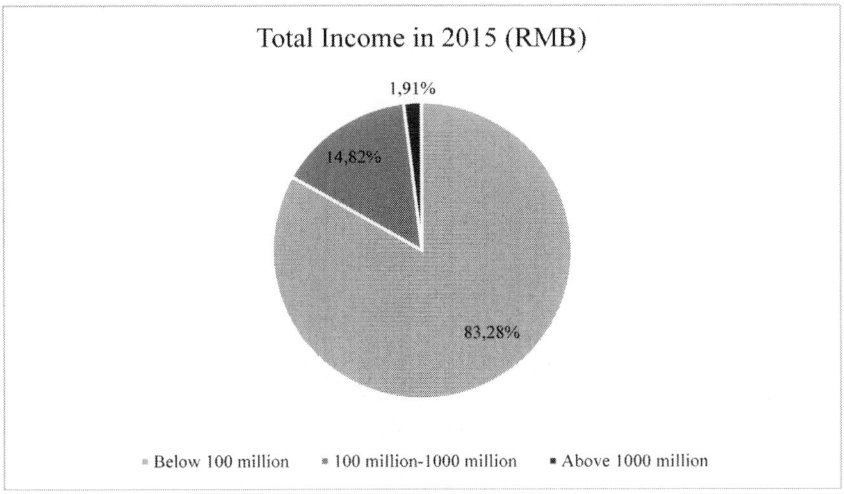

Total Income in 2015 (RMB)

1,91%

14,82%

83,28%

▪ Below 100 million   ▪ 100 million-1000 million   ▪ Above 1000 million

Source. (Yang ed. 2017, 54).

By the end of 2015, the vast majority of Chinese foundations had a relatively small total income of fewer than 10 million yuan, and only seventy-two foundations had total revenue of more than 100 million yuan in 2015, accounting for 1.91 percent of total income in 2015.

Table 4-4: Income source percentage of PFFs and NPFFs in 2015

	Income Source	Numbers	Percentage
NPFFs	Donations	2,520	71%
	Investments	2,520	10%
	Government subsidies	2,520	2%
	Others	2,520	17%
PFFs	Donation	1,269	58%
	Investments	1,269	11%
	Government subsidies	1,269	10%
	Others	1,269	21%

Source. (Yang ed.2017, 068).

Donations were the main source of income for both PFFs and NPFFs, accounting for 58 percent and 71 percent of their total income, respectively, by the end of 2015. However, PFFs received more funding from the government than NPFF.

One representative[15] from an influential nationwide PFF commented on why her foundation had been able to raise funds in recent years. First, she said that a large percentage of special donations were made for special-purpose projects (zhuan xiang zi jin, 专项资金). Second, the foundation was highly active and well-prepared during 99 Public Welfare Day,[16] when they raised funds from the public. They have been ranked in the top five organizations for money raised every year since 2016. Third, she said that the foundation still benefits from being a "national level PPF." Thus, the public and enterprisers are more inclined to donate to them, especially those companies that want to donate money to earn a reputation.

---

15 An interview with project officer of a government-background foundation, Foundation L, Beijing, 17 April, 2019.

16 99 Public Welfare Day is an annual public welfare activity that Tencent Charitable Foundation and hundreds of public welfare organizations call for the public to make online donations. It began in 2015, and was jointly launched by Tencent, celebrities, enterprises, and other social and marketing organizations.

4.3.4 Total expenditures of Chinese foundations: PFFs' expenditures are still greater than NPFFs'.

Figure 4-8: Total expenditures and growth rate from 2008 to 2017 (billion/year)

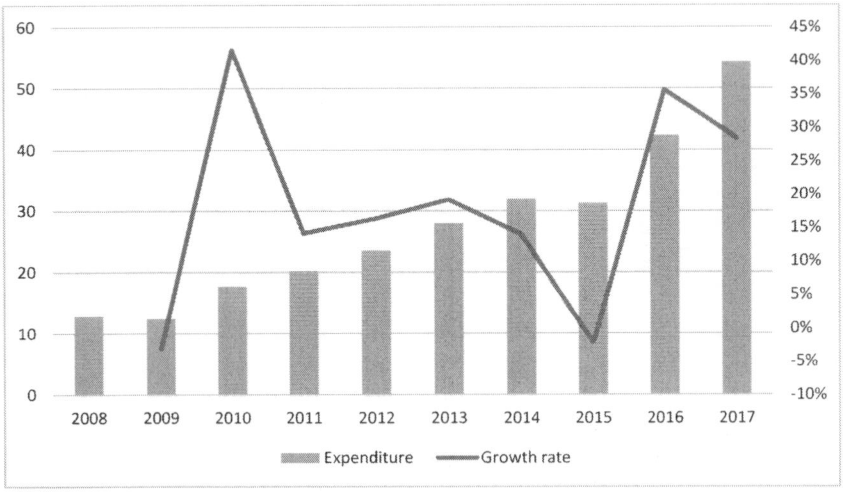

Source. (Yang ed. 2017, 111; Yang ed. 2018, 114).

Note: The expenditures for 2008–2011 are from the *Annual Report on China's Philanthropy Development* 2017 (Yang ed. 2017). The data for 2011–2017 are based on those for 2011–2016 from *Annual Report on China's Philanthropy Development* 2018 (Yang ed. 2018), the latest version published. There are some differences between the two annual reports, thus I adopted the latest version.

Interestingly, the differences between PFFs and NPFFs, regarding their total assets, expenditures, and income, are noteworthy, as they provide a keen understanding of the developmental trends and transformation of the two entities.

Table 4-5: Average expenditures of PFFs and NPFFs in 2015

	Numbers of foundations	Average expenditure (million RMB)
NPFFs	2510	4.5
PFFs	1269	15.4

Source. (Yang ed. 2017, 80).

Note: These data were collected until December 31, 2015. A total of 3,779 foundations in China had disclosed fundraising qualification types and net assets.

The average expenditures of PFFs (15.4 million RMB) were much higher than the average expenditures of NPFFs (4.5 million RMB) by the end of 2015, although the total number of NPFFs exceeded that of PFFs. Similar to income, foundations' expenditures were also likely related to the regulations of foundations. Article 29 of RMF-2004 stated, "The amount of money spent annually by PFFs on the public benefit activities stipulated in their charter must not be less than 70 percent of the previous year's income; NPFFs annual expenditure on the public benefit activities stipulated in their charter must not be less than 8 percent of the surplus from the previous year."

4.3.5 Uneven geographical distribution of Chinese foundations: East over West

Foundations are not equally distributed in China. There are a large number of foundations in the eastern region (such as the provinces of Guangdong, Jiangsu, Zhengjiang, and Shanghai) and a small number in the northwestern region (*Blue Book of Foundation: Annual Report on China's Foundation Development* 2019, 112). The top five places (Guangdong, Beijing, Jiangsu, Zhengjiang, and Shanghai) have 3,429 foundations, accounting for more than half of all Chinese foundations. Given that the number of foundations was influenced by policies and the political environment in the 1980s and 1990s, changes in the total number of Chinese foundations related positively to the economic situation of the times.

Figure 4-9: Number of Chinese foundations in different provinces on December 31, 2017

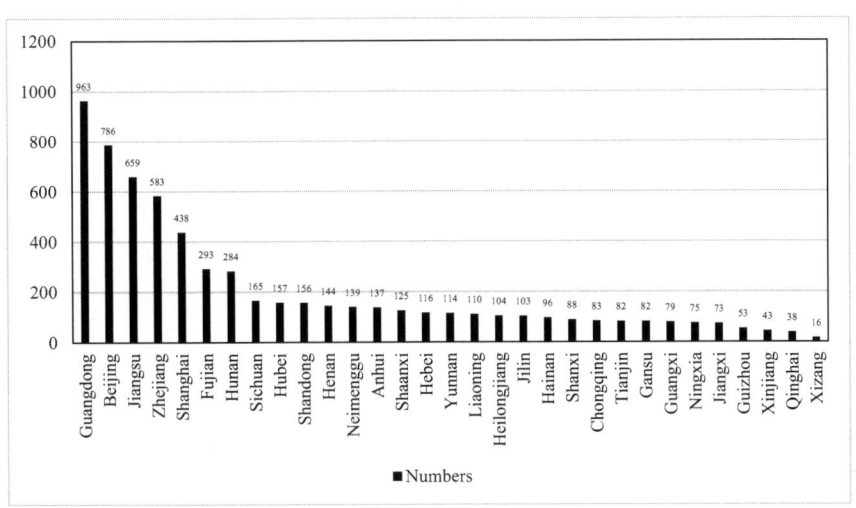

Source: Cheng and Han (2018, 109), adapted by the author.

4.4.6 Working areas of Chinese foundations: Much the same as the government's working priorities

Past studies (e.g., Chan and Lai 2018; Lai & Tao & Spires 2015) have concluded that Chinese foundations work mostly on projects related to improving education, alleviating poverty, enhancing medicine and health, and so on—that is, the traditional charitable activities—rather than development and social change. Nevertheless, here I focus on areas related to foundations' decisions on the number of funds they grant to grassroots SOs and the life cycle of those grants.

Implementing a public welfare project that is compassionate and familiar is the most effective way for foundations to raise funds in China (Xu 2010, 67). This is especially the case for education. For Chinese foundations, especially those that need to raise funds to carry out public welfare activities, focusing on education, especially in poor and remote areas, is one way they can easily gain extensive social support and public attention. Table 4-6 lists foundations' work areas, with education accounting for more than 50 percent of all foundation projects in China.

Table 4-6: Working area distribution of Chinese PFF and NPFF projects in 2014

Working area	PFF		NPFF		Total	
	No.	Percentage	No.	Percentage	No.	Percentage
Education	2141	37.77	4148	61.97	6289	50.87
Public welfare development	862	15.21	530	7.92	1392	11.26
Poverty alleviation & community development	419	7.39	393	5.87	812	6.57
Medical and health	460	8.12	341	5.09	801	6.48
Social services	259	4.57	290	4.33	549	4.44
Culture & art	289	5.10	251	3.75	540	4.37
Environmental Protection	217	3.83	106	1.58	323	2.61
Disaster relief	112	1.98	123	1.84	235	1.90
Scientific research	66	1.16	90	1.34	156	1.26
Sports	90	1.59	41	0.61	131	1.06
Volunteering	58	1.02	65	0.97	123	0.99
Policy advocacy	56	0.99	37	0.55	93	0.75
Law & civil right	49	0.86	5	0.07	54	0.44
others	590	10.41	274	4.09	864	6.99
Total	5668	100.00	6694	100.00	12362	100.00

Source. (Anonymous 2016, 067).

Table 4-6 shows that the top five fields of workings in Chinese foundations were education, public welfare development, poverty alleviation & community development, medicine and health, and social services. This remained the same for most donations 2017: education (27.4%), medicine and health (24.1%), poverty alleviation (21.2%), public welfare (7.56%), and social services (7.21%) (Ma, Liu & Jin 2017, 16). PFFs had a greater percentage on public welfare development, medicine and health, poverty alleviation & community development than NPFFs in 2014.

As mentioned earlier, most governmental foundations actually are created and serve as "subsidiaries of their affiliated government agencies and usually work to help fulfill the government's social welfare responsibilities" (Chan and Lai 2018, 11). The major activity of the Chinese foundation is still relief, particularly for poverty alleviation and meeting basic needs and, more rarely, protection (7%) and social change (2%).

At the international level, the philanthropic work areas are somewhat different. For example, in Germany, four working areas are prioritized: social services (58% of foundations), primary and secondary education (37%), arts and culture (36%), and higher education (32%). Other areas include environmental protection (14% of foundations), sports (11%), religion (8%), animal welfare (5%), and developmental cooperation (3%) (Anheier et al. 2018, 1644–1646). Some American foundations focus on humanistic and developmental activities and programs, such as global health, global development, ending extreme poverty, and health-related research and awareness, which are the focus of the Bill & Melinda Gates Foundation. Global medical and health issues, development of agricultural technology, theater, music, and other cultural fields are the Rockefeller Foundation's grant-making themes.

In addition to addressing primary areas of interest, foundations must function under the government's current management system, including its dual registration management system.

Corporate donors expect that their donations will be used on short-term projects that will give them credibility at low cost and that will help them promote corporate social responsibility and generate sound marketing. Donations to government-linked groups may be used as tax deductions, but not donations to non-governmental organizations.

According to *China Philanthropy Times*, the top ten NPFFs in 2018 were Tencent Philanthropic Foundation, Guangdong He Foundation, Tsinghua University Education Foundation, Beijing Jingdong Philanthropic Foundation, Ningxia Yanbao Philanthropic Foundation, Fanhai Philanthropic Foundation, Ai You Foundation, Laoniu Foundation, Zhejiang Mayun Philanthropic Foundation, and Heren Charity Foundation. One-third of these NPFFs are university foundations, which raise funds and operate projects but have no interactions with grassroots SOs.[17] Their main focus in on areas such as education, disaster relief, and poverty alleviation, while they focus less on health care, art, culture, public services, community development, and policy advocacy.

---

17 Found at http://www.gongyishibao.com/html/yaowen/13806.html, accessed November 2, 2019.

4.4 Discussion on the characteristics of Chinese foundations

Based on the data presented in this chapter, it can be seen that Chinese foundations are developing steadily over the past decades. Each period leaves a legacy for the period that follows it and influences and helps shape the characteristics of the later period. This section concludes the characteristics in different periods and sees how those characteristics affect the current foundations.

4.4.1 Characteristics of Chinese foundations from 1949 to 2007

It has happened for foundations since their appearance in China, which has resulted in a type of top-down mechanism that has not encouraged foundations to play a role in grantmaking and in supporting the third sector. Nor has cooperation between foundations and grassroots SOs been considered. This lack of development has created problems for foundations, and it has also affected the development of grassroots SOs, which in turn has affected the independence of the third sector.

On the other hand, the early, decade-long development of government-affiliated foundations produced a broad understanding of how foundations operate in China. One of the most apparent innovations of RMF-2004 was its distinction between PFFs and NPFFs, in which it was clear that NPFFs were expected to play more roles than PFFs in promoting the third sector. However, this fact along with the previous, divergent views on foundations produced considerable difficulty for NPFFs in terms of becoming grant-making foundations. Moreover, the government-affiliated PFFs still enjoyed more advantages in charitable funding and were still in charge of mobilizing most resources. Also, NPFFs and PFFs remained consistent in the short term, both in the operation of projects and in the choice of project areas.

Little interaction occurred between foundations and grassroots SOs from 2004 to 2007, even after the appearance of NPFFs, which had been promising for SOs regarding grantmaking. There was still no need for interactions between them due to the dominant operating approach of Chinese foundations. The appearance of NPFFs at this time did involve making grants to grassroots SOs, let alone the PFFs that raised funds from the public. The long-established operating approaches and the public donors' view of Chinese foundations made it difficult to change the use of foundations' funds in a short period.

4.4.2 Characteristics of Chinese foundations from 2008 to 2017

In China, foundations are still small, even with the sustained growth of assets, income, and expenditures due to an increase in the number of Chinese foundations. Based on that growth, the total number of NPFFs surpassed the number PFFs starting from 2011. The former is still growing, while the latter is stagnating. However, from a different perspective, the total assets, income, and expenditures of PFFs are more than those of NPFFs. The rapid growth of NPFFs after 2004 contributed much to the development of foundations.

However, under the strong influence of PFFs for many years and management under the government, NPFFs continued to work similarly to the way PFFs did; that is, within a government-organized philanthropic ecosystem, such as work areas, operating approaches, and so on. As one study noted, "This government-organized philanthropic ecosystem dominated China's philanthropy scene" (Shieh 2017, 1793). This was the case from the appearance of Chinese foundations in the 1980s until the appearance of NPFFs in 2004. Moreover, the previous thinking on foundations in China continued to strongly influence the development of all philanthropic foundations in various ways.

Whether it be PFFs, NPFFs, or family foundations, as mentioned earlier, education remains the priority working area, followed by other traditional charitable areas such as relief, poverty alleviation, children and women, and so on. Some sensitive areas and developmental fields still have difficulty attracting the attention of domestic foundations, areas such as labor, AIDs, and environmental protection. Xu (2010, 121) pointed out that whether supervisory units support foundations' work or not largely depends on the influences produced by foundations. If a foundation has a positive impact on a supervisory unit, the supervisory unit will support the foundation's work; if not, or if sensitive areas are involved, the unit will not support the foundation or intervene in any way. Similarly, under such circumstances, foundations' working areas are, positively related to their supervisory unit and civil affairs department. Xu (2010, 117-119) added that self-interest is the most influential factor affecting a supervisory unit's attitude toward a foundation. The basis behind this behavior is still to place the foundation in a position that is subordinate to the supervisory unit; this also applies to civil affairs departments and even finance bureaus. Chinese foundations' working areas are still influenced by top-down, government-influenced approaches, which is inconsistent with independence as the most important feature in the third sector.

From their inception, Chinese foundations did not directly or indirectly interact with grassroots SOs during their development due to government dominance. Moreover, after many years' experience, government-affiliated foundations formulated their own approaches to fundraising and their own operating model. Under such a government or quasi-government system, Chinese foundations excluded grassroots SOs in their operating mechanism. Although the promulgation of RMF-2004 encouraged the development of NPFFs, their growth in numbers did not change the thinking of how foundations spent their funds, that is, without dependence on the administrative systems. The original intention of RMF-2004 was to encourage the establishment of nonpublic foundations and through them make direct grants to grassroots SOs. Although this approach was one possibility from the viewpoint of policy, it was not a common practice. After years of development, it turns out that NPFFs used the same approach as PFFs. That is to say, changes in policy were not inevitability put to practice (Xu 2010, 174; Lai 2017, 65).

4.4.2.1 Political restrictions on foundations' registration and evaluation

Before 2004, when specific government agencies established PFFs, those agencies became the supervisory units for the PFFs they established. However, most government agencies were reluctant to take responsibility for supervising NPFFs, especially when their activities or fields of workings were different from those of the supervisory units. One influential scholar claimed, "Thirty years after the reform and opening up, Chinese people currently have a strong charitable motivation and a strong desire for self-organizing. But the dual registration management system has become an obstacle to this motivation and desire" (Zhu 2009).

It is a double-edged sword for government departments to become supervisory units for foundations: on the one hand, units would be considered irresponsible if they did not properly oversee the activities of foundations; on the other hand, too much oversight created an impression of interference. Also, most government officials do not fully understand the activities and roles of foundations. The Civil Affairs Department explored allowing foundations to register directly without a supervisory unit. In March 2013, the State Council promulgated the "Institutional Reform and Functional Transformation Plan," which explicitly proposed focusing on the development and prioritization of industry associations, chambers of commerce, science and technology, public welfare and charity, and urban and rural community service social organizations. Such organizations were qualified to apply for registration directly to civil affairs departments without the approval of a supervisory unit. However, shortly thereafter they were prevented from registering directly because of tightening policies, and foundations that had already registered without supervisory units were required to find one. It just so happened that one of the foundations I interviewed on March 29, 2019 (Foundation I) was not able to find a supervisory unit until mid-2019.

Also, government agencies use a grading system to evaluate foundations (e.g., the agencies look at internal governance, job performance, social impact, etc.), which further restricts their development. The higher a foundation's score, the higher its degree of transparency and the public's corresponding credibility. Transparency and credibility matter greatly when raising funds from domestic individuals and entrepreneurs. In 2008, the Foundation Evaluation Committee of the Civil Affairs Department issued the 2005–2006 Foundation Evaluation Level Results Announcement, which was the first evaluation of foundations in China.

4.4.2.2 Political Restrictions on foundations' tax and independence

After the promulgation of RMF-2004, it has reflected the need for NPFFs by that time under the socio-economic and political context and has positively promoted the development of foundations, especially the rapid growth of NPFFs. Related policies and regulations, however, have not improved accordingly. Similar to the first regulation in 1988, which occurred after the appearance of foundations in the early 1980s, in 2004, the challenges still related mainly to tax-related laws and issues around RMF-2004. Feng (2015, 146–147) mentioned that there was no comprehensive and integrated tax system in China and that the legislation was scattered and vague, which was not advantageous in terms of finding potential donors. Although foundations enjoy tax exemptions in principle, there are certain deficiencies in the stipulations for direct action. First, individuals must go through a very complicated and tedious, sometimes unpleasant, procedure to claim a tax deduction, which includes many administrative stamps and certificates showing that the funds' sources of his donation were legal. Also, foundations must apply each year for tax-deductible status or discuss the tax status of every donation (Feng 2015).

Second, RMF-2004 restrictes employment of a professional staff and thus the professionalization of foundations. for example, ten percent of the cost for salaries and administrative needs was not enough; hence, some foundations had to hire government officials on a part-time or temporary basis (gua zhi) and operate their projects through the local governments. In this way, foundations became more dependent on the government's officials and financial support. Low salaries meant that foundations could not hire a more skilled staff in the long run. Also, as stipulated in their charter, the amount of money PFFs spent annually on public benefit activities must not be less than 70 percent of the previous year's income, which was too inflexible. This rule did not take into consideration the foundations' sustainability. For example, if a foundation were to raise a lot of funds in a specific year, it would want to use the money in a planned and effective way, instead of in a stressful and unexpected way based on a rule. In addition, local foundations have always found it difficult to raise funds in areas of poverty, so spending 70 percent of the previous year's income is not sustainable.

4.4.2.3 The changing role of Chinese foundations in supporting grassroots SOs

In the early 1980s, foundations were created as subordinate agencies of the government headed by government officials, through which foundations received administrative benefits and provided social welfare services to help children, enhance education, and alleviate poverty, all of which supplemented the government's responsibilities in those areas. In 1988, RMF-1988 began to see foundations as social associations under a triple-management system; that is, they were managed by supervising units, approved by the People's Bank of China, and administrated by civil affairs departments.

In the late 1990s, foundations began to assume independent social responsibility and became an important supporting force in promoting social development. After the promulgation of RMF-2004, it was expected that Chinese foundations would raise more private funds and still redistribute them for public purposes under the government's dual management system. In summary, Chinese foundations mainly function as complementarity entities, providing and supporting public welfare and social services to supplement the government's responsibilities in those areas.

5 Understanding cooperation from the perspective of both foundations and grassroots sos

Based on the previous discussion of foundations' historical development and characteristics, it can be concluded that grant-making foundations did not automatically appear with the emergence of foundations in the 1980s, nor did they appear in 2004 with the emergence of NPFFs—because there was neither space nor necessity for foundations and grassroots SOs to interact with each other. Even the various developments in recent years have been unreasonable and challenging, with the result that grant-making foundations have not yet emerged in China. Instead, under the stimulation of the Wenchuan earthquake disaster in 2008, some foundations noticed the role that grassroots SOs played and began a decade-long interaction characterized by friction, which leads to certain questions: Under what circumstances will cooperation happen? How will cooperation be started? What kinds of dilemmas might arise from cooperation? This section answers these questions in sequence by combining the above-mentioned theories and the analysis of a large number of secondary data.

5.1 Under what circumstance can cooperation begin between foundations and grassroots SOs?

China has gradually recognized the important role that grassroots SOs play and the third sector as a global trend in contemporary society. However, due to anxiety and worry, the relevant official departments have been in a skeptical attitude. Thus, grassroots SOs cannot be supported by the government's financial resources and policies. Because grassroots SOs have, for a long time, been in a difficult position in terms of government recognition, their resources are insufficient and they lack motivation. This situation makes it difficult for them to stimulate social activities and acquire resources. Conversely, though numerous, SOs are generally seen as being incapable. In the case of grant-making foundations that are already in practice, their overall size is still small in terms of funding amounts and periods. The biggest problem for SOs, therefore, continues to be acquiring the funds they need to survive and function.

The rapid growth of Chinese foundations gives them a corresponding advantage in securing funding. Also, foundations provide funding resources to others, such as grassroots SOs, and the SOs implement the foundations' projects in exchange. In the third sector, this symbiotic relationship is regarded as the best resource allocation structure for achieving broad goals and far-reaching results.

5.1.1 Why grassroots SOs need to cooperate with foundations, especially on funding resources

In the interviews conducted for this dissertation, I formulated one question for grassroots SOs to explore all types of resources that they need to receive from domestic foundations. Their answers were also used to determine whether grassroots SOs actually ing from domestic foundations. The question I asked is as follows (I also discuss this question in the following section):

> *Which kinds of resources do your organization need from domestic foundations? Please describe.*

All thirteen interviewed representatives from grassroots SOs expressed a need for financial resources from domestic foundations. One representative (SO 8, see Chapter 7 for details) expressed her need for domestic funding in the following way:

> *My grassroots social organization cannot survive without domestic foundations. Foreign foundations have already withdrawn from China gradually since 2010 and could not fund grassroots SOs anymore if they do not register in China according to the requirements from the Overseas NGOs Law which was enacted in 2016.*

The preceding response shows that grassroots SOs count on domestic foundations as the major funding resources, particularly as overseas foundations gradually stopped funding Chinese grassroots SOs. Furthermore, the government always saw overseas funding as unsafe because it perceived them as having political or religious purposes, a fact that was supported by some interviewees that received funds from foreign foundations or international organizations (including grassroots SOs 1, 2, 4, 7, 8, and 10).

There are four main funding sources for grassroots SOs in China: the government, public donations, domestic foundations, and overseas organizations, respectively. Given that the government and Chinese foundations are grassroots SOs' main donors in China, the following discussion focuses on the distribution of domestic donations. This approach allows me to explain why it is hard for grassroots SOs to acquire donations in China and the changing context that occurred when overseas organizations, which had provided great support, began withdrawing their support in the 2000s.

5.1.1.1 Why do grassroots SOs have difficulty raising funds?

As demonstrated, Chinese foundations mostly operate their own projects, only a few of which support grassroots SOs. Even some private and corporate foundations that developed quickly after 2004 were reluctant to fund grassroots SOs because they were under the influence of previous foundation mechanisms. In addition, why grassroots SOs find it so difficult to raise funds, through donations directly and from the public indirectly, can be viewed from three perspectives.

First, grassroots SOs have had difficulty raising funds from the public because they have no qualifications to do so and lack professional fundraising personnel. Furthermore, they seldom receive direct donations from the wealthy or enterprises because they are for the most part registered as CNIs and thus are not recognized as general charitable organizations by the public. The representatives interviewed had almost no direct contact or communication with entrepreneurs. Even the Charity Law of 2017 made it possible for grassroots SOs to raise funds from the public only after they were accredited as charitable organizations by the Civil Affairs Department, while in reality small and local grassroots SOs hardly ever gained certification. Even the few that were approved are comparatively weak in extending their influence in practice, as the majority of local grassroots SOs are small and lack professional staff, let alone professional fundraising skills.

Second, extremely limited donations flow to grassroots SOs because government-organized organizations monopolize the allocation of donations and because grassroots SOs have never been a priority, especially organizations that have nothing to do with government. The interviews conducted for this dissertation indicated that if individuals at grassroots SOs have good interpersonal relationships with the government, they may be able to gain information about donations and apply in a timely way. The interviews also showed that if the relationship between grassroots SOs and the government was limited to administrative stamps or supervision (which was most often the case), grassroots SOs were not even aware of the donation information.

In many cases, such as in the event of disasters, it is also difficult for grassroots SOs to allocate donations. If the donations are substantial, foundations or large SOs with close links to the government are more likely to gain access to donation channels and obtain qualifications than grassroots SOs. Moreover, when a disaster occurs, the government may take measures to control donations and open this opportunity only to government-backed foundations. The state gives favor to government-linked charities to protect its dominant position, instead of letting grassroots SOs allocate a greater percentage of financial resources.

Third, the public does not realize the cost of administration and staff and hopes that all donations are used directly for the beneficiary. This was underscored in the interviews when the representative from Foundation M, who had rich experience in fundraising from the public in China, indicated that donors expect that funds raised from the public are used completely for the beneficiary, without consideration of operational expenses or short-term projects producing significant results. Foundation M is not an isolated example; many other foundations have difficulty explaining the cost of administration and staff to their donors. Not to mention grassroots SOs, they are more difficult to explain the organization's operating expenses to the public.

5.1.1.2 Yet, the question worth asking is, where do Chinese donations go if not to grassroots SOs?

Although the number of grassroots SOs has increased greatly over the past decades, a significant amount of Chinese donations flows to the government or government-affiliated agencies and charities linked to the government, as indicated by the distribution of donations in 2010 and 2017.

In 2011, the China Charity Donations Information Center (中民慈善捐助信息中心) issued the 2010 *Report of China Charity Donations* 《2011 中国慈善捐助报告》, which indicated that in 2010, 58.3 percent of Chinese donations went to the government or government-affiliated agencies, charities linked to the government, and the Red Cross, broken down, as 20.6 percent going to civil affair departments at all levels, 9 percent going to other party agencies and mass organizations (excluding civil affairs departments), and 6.7 percent going to the Red Cross or Red Cross-linked organizations. Only 1.3 percent went to social associations, CNIs, and other social welfare-related organizations, of which some were surprisingly still government-backed SOs. According to the analysis of Xu (2014, 168), the total amount of charitable donations in 2010 was 70 billion RMB. With only 1.3 percent of total donations in China going to social associations, CNIs, and other social welfare-related organizations, it is clear that 910 million RMB went to nonprofit organizations without government links. It should be noted that far fewer donations went to nonprofit organizations because of the inclusive government-run shelters and nursing homes, charity federations and Red Cross at all levels, and so on.

Chart 5-1: Proportion of donations received by different bodies in 2017

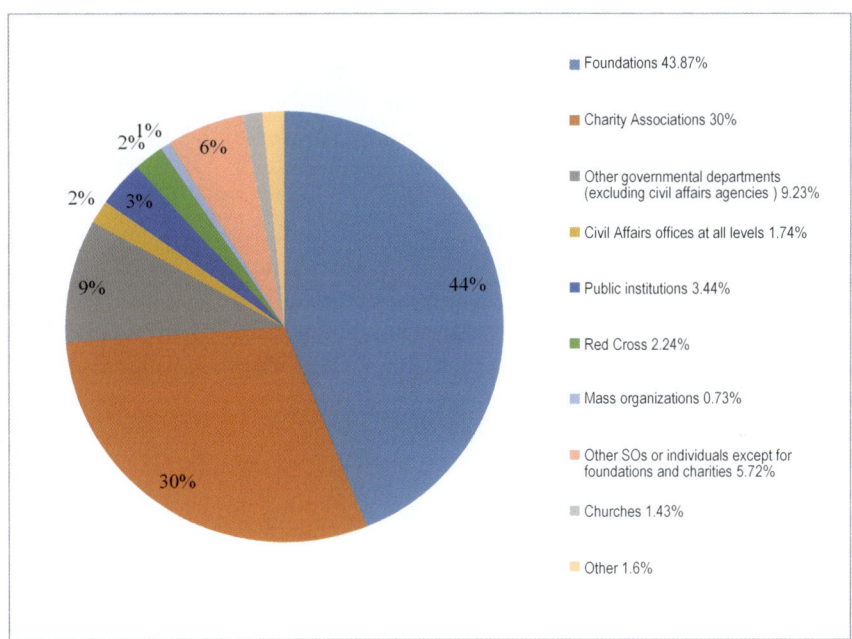

Source: From the 2017 China Charity Donation Report (Ma, Liu and Jin, 2018,15) and adapted by the author.

Chart 5-1 shows that the flow of donations changed in 2017, and only 5.72 percent went to other social organizations (excluding foundations and charities), while the percentage for grassroots SOs without government links was less than 5.72 percent because a considerable percentage of social organizations were GONGOs.

Of course, not only is the de facto boundary between the government and charity organizations often hard to determine in China, but it is also difficult to collect data that distinguishes between government-affiliated organizations and non-government-affiliated organizations.

5.1.1.3 Why international foundations drastically lowered their once abundant funding to Chinese grantees

International funding refers to the grants made by foundations and organizations outside mainland China, including Hong Kong, Macau, and Taiwan. Chinese people sometimes refer to these grants as "foreign milk" (yang nai), a take on "breast milk" (mu ru). The data collected supports the logic behind explaining the Chinese grassroots SOs' change from heavy dependence to the decline of overseas organizations' funding.

Although the existing literature emphasizes China's heavy reliance on international funding (e.g. Spires, Tao, and Chan 2014, 69–72; Shieh 2017, 1797–1799; Lai 2017, 3-4), it is hard to figure out exactly how much international funding China receives.[18] Empirical studies suggest that, in their stages, many grassroots SOs rely heavily on international funds, or are even created with the support of international organizations. Take SO 1, for example. It was established by an American foundation in the early 2000s and then was supported completely by funding from European and American foundations.

According to Professor Ming Wang, president of the Institute for Philanthropy Tsinghua University, more than 90 percent of Chinese grassroots SOs have received funding from overseas groups (Li 2018, 114). Take US-based foundations as an example. They made 188 grants totaling $24,862,257 to Chinese grassroots organizations from 2002 to 2009. Additionally, "Hong Kong is also a regular source of funding for numerous programs in mainland China through organizations such as Greenpeace, Oxfam Hong Kong, and Partnerships for Community Development" (Spires 2011b, 316). Then a study by Spires, Tao, and Chan (2014) provided anoth-

---

18 For example, Spires Tao and Chen (2014) found that some international funding eventually goes to grassroots SOs through a handful of intermediate organizations, especially funding from sensitive foreign foundations or to sensitive fields or organizations that deal with issues such as labor rights and HIV. Additionally, some foreign funds flow into Chinese government agencies first and then go to SOs through those government agencies (70–71).

er insight on where the funding resources for Chinese grassroots SOs came from, based on a large sample of grassroots organizations from 2009 to 2011 in three regions (Beijing, Guangzhou, and Yunnan). The results showed that Chinese foundations still were not the main funding source for China's grassroots SOs but that overseas funding was.

5.1.1.4 Government's attitude toward overseas organizations

Although some overseas NGOs "only help and do not disturb" (Yang and Wang 2014), the government has not yet established a legal system to manage different categories of foreign NGOs. Instead, to prevent the challenges and damage caused by overseas NGOs, a more severe and cautious attitude was adopted by the government. Moreover, the term civil society has become an issue in practice and with academics. It is often claimed that the state must not allow the third sector to fall into the so-called civil society trap. In consideration of governmental and national interests, the government has adopted all possible measures to consolidate its leading position, maintain the long-term security of the country, and ensure that the people live and work in peace and contentment. So far, the legal status of overseas NGOs has not been recognized by the government, and its space for activities has also been severely restricted. Also, government agencies, from the national to the local level, are always worried that deregulation will result in the proliferation and loss of control of overseas NGOs, which causes huge difficulties in supervision.

Studies (Liu and Ma 2012, 297; Zhu 2012; Lai 2017, 4–6) have shown that the Chinese government's attitudes and policies toward international NGOs over the past thirty years mainly have been tolerated and accepted, while no clear laws and regulations have been enacted to manage their activities. There are two probable explanations for this (Mann 2013, 23–25). On the one hand, the government has gradually realized its important role in providing funding as a supplement to social services, and as a result, the relevant departments have been just waited to see what would happen to social organizations before reacting. On the other hand, because of various doubts and worries over the possibility of international NGOs harming national security, the Chinese government has always avoided recognizing the legitimacy of these organizations and providing a legal basis for their actions. Of course, this policy-free strategy is convenient for government agencies.

Until the end of 2009, the *Notice of the State Administration of Foreign Exchange on Issues concerning the Administration of Foreign Exchange Donated to or by Domestic Institutions* (hereafter *Notice*) was deemed the first policy intervention in overseas NGOs' activities in China; it showed the Chinese government's cautious attitude toward overseas NGOs through the restriction of overseas funds (Lai 2017, 4; Jia 2017, 38). The *Notice* categorized the income and expenditures of foreign exchange donated to or by domestic institutions. The most stringent article is given here as an example. In accordance with the *Notice*, when a domestic enterprise accepts donations from or makes donations to any nonprofit overseas institution, the enterprise should submit the "donation agreement which is notarized and has indicated the purpose of funds" and "certification documents showing that the overseas nonprofit institution is registered and formed abroad according to the law" (a Chinese version should be attached; both are included in Article 5) along with other application documents. One reason for this stipulation was that many overseas nonprofit organizations were registered as enterprises, and it was difficult to prove that they were nonprofit organizations. Still, many donations came directly from overseas enterprises. Another reason is that it was unrealistic for many overseas NGOs to show their original documents of registration to a Chinese notary office. In addition, many other government restrictions made it difficult for overseas NGOs in China to survive. Some overseas organizations simply withdrew from China, and some of the remaining overseas organizations faced difficulties in funding grassroots organizations. At the end of 2012, only eighteen overseas foundations had obtained qualifications of working in China upon the registration of representative offices. The implementation of this law quickly inhibited China's grassroots organizations, especially the "business registered" or non-registered grassroots organizations, which encountered a critical funding shortage.

The development of overseas organizations in China gradually began to suffer setbacks in the late 2000s. Overseas organizations believed that with the development of China's economy, China had become a wealthy country. Therefore, China no longer met the standards set for developing countries to receive foreign economic assistance (Lai 2017, 4). Furthermore, the financial crisis in the United States and Europe affected the fundraising of overseas organizations, which in turn reduced the funding of grantees by overseas organizations. China also began to see some of the negative effects of overseas organizations and took strict measures in terms of internal governance and supervision. In a study, Zhao (2013, 28–31) pointed out that foreign NGOs have endangered the country's national security by threatening China's unification, national interests, and political stability. As a result, the Chinese government strengthened its management of grassroots SOs that receive overseas funds, and it has now become more difficult for grassroots SOs to obtain such funds.

At the beginning of 2017, the Overseas NGO Law came into force, which in practice made the life of overseas NGOs even harder regarding registration and activity in China. At the time I interviewed two representatives from a European foundation, they had been seeking a supervisory unit in Beijing since 2017 and had not found one by the beginning of 2019, and thus still had not been approved for registration.

Overseas NGOs still working in China have two possibilities: to register a representative office in China or to request approval to conduct temporary activities from the Ministry of Public Security or its appropriate provincial department. When overseas NGOs register their offices in China, they need to find their supervisory department and then register in "the public security organs of local governments at the county level or above" (Article 7). In other words, their representative Chinese offices are required to function in a dual management system. If overseas NGOs do not register in a representative office in China, they are required to report to the police department all their temporary activities and each organization they will cooperate with for various restricted activities, such as religious and political activities. The registration process is not only complex but also highly variable. Some overseas NGOs cannot find a supervisory unit at all. As a result, most overseas NGOs have gradually withdrawn from China.

5.1.2 Why Chinese foundations do not make grants to grassroots SOs

Together with the development of Chinese foundations as previously described and driven by grassroots SOs, the transition of Chinese foundations from operating to grantmaking is on the way. With the rapid development of China's economy, the government has become wealthy, and foundations have entered a non-administration period. Now the purpose of foundations is not to make up for the financial shortage of government agencies. As the third sector, foundations should be independent, rather than depend on the government's system. In their past fundraising, foundations relied on a single channel within the government, but this approach is no longer an advantage when raising public funds. In addition to the rapid emergence of NPFFs, operating foundations have also begun to encounter a resource shortage. Specifically, they are experiencing a shortage of single funding sources, heavy reliance on the government's mechanism, and unprofessional personnel, which have all led to unprofessional project management, which in turn has led to financial difficulties. However, different from grassroots SOs, foundations still see the qualification to raise funds from the public as an advantage. What foundations need to consider is how to implement projects through grassroots SOs, how to strengthen project management, and how to enhance the utilization of grants. Then they can spend more time and energy raising funds.

A case study of one local NPFF: Why it did not want to make grants to grassroots SOs

A representative from a small local nonpublic fundraising foundation explained why her foundation does not make grants to grassroots SOs and why its leaders do not want to make such grants (Foundation A, interviewed March 12, 2019):

> *The managers' biggest consideration is that the foundation is legally run, and then the next consideration is to complete various poverty alleviation projects according to the guidance of one government agency, such as subsidizing individuals or a village. The annual budget in our foundation is very small, around 4 million RMB. The daily activities, as a rule, are run by the donations from specific members or philanthropist, but the people in this government agency do not seem to want to develop the foundation as a career, but hope that "Just do something safely." Even if we (our managers) want to make the foundation bigger or better, we are not free to make any decision.*
>
> *We can only fund specific target groups or individuals, according to the willingness of donors or members. The funding is normally restricted, or even specific donation or specific activities to a village. It happens that the donor donates money to the village where he is from through our foundation. If the donors do it by themselves, they normally cannot make enough influence or reasonably spend the money. If the foundation is supported by our foundation, those donors' enterprises will have certain benefits, such as tax exemption and reputation. When the donation information is released to the public, it also has a positive influence on the donors, and it feels like more "decent." In case of any emergency, even if the size of our foundation is very small, it still enables us to mobilize various resources as a philanthropic foundation or through the liked government agency. For example, during one earthquake, in the name of the foundation, a donation of more than one million was raised in a short period.*

As the country's poverty alleviation work is about to end, our foundation will also change. Even if we are doing poverty alleviation work for many years, we are worried that there will be many cases of returning to poverty due to illness, education, etc. But this is not something we can decide, anyway.

This 2013 founded local NPFF is an operating foundation functioning as an additional subsector doing "reputation projects" for a government agency. It raises funds from its members and then undertakes administrative purposes in poverty alleviation as the government department's political achievements. Although the staff is not civil servants, they still have inextricable links with provincial government agencies and local departments. Undoubtedly, they insist on being an operating foundation rather than a grant-making foundation.

Chinese foundations, especially PFFs, operate their own projects through a governmental administrative "closed way" system of funding distribution (Xu 2010 198–199), as discussed earlier. On the one hand, foundations think that it is safe to spend money within the official systems and are cautious of grassroots SOs that they do not trust. On the other hand, funding shortages and insufficient capacities are two contradictory aspects of grassroots SOs, which seriously affects their organizational development. To be more specific, the main difficulties grassroots SOs face in their early stage is lack of funding, which makes it difficult to hire professional staff, carry out effective projects, and improve their own governance structure. As a consequence, foundations are struggling to find capable grassroots SOs to work with, while grassroots SOs are trapped in their own vicious circle due to funding shortages and insufficient capacities.

In organizations' institutional environment, the lack of normative grant-making of foundations and a shortage of professional human resources in the field of grantmaking have caused tension. In a recent study, Lai (2017, 136) showed that the unequal organizational power based on the grassroots SOs' resource dependence on foundations is the main reason for the conflict between the two parties. In short, the appearance of grant-making foundations brings opportunities for grassroots SOs to get out of the dilemma caused by funding shortages. At the same time, several recent studies have shown that the growth of domestic NPFFs will be an important source of grassroots SOs (Chan 2010; Shieh 2017; Lai 2017).

5.2 How cooperation is initiated between foundations and grassroots SOs in China

Because of their developmental characteristics, the struggle for Chinese foundations has not been making grants to grassroots SOs but accumulating funds. However, because of marketing forces, once NPFFs arose, they were able to break through this issue and accumulate the funds and resources they needed to address social interests.

In this section, I explore the ongoing interactions between foundations and grassroots SOs. I look at events since 2008 when the Wenquan earthquake disaster prompted cooperation between the two. I then examine the obstacles they face in working together from the perspective of the cooperation theory to provide a deeper understanding of those obstacles.

The Narada Foundation, founded in 2007 as the earliest domestic grant-making foundation dedicated to providing financial support to grassroots SOs in China, has played an important role and set the tone for making grants to grassroots SOs (Shieh 2017; Lai 2017; Woqi Foundation 2018). The Wenchuan earthquake was "a watershed event for China's associational atmosphere" (Shieh and Deng 2011, 194). This event led to the widespread participation of volunteers and associations, which also brought together foundations and grassroots SOs. During the NGO Cooperation Forum for 512 Post-Disaster Reconstruction in 2009, Yongguang Xu, as Narada Foundation's president and co-founder, presented the developmental ecosystem of the public welfare sector: "Only when you live well, can I live better," which implied cooperation between foundations and grassroots SOs. This notion is theoretically supported by Axelrod's live-and-let-live system.

5.2.1 Successful examples of foundations and SOs working together

To understand how Chinese grant-making foundations work, the section takes a glance at several leading grant-making foundations in China. The characteristics of the leading grant-making foundations listed in Table 5-2 below are due to their diverse modes of establishment and backgrounds, which shaped their fundraising and funding schemes, for example, government-affiliated foundations' relationships with the state and entrepreneur-created foundations' relationships with entrepreneurs or companies. Foundations' connections with founders and founding bodies are among the important factors affecting their independence in decision-making and operating mechanisms.

Table 5-1: A glance at several leading grant-making foundations/foundations which make grants to other organizations/individuals in China

Foundation	Background	Grant-making strategies
China Foundation for Poverty Alleviation	Established in 1989 Working areas: China/Asia, Africa, Latin America Expenditure: RMB 415m (2016 Annual Audit Report) 130 full-time Staff	In 2005, this foundation started its attempt to fund SOs through bidding and invitations for bids. After the 2008 Wenchuan earthquake, CFPA gradually developed its own mechanism for grantmaking. The transition from operating to grantmaking was a logical progression based on its extensive experiences in rural development (poverty alleviation and disaster relief), which was CFPA's funding focus at the time. Drawing on its expertise and brand, CFPA's current emphasis is in cooperation with SOs.
China Charities Aid Foundation for Children (CCAFC)	Established in 2010 Working area: nationally Expenditure: RMB 105m (2015 Annual Audit Report) 20 full-time staff	CCAFC mobilizes resources via "united fundraising." Learning from United Way, CCAFC shared its public fundraising qualification with grassroots SOs, jointly launched the "Tongyuan United Fundraising Plan," and opened up a new way to raise funds from individuals.
Beijing Warm Foundation	Established in 1995 Working area: Beijing Expenditure: RMB 19.5m (2015 Annual Audit Report) 4 full-time staff	As a government-affiliated foundation, Beijing Warm Foundation was the first foundation to develop workers' community organizations in China. Another highlight was the requirement that such organizations work with two trade unions at the ground level. Beijing Warm Foundation takes advantage of its governmental affiliations and links the resources and activities of SOs and trade unions.
Narada Foundation	Established in 2007 Working area: nationally Expenditure: RMB 33.67m (2016 Annual Audit Report) 23 full-time staff	Narada Foundation's strategies have gone through a series of transformations, from investing in projects and certain fields to investing in people, and eventually to investing in the impact and scaling-up of effective philanthropic products by creating the China Effective Philanthropy Multiplier jointly with other leading organizations in the sector. Narada Foundation's final strategic plan for 2017 to 2019 was to "build the Ecosystem of the Philanthropic and nonprofit sector, and promote cross-sector collaboration and innovation."

Foundation	Background	Grant-making strategies
SEE Foundation	Established in 2004 Working area: nationally Expenditure: RMB 61.6m (2016 Annual Audit Report) 55 full-time staff	From the funders' perspective, SEE Foundation experienced several phases of organizational development. It struggled in the beginning until the secretariat honed its grant-making skills and allowed professional environmental practitioners to select, design, and deliver projects. It has reconnected with its inherent entrepreneurship and business resources and enhanced its use of those advantages. JinCao Tong Xing and Greenmaker Plan have become very influential signature projects.
Fujian Zhenro Foundation	Established in 2013 Working area: nationally Expenditure: RMB 7.6m (2016 Annual Audit Report) 7 full-time staff	This foundation supports start-up SOs via micro funds, works with platforms in second/third tier regions, and mobilizes and cultivates SOs through trial and error where the nonprofit sector is underdeveloped. By fueling the collaboration of funders (foundations) and upgrading its program, the Zhenro Foundation helps SOs acquire diverse funding sources, brings more perspectives and resources together around the same goal, and amplifies its impact on the nonprofit sector.
Alibaba Foundation	Established in 2011 Working area: nationally Expenditure: RMB 136m (2015 Annual Audit Report) 6 full-time staff	Two distinctive characters of the Alibaba Foundation: dependence on the Internet company Alibaba Group and close relationship with its CSR department. Alibaba Group employees' participation in environmental protection funding assessments; that is, a philanthropic panel is selected by employees to make funding decisions. The organizational structure—a philanthropic panel as a decision-making body and the foundation secretariat as a professional consultant and executive organ—is rare among Chinese foundations.
Guangdong Harmony Foundation	Established in 2009 Working area: Pearl River Delta Charitable Expenditure: RMB 10.5m (2015 Annual Audit Report) 7 full-time staff	As one of the few community foundations that developed from the bottom up, this foundation operates by fundraising in targeted communities and providing funds to organizations in the same community so that they can respond to critical issues. GHF has its own organizational culture regarding relationships with grantees, funding directions, and sustainable governance. It considers grantees as strategic partners and stresses equality, respect, and mutual growth, and sound grant-making—officer-training principals are in place within the foundation. Its funding targets are regional rather than across the country.

Foundation	Background	Grant-making strategies
You Cheng Foundation	Established in 2007 Working area: nationally Expenditure: RMB 50m (2016 Annual Audit Report) 24 full-time staff	This foundation typically focuses on high-engagement grantmaking (can yu shi zi zhu 参与式资助). Apart from financial support, it emphasizes more intense participation in the development of grassroots SOs and offers platforms for advocacy, capacity building, and other resources.
Ai You Foundation	Established in 2008 Working area: nationally Expenditure: RMB 318m (2016 Annual Audit Report) on grantmaking: 26m 24 full-time staff	Through exploration and development over the past decade, Ai You developed two charity chains: a project to aid orphaned and poor children (operating program) and a venture philanthropy project. Ai You implements enterprise-style management. Through the Venture Philanthropy Program, it supports and influences social enterprises and charity organizations with funding, resource development, strategic guidance, and management (HR, finance, and IT), as well as brand activation in virtue of the experience and resources it accumulated over the past decade.
Shanghai United Foundation (SUF)	Established in 2009 Working area: nationally Expenditure: RMB 33.8m (2015 Annual Audit Report) 15 full-time staff	This foundation raises funds from the public and uses the funds to support grassroots SOs with clear marketing goals when operating and managing projects. The foundation's most distinctive characteristic is its sensitive "customer relations management" of uncertain upstream donors and uncertain downstream beneficiaries in the grant-making chain and its efforts to link the two. In particular, by sharing decision-making with donors, the foundation created a brand-new project assessment mechanism. In the grant-making market, SUF offers market-based services to nonprofit organizations (primary customers) and nonprofit talents (secondary customers) in Shanghai and across China.

Source: Mainly from Woqi Foundation (2018). The Ai You Foundation was added due to its recent, leading contribution toward grantmaking to grassroots SOs.

Zhenro Foundation and Narada Foundation, both entrepreneur-based foundations, phased out the link with their business initiators at the very beginning to ensure their independence and avoid being reduced to a brand-building CSR tool. However, the relationship between the Alibaba Foundation and its corporate founders is an important issue for foundations with business backgrounds. You Cheng Foundation, one of the earliest grant-making foundations, especially focuses on engaging grantmakers in grantees' project implementation and organizational development. This kind of high-engagement grantmaking can be regarded as a mixture of operating and grantmaking approaches.

Government-affiliated foundations are making strategic efforts to transition from an operating model to a quasi-grant-making model. CFPA exemplifies the point of this case. As a highly influential operating foundation in the field of poverty alleviation and disaster relief, CFPA's dependency on existing resources and its project-operating norm somewhat burden its transition to a grant-making foundation. Currently, CFPA is unlikely to become a foundation focusing on grantmaking and no longer stresses grantmaking. Based on its expertise and brand, its current emphasis is on cooperating with grassroots SOs.

A united fundraising approach was adopted by two recently established PFFs, namely CCAFC and SUF. A united approach means that foundations share their public fundraising qualification with grassroots SOs, and as a result, grassroots organizations can raise funds for one or more specific projects. Initiated by a grassroots organization called Non-Profit Incubator (NPI) and with rich business experiences, SUF takes both fundraising practices and grant-making practices as guidance, through developing its market, educating and guiding donors, helping grantees gain new perspectives on donors, and improving the design and delivery of their projects. SUF created a series of brand projects, for example, the One Egg Program and the Handwashing Project.

Interestingly, Chinese foundations have learned or are still learning from the grant-making experiences of overseas foundations, for example, the Narada Foundation from the Ashoka Foundation and Ford Foundation, the You Cheng Foundation from the Ford Foundation, the SEE foundation from the Rockefeller Brothers Fund, the Harmony Community Foundation from the Rockefeller Brothers Fund, and the He Yi Lv Foundation from the Global Greengrants Fund (GGF). Although they are deeply imprinted by the overseas foundations' operating model, the Chinese foundations form their unique characteristics and do not completely replicate the funding logic of foreign foundations. A typical example is the

You Cheng Foundation, which uses a high-engagement grant-making approach. In the beginning, the You Cheng Foundation aimed to work as a grant-making foundation similar to that of the Ford Foundation. The establishment process was affected by the domestic environment and policies at the time, such as the failure to find suitable partners and advice from the China Foundation for Poverty Alleviation. Afterward, the You Cheng Foundation became a unique high-engagement grant-making foundation in China.

The You Cheng Foundation first used high-engagement grantmaking (can yu shi zi zhu 参与式资助) in 2008, in which, in addition to providing funding, it advocated for intense participation in its grantees' development and for building platforms that would influence expansion, capacity building, and other resources. In 2009, Ping Wang, Founder & Chairperson of You Cheng Foundation, gave a speech entitled "High-Engagement Grantmaking Approach, You Cheng Foundation's Exploration on the Operating Model of NPFFs," at the first annual meeting of NPFFs:

Specifically, high-engagement grantmaking consists of three categories :
- *The first category refers to participation-oriented projects, which meet the long-term development needs of You Cheng Foundation and are strategic public welfare projects of You Cheng Foundation. You Cheng Foundation will undergo a thorough feasibility demonstration on such projects, which are implemented by our own team. In the implementation process, other partners/grantees are also funded to participate together. The "You Cheng Poverty Alleviation Volunteer Action Plan" and "Social Innovation" that we are currently implementing are such projects. Within You Cheng Foundation, we liken such projects to industrial investment, which is described in the language of business investment.*
- *The second category refers to socially innovative nonprofit organizations and their projects that are still in the development or start-up period. When funding such projects, You Cheng also invests in its own team and external experts in addition to funding. The team participates in the pilot project of the funded project, and guides or assists grantees to carry out in-depth research and development, strategic planning and strategy formulation of public welfare products to comprehensively improve the ability of grantees. At the same time, the You Cheng Foundation will also invest in other mobilized resources, including volunteers, to assist in the incubation of the project. This type of project is to some extent similar to VC (Venture Capital) in the business sector. The "two village projects" funded by You Cheng and some of the practices of last year's 512 Wenchuan earthquake relief fall into this category.*

> – *The third category refers to public welfare projects that already have a
> certain scale and are relatively mature, but require funds during the de-
> velopment. We will provide funding for the project on the premise of ac-
> curately assessing the project. This kind of funding is equivalent to PE
> (Private Equity) in the commercial field, except that we do not obtain
> the equity of the funded organization. You Cheng Foundation's grants
> for "collaborators" is typical of such projects. This is also a type often
> done by many other grantmaking foundations.[19]*

This high-engagement grant-making strategy has influenced other Chinese
foundations. From a positive perspective, foundations can comprehensively guide and help their recipients develop. However, too much interference may not allow recipients to develop according to their own wishes.
Based on the resource interdependence theory, in which trust and common goals must exist in unison, conflicts can have adverse effects on recipients, for example, their funding might be cut off.

5.2.2 Transition from an operating foundation to a grant-making foundation: A case study of one local PFF

To understand the interactions between foundations and grassroots SOs, it
is necessary to understand the early nature of PPFs. If they grew from government agencies or quasi-government institutes, the majority of their
leaders will have worked and may still work as government officials. This
affects the PPFs' perspective on expenditures and purpose. They may be inclined to work with local administrative units at the governmental level
and, when considering the risks of cooperation, take only those risks that
are within their control. Besides, when considering the cost of a project, if
a foundation's leader is a former or retired government official, communication with local administrative units will be easier and less expensive.

In a study, Ni and Zhan (2017) noted that political connections with the
state can still enable foundations to receive priority on the legalization of
dual management and to obtain more financial resources from government subsidies and public and marketing fundraising. A similar case arose
during my interview with a local foundation, Foundation B, that raised
funds for environmental causes. Foundation B's representative explained

---

19 You Cheng Foundation website, http://www.youcheng.org/share.php?id=172,
    accessed September 30, 2019.

their worries and difficulties when considering whether to work with local SOs.

The director of the board of one foundation interviewed (Foundation B) had worked for a government department for many years. Similar to what PFFs did in the beginning, this foundation had been operating its projects and funds through local low-level government agencies in different communities and villages under a very low administration cost. Its team had been thinking about and planning to shed its strong dependence on government agencies because of the limitations the government placed on them. Also, the founder, who had worked for the government and would soon retire, did not have a lot of power in the government. Therefore, it would not only be hard to operate their projects using the old approaches, but it would also be difficult to be managed strictly by the government due to the pressure arising from its non-administration and de-institutionalization policies. In consideration of the current unstainable working model and the blurred lines between the foundation and the government, the foundation's leaders and stakeholders were thinking about separating from the government completely. Its "fresh blood" staff (young, creative people who were recruited directly through job advertisements and had never worked in the government, but had years of experience with cooperation) thought they could serve as administrative arms with government agencies. However, when they started thinking about how to work with grassroots SOs, they realized that, compared with their trust of local administrative units, they hardly trusted grassroots SOs and had concerns about grassroots SOs' qualifications, abilities, and mode of funding. In the end, it appears that foundations continue to believe that it will be easier to cooperate with their old partners in government systems.

Additionally, after many years' work with local governmental units, the representative from Foundation B said,

> Some of our foundation's inherent and traditional projects, such as afforestation, protection of wild animals, still rely on government administrative resources to complete. For example, the foundation needs to work on a newly planted land, which must be approved by the forestry department. Part of the work is assisted by special professional research and experts such as the Chinese Academy of Sciences, including scientific examinations and subsequent technical training. Because of the foundation's own field of work, the operation of the projects and the requirements for professionalism still rely heavily on the government system.
>
> Now, considering the foundation's perspective, we hope to play the role of working together with other grassroots SOs and society. However, there are

many good grassroots SOs in Y province where our foundations locate. How to work with other local organizations is what our foundation wants to consider and plan next. In addition, our foundation hopes to mobilize the public's resources to do some charitable activities, public welfare donations and other charitable activities together. The will of the public is fragmented, which requires our foundation to design some attractive activities. These activities are just an external manifestation. Some of the ideas behind them, such as the concept of sustainable living and environmental protection, require us to work with the local organizations. That is to say, some of the scientific research professional's highly demanding tasks need to be done by professional scientific research institutions, while other works to promote public participation are hoped to cooperate with some local organizations, which is also the advantage of local organizations. Previously, our foundation did not cooperate with local organizations, mainly because of foundation grants. The foundation respects the wishes of donors and then carries out projects accordingly. The original working model did not involve local organizations. Moreover, the foundation does not have the right to speak and to make decisions on its own.

Again, we can see that cooperation between this foundation and grassroots SOs was still in the trial stage. Two facts can be derived from the above passage. First, this local PFF had no advantage in the government system and needed to mobilize social resources for fundraising and implementing projects. Second, however, were the difficulties facing this foundation during the transition, whether it was the limitation of fundraising or the long-term working model of dependence on government agencies or quasi-government institutions.

From the perspective of political connections with the state, the founders of the abovementioned foundation have worked with the government for a long time, which is the exact reason the relevant government agency would like to be its supervisory unit. If the main founders are still working in a government agency in a leadership position, the foundation may receive significant benefits from the government, such as government subsidies and project implementation through local administrative sectors. However, when the founders retire from or have no power in the government agency, the foundation may find it difficult to obtain resources from the government and find itself in an awkward position. Moreover, in terms of institutional development, the foundation needs to turn to society and the public to obtain more resources, and in this case, its independence becomes particularly important in terms of funding sources, internal governance, and project activities. Overall, the previous shaping behavior of foundations continues to have a strong influence.

5.2.3 How many Chinese foundations are supporting grassroots SOs?

Although the figures for funding from Chinese foundations to grassroots SOs are not available, on the one hand, the boundaries of quasi-cooperation are blurred by issues such as the flow of funds between foundations are made hastily or happen only once (e.g., one-time exchange or they work together on a specific activity for a short time). On the other hand, the number of grassroots SOs is difficult to count, for example, due to unregistered grassroots organizations.

Confusion of grant-making programs and grant-making foundations in China
Regarding the interactions between foundations and grassroots SOs in China, one big challenge is the lack of even basic information and data on Chinese grant-making foundations. The previous literature review and the following discussion on definitions show that it is difficult to present with any confidence a general study on SOs and the third sector. Also, given the numerous unregistered grassroots SOs in China and the problem of legal supervision, it is hard to determine how many grants are given to support unknown organizations. Nonetheless, it is possible to use data from observations as a systematic way to fill in the gaps and prepare general, if somewhat limited, reports. For necessity, at times, I included specific data, as exemplified here:

> *As early as 2010, studies were saying that the donation income of PFFs throughout the year was 15,171,778,585.45 RMB, and their expenditures in public welfare were 12,745,629,492.00 RMB. If PFFs are supposed to spend 10% of their expenditures in cooperating with grassroots SOs, it would be 1.27 billion RMB of providing considerable funding to grassroots SOs. However, the author [of Blue Book of Foundation: Annual Report on China's Foundation Development 2012] thinks that the funding support of PFFs to grassroots SOs' projects in 2010 did not exceed 1% of foundations expenditures. (Xu 2012, 129–130, in Blue Book of Philanthropy: Annual Report on China's Philanthropy Development 2012, translated by author)*

In general, funding of grassroots SOs had already changed significantly before 2008. Organizations that had received funding from foreign organizations had a sharp reduction in funding, and the number of grants and the amount of funding from domestic foundations was far from enough for grassroots SOs. The biggest problem for grassroots SOs was, and still is, survival due to limited funding resources. Moreover, grassroots SOs find very little funding that they can apply for successfully, particularly for development and politically sensitive projects.

When analyzing and evaluating interactions between foundations and grassroots SOs, the best approach is to first understand how many Chinese grant-making foundations interact with grassroots SOs, as well as the process involved in their ongoing interactions

In the existing literature on Chinese foundations, there is confusion, especially in recent studies, about how many grant-making foundations exist in China, including, for example, in research papers and the public media. This issue relates to how Chinese scholars and practitioners define and classify Chinese foundations. Their different definitions and classification methods cause the numbers to vary greatly. For example, here are various statements about the number of Chinese grant-making foundations in China:

Statement 1: According to statistics in *Development of Chinese Foundation: An Independent Research Report* (2014, 125), among 3,610 foundations only 1.71 percent were grant-making foundations at the end of 2013.

Statement 2: When looking for domestic grant-making foundations to launch, the China Donors Roundtable (CDR, founded in 2015), they found approximately twenty to thirty, but no more than forty, grant-making foundations, according to a speech by Zhiyan Li (current secretary-general of CDR) on grantmaking (Li, 2019).

Statement 3: Similar to statement 2, a study by Lai (2017) listed twenty-six grant-making foundations, based on those listed in the China Foundation Rankings in 2013 and 2015 (ji jin hui ping jia bang 基金会评价榜 2013 and 2015). The Beijing Woqi Foundation (2018) wrote a book that included an analysis of eleven well-known grant-making foundations. However, what needs to be emphasized is that all eleven foundations were mixed foundations; that is, they mixed their own operations and programs and engaged in grantmaking (Woqi Foundation 2017, 5).[20]

---

20 Mixed foundations include China Charities Aid Foundation for Children (CCAFC), China Foundation for Poverty Alleviation (CFPA), Beijing Warm Foundation, Zhenrong Foundation in Fujian Province, Shanghai United Foundation, Alibaba Foundation, SEE Foundation, Xin Ping Foundation, China Social Entrepreneur Foundation, Guangzhou Harmony Community Foundation, and Narada Foundation.

Statement 4: Yongguang Xu (Woqi Foundation, 2018) stated that the total number of grant-making foundations—including foundations whose organizational orientation is to make grants (i.e., use their funds to finance the development of the public welfare sector)—that make grants to grassroots SOs is less than 1 percent of foundations.[21]

The preceding four statements illustrate the fact that grant-making foundations are rare, but it is always a very vague number. The following table 5-3 contains a total of 17 grant-making foundations in China by the end of 2018, including foundations that include the word of "grant-making" in their intuitional strategy and those directly positioned themselves as grant-making foundations. This statistic is based on the analysis of my field research and the verification of a large number of second-hand data as follows. First, I spent four years, from 2014 to 2018 ,collecting information on grant-making foundation while I worked in a grassroots SO. Additionally, during the field research process, I asked experts and representatives from grassroots SOs & foundations about which foundations are grant-making foundations and which foundations actively do grant-making activities and then verified them. The second is to search for partners in CFF and China Donors Roundtable, which are two influential networks of working with grant-making foundations. The third is to re-determine the list of foundations shown in the 2013 and 2015 China Foundation Rankings and then go to the foundation's website for verification and screening one by one.

Table 5-2: Profile of Chinese Foundations with missions of grant-making as stated in the foundations' website

No.	Registration Level	NPFF/PFF	Year	Interaction with Grassroots SOs	Others
1	Local	PFF	1995	Y	Government-affiliated; both operation and grantmaking
2	Local	NPFF	2004	N	Family Foundation
3	National	NPFF	2007	Y	Entrepreneur
4	National	NPFF	2007	Y	Entrepreneur
5	National	NPFF	2008	Y	Entrepreneur
6	Local	PFF	2008	Y	Entrepreneur; changed from NPFF to PFF
7	Local	NPFF	2008	Y	Community Foundation

---

21 See China Development Brief: http://www.chinadevelopmentbrief.org.cn/news-2 1592.html, accessed July 1, 2019.

No.	Registration Level	NPFF/PFF	Year	Interaction with Grassroots SOs	Others
8	Local	PFF	2009	Y	United fundraising approach
9	National	NPFF	2009	Y	Government-affiliated
10	National	PFF	2010	Y	Government-affiliated
11	Local	NPFF	2010	Y	Entrepreneur
12	Local	NPFF	2012	Y	Entrepreneur
13	Local	NPFF	2013	N	Entrepreneur
14	Local	NPFF	2013	N	Family Foundation
15	Local	NPFF	2015	N	Co-founded by foundations
16	Local	NPFF	2017	N	Family Foundation
17	Local	NPFF	2017	Y	Entrepreneur

Additionally, looking further into their cooperation, we can see that, in reality, very few grants are made to grassroots SOs (likely because there are only a few grant-making foundations in China). Take two Chinese grant-making foundations as examples: the Narada Foundation and the He Foundation, both of which are discussed in upcoming case studies. The Narada Foundation spends only part of its budget to support grassroots SOs), and the He Foundation, which has assets of 6 billion RMB, does not fund grassroots SOs at all but makes grants to several small-size foundations or directly to big-size governmental-background social organizations.

A case study on Narada Foundation's grantmaking approach
Narada Foundation was established in 2007 as the first Chinese grant-making foundation, predominately seeking to construct sound philanthropic infrastructures in China. Starting with its commitment to foster civil society, it makes grants to excellent nonprofit projects and nonprofit organizations nationwide. In a speech in 2007 during the first Narada Foundation Board of Trustees meeting, Qingzhi Zhou, honorary president and one of the organization's founders said,

> *To achieve the goal of ultimately benefiting the disadvantaged groups and promoting social change, we must work with numerous social organizations' partners to jointly achieve our goals by supporting their projects and helping to enhance their organizations' capabilities. For the selection of partners, attention should be paid to those organizations and entrepreneurs who have truly grown up in the private sector and who have the spirit of innovation*

and social ideal. They are our most important partners to achieve our foundation's goals.[22]

This speech shows that the fostering of civil society has become the Narada Foundation's mission and was embedded in its values from the beginning. Thus, the foundation developed four grant-making strategies at different stages: the New Citizen Program in 2007, the Ginkgo Fellow Program in 2010, the Jingxing Plan in 2010, and the China Effective Philanthropy Multiplier in 2016. According to Narada Foundation's statistics, from 2007 to 2016, its total expenditure was nearly 230 million RMB. It had provided funds for 783 projects conducted by 451 organizations or individuals. More than 60 percent of the grants were spent to build philanthropic infrastructures,[23] supporting more than ten influential networks, platforms, and professional supporting organizations. Examples of the platforms that Narada Foundation has created or jointly supported include the China Private Foundation Forum in 2008 (which was registered as an independent organization in 2016), Non-Profit Incubator (NPI) in 2009, the China Donors Roundtable (CDR) in 2015, and the Effective Philanthropy Multiplier in 2016 to support scaling-up the impact of proven solutions to social problems.[24] These platforms focused on how to lead cooperation between foundations and grassroots SOs. Most noteworthy is that CFF created a serious brand platform to strengthen communication and cooperation among Chinese foundations, as indicated in a speech by CFF's secretary-general at the annual National League of Cities (NLC) City Summit meeting.

5.2.4 Grant-making is important, but alone is far from sufficient

The preceding statistics show that, from 2007 to 2016, fewer than 40 percent of the grants (92 million RMB) were made to organizations or individuals by the Narada Foundation. Ginkgo Fellow Program and Jingxing Plan are taken as two of the most representative grant-making programs due to their pioneering practices in the Chinese foundation sector. The

---

22 See Narada Foundation website, http://www.naradafoundation.org/Uploads/edit or/20140909/14102550251853.pdf, accessed July 1, 2019.
23 See Xinhua News, http://www.xinhuanet.com//gongyi/2017-05/22/c_129612558.h tm, accessed July 1, 2019.
24 Effective Philanthropy Multiplier website, http://www.haogongyi.org.cn/home/e nglish/index.html, accessed July 1, 2019.

former subsidizes individuals and allows those working in nonprofit sectors to live a decent life, thereby expanding and strengthening recipients' organizations through supporting individuals and finally promoting the prosperity of the philanthropic sector. The latter provides unrestricted grants to leading grassroots SOs.

The Ginkgo Fellow Program, one of the Narada Foundation's best-known brand projects, aims to achieve personnel and career breakthroughs for its fellows by offering them grants of 100,000 RMB per year for three consecutive years. Since 2010, it has been one of the most influential fellow programs for people working in the nonprofit sector, including grassroots SOs and foundations. From 2007 to 2016, the Ginkgo Fellow Program funded eighty-one people, with total funding of 41.49 million RMB.

The Jingxing Plan is regarded as grassroots SOs' most influential program in China because of its three-year support plan and the number of unrestricted grants it has awarded, which, from 2011 until 2016, totaled 19,650,371.00 RMB in grants to sixteen grassroots SOs to foster their grantees' work on organizational development manuals, team leadership training, fundraising skills, and capability strategies for product development.

The Jingxing Plan's selection criteria are critical to grantee organizations, that is, the presumed excellent and leading SOs in the philanthropic sector or platform-based institutions. Once grassroots SOs meet that criteria, they become a partner with Jingxing, and each organization can receive an annual grant of 300,000 RMB to 500,000 RMB for no less than three years. These grants are flexible and can be applied according to the grantees' preferences, such as for business research and development, team building, summarizing experiences, strategic planning, fundraising, communicating a brand, constructing financial and management systems, and administrative costs.

Three examples illustrate that point. The funds that Shanghai Xintu Community Health Promotion Agency received from the Jingxing Plan were used for the salaries of its leaders and fundraising staff, for capacity building of teams and fundraising activities, and to support new city development projects. The funds obtained by the "I You She" organization were used mainly to optimize job allocation, to systematically review the organizational experience, and for research and development of new projects. The funding received by Natural University was used for the cost of the executive team, for office expenses, for the construction of its website, and for part of the expenditures for the annual meeting.

Investments in grantee organizations that do not place restrictions on methods and other processes give grantee organizations the flexibility they need to make the funding decisions they deem best. This flexibility is an important factor for organizations such as Nature University,[25] I You She, and Green Hunan.

Understandably, Jingxing Plan was regarded as pioneering work in the grant-making process, especially when the idea of grantmaking to grassroots SOs was still an unfamiliar one in China, in terms of both the length of a funding project and the number of funds granted. Unfortunately, Jingxing Plan ceased in 2016. Nevertheless, in the interviews I conducted, when grassroots SOs were asked to name one or two sustainable funding foundations, it was the one most frequently mentioned. It is worth noting that this program greatly enhanced and promoted the development of the organizations it funded. However, the program was not large in scope. Only one eligible grantee was selected in 2013, and at most there were only four eligible grassroots SOs in 2012 and 2015. Still, the Narada Foundation constantly emphasizes its influence in the philanthropic sector, claiming to actively "guide and promote more foundations to fund grassroots SOs." Alternatively, the program is seen as a model for the success of other foundations, which can encourage more other foundations to make grants.

Table 5-3: Numbers and amounts of Jingxing Plan from 2011 to 2016

Year	Number of approved organizations	The total amount of approved grants (RMB)
2011	2	1,670,485.50
2012	4	5419,700.00
2013	1	1,200,000.00
2014	3	4,270,000.00
2015	4	5419,700.00
2016	2	1,670,485.50
Total	16	19,650,371.00

Source: Narada Foundation website, http://www.naradafoundation.org, accessed November 17, 2019; adapted by the author.

---

25 Nature University is not a true university, but an environmental protection project based in Beijing.

5.2.5 A case study on how capital flows in grant-making foundations—He Foundation

The He Foundation is a large private foundation that focuses on grantmaking and supporting organizations in the philanthropic sector. However, an analysis of this foundation shows that it does not seriously consider grassroots SOs for funding, so they hardly ever directly receive funding support. The He Foundation has its own approach to grantmaking; for example, it grants funds to large and small foundations that operate projects by themselves or through indirect grants to grassroots SOs. Most of its recipients, e.g. Guangdong Charity Federation and Shunde Charity Federation, are government-affiliated organizations. Its grant-making process also increases operating costs because of their indirect way of funding intermediate organizations or foundations.

Figure 5-1: He Foundation charity plan

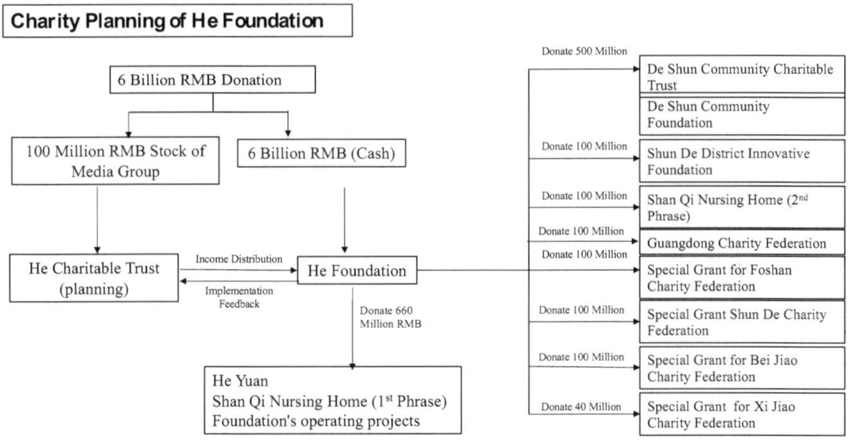

Charity Planning of He Foundation

		Donate Amount	Recipient
6 Billion RMB Donation		Donate 500 Million	De Shun Community Charitable Trust
			De Shun Community Foundation
100 Million RMB Stock of Media Group	6 Billion RMB (Cash)	Donate 100 Million	Shun De District Innovative Foundation
		Donate 100 Million	Shan Qi Nursing Home (2nd Phrase)
		Donate 100 Million	Guangdong Charity Federation
He Charitable Trust (planning)	He Foundation	Donate 100 Million	Special Grant for Foshan Charity Federation
		Donate 100 Million	Special Grant Shun De Charity Federation
	Donate 660 Million RMB	Donate 100 Million	Special Grant for Bei Jiao Charity Federation
He Yuan Shan Qi Nursing Home (1st Phrase) Foundation's operating projects		Donate 40 Million	Special Grant for Xi Jiao Charity Federation

(He Charitable Trust—Income Distribution / Implementation Feedback—He Foundation)

Source: Xie (2017, 30-31), adapted by the author.

As shown in figure 5-1, grassroots SOs are excluded under such funding schemes. In the transfer of the above foundations' funds, there is no space for grassroots SOs throughout the entire grant-making process, whereas there is space for the grants that flow from large foundations to smaller foundations or directly to government-affiliated charitable foundations and organizations.

Given the effect that large foundations have on grants to small foundations and corporate- or company-sponsored foundations' support to large public fundraising foundations, celebrity foundations, and university foundations, it is not surprising that roughly 60 percent of the grants go to different foundations, as indicated here:

> *According to the items of "Donations from Other Foundations" and "large payment of major public welfare projects" in the annual reports, 106 (57%) of the 184 foundations have been donated among the circle of different foundations through rough and conservative statistics. The donations of those foundations with very strong professionalism are the least as a result of their few associations with other foundations; and the amount of donations is proportional to the level of activity of the foundation (Source:* Wang 2018).

Based on the He Foundation, which is one of the most influential grant-making foundations in China, it can be concluded that significantly fewer grants are made to grassroots SOs.

The preceding two examples show that in China grant-making foundations are still very rare and that, in reality, the funding grassroots SOs receive from those foundations is not enough to cover their financial demands.

5.3 Problems and complaints during interactions

The following passage is from an opening speech by Yongguang Xu during the 5/12 Post-Disaster Reconstruction Cooperation Forum: Achieving Local SO and Foundation Cooperation in 2009.

> *Entering the era of cooperation between foundations and grassroots SOs is a major change in China's philanthropic infrastructure. In the supply chain of the philanthropic infrastructure, PFFs and NPFFs are funding providers, and various types of non-profit organizations (grassroots SOs and non-profit organizations separated from state institutions) are terminals in the philanthropic infrastructure.* (Xu 2009)

However, the question is, have foundations and grassroots SOs entered an era of cooperation as XU suggested one year after the Wenchuan earthquake in 2008? Although many people think foundations and grassroots SOs can work with each other smoothly, in reality, that has not been the case. Furthermore, both parties have criticized each other for a long time.

Since 2009, CFF has held national conferences every year that focus on the interactions between foundations and grassroots SOs in China. In 2011, a CFF panel discussed an interesting topic, "NPFFs 'no shortage of money' and grassroots 'only shortage of money.'" This topic, which was discussed from two perspectives, was initiated in the process of preparing the conference and was based on opinions solicited from many organizations. The first perspective is that of foundations. Many foundations said that they have a significant amount of money left near the end of the year. The second perspective is that of grassroots SOs. When CFF collected their opinions, the grassroots SOs thought that they had not received sufficient funding.

During the 2012 Research Report of Cooperation and Innovation of Chinese Non-Governmental Organizations and Foundations: Strategic Cooperation and Promoting Social Innovation (Bao 2012), I use the two following quoted sentences to explain the problems faced by foundations and grassroots SOs during the process of their interactions.

> *There are more than 2,000 foundations in China, but very few of them are grantmaking foundations. If there are more grantmaking foundations, private public welfare organizations (min jian gong yi zu zhi, 民间公益组织) will have more opportunities to choose suitable foundations according to their own goals, but they still can't do it now.* (7)
>
> An Interview with the focus group of private non-profit organizations
> *We originally planned to bid for 10 million RMB in Yushu, but there were not so many projects that meet the funding requirements. Finally, we only selected the projects with 7.5 million RMB.* (7)
>
> By China Foundation for Poverty Alleviation, Jun Wang

The former sentence means that grassroots SOs expect the appearance of more "suitable" foundations in accordance with their goals, while the latter one means that foundations have a lot of funding resources but cannot find enough "qualified" recipients to meet the foundations' requirements. Although the two entities seem to have different needs, they face the same problem, which is that both of them cannot find "capable partners" even when they attempt to work with each other, as both foundations and grassroots SOs grow in size and numbers.

Additionally, China Foundation Ranking (ji jin hui ping jia bang 基金会评价榜) is an event in China in which grassroots SOs who have been funded by overseas and domestic foundations evaluate the grant-making behavior of the foundations, and in which the awards are given to foundations. The award is based on three factors: to produce independent evaluations of foundations from the perspective of grassroots SOs and call on foundations to establish good cooperative relations with grassroots SOs, to promote foundations' enthusiasm for supporting grassroots SOs, and to assess the effectiveness of funding activities, and thereby enhance the development of China's philanthropic sector. It has been held in 2013 and 2015.

What grassroots SOs expect is the focus of this research. Their expectations for 2015 are shown in the following table.

Table 5-4: What grassroots SOs expect from foundations in China

	Comments from grassroots SOs (2015)
Financial disagreements are the most common problem	"Cut the budget without giving reasons." "The salary budget is always reduced, and XX foundation does not support the insurance budget." "When XX foundation first launched the bidding project, it did not include administrative expenses. Under the joint appeal of experts and many organizations, I am willing to provide 10% of project management costs, and the project funds are only 20,000 yuan, which does not work well." "XX foundation always requires us to purchase products under their "price platform," which obviously affects the quality of our projects. In addition, the foundation only accepts invoices, but sometimes we can only get the receipt instead of the invoice. In that case, we are required to use the invoice of the same categories together with the real receipts. Our financial staff and auditing company think that we are forced to make fraud, and we publicly inform the auditing company that we have made fraud. Our communication did not help in the end." "XX foundation deliberately cut the project budget. The maximum (we are informed to make the budget under 150,000 RMB during application) budget is 100,000 RMB (we get the notice directly with the negotiation process). As a result, the necessary activities and personnel expenses are cut regardless of whether the project budget is reasonable or not. Additionally, we, as a grantee, have to supplement the project expenses through fundraising." "Too many project activities, high expenses of office supplies, lots of documentaries and project reporting, and very strict financial expenditures." "No compensation for project administrators. The project is very exhausting." "When we cooperate with the government for saving some costs and resources during project implementation, it is rejected to be part of the project activities by the XX foundation, so that this activity expenditure."
Foundations' professionalism	"XX Foundation pretends to understand the project, but in fact not. They sit up high in a leading position and do not accept our suggestion, accuse and complain [about] us in the end." "XX Foundation did not understand the social work organizations and did not respond effectively to the problems that we told them."
Professional skills	Frequent staff turnover in foundations. Project official[s] are not professional but pretend to be professional.
Strong administrative influence, but weak on implementation	The project on the community's vulnerable group with X Foundation is not pragmatic. The project funding is paid late and the project is not sustainable. Even though the project was finished well finally, the cooperation was not pleasant because the project was separated from the community."

	Comments from grassroots SOs (2015)
Excessive interference with grantee organizations	"The grantee mostly enforces the orders from the foundation with limited initiatives." "We only cooperate[d] with the XX foundation once. We are required to submit the progress report every month, and the evaluation is conducted by a third party regardless of the actual implementation of the project. So we spend a lot of energy on that project."
Others	"The project officials of XX Foundation visited our organization and decided to fund our organization. We then submitted the letter of intent, but did not get any response and feedback in the end." "The project proposal and planned activities were handed over to the foundation, who suddenly changed and did not fund us."

Although some grassroots SOs argue with foundations, most of them prefer to keep silent when they have conflicts with foundations. Unpleasant conflicts will affect cooperation with other foundations as well.

What kinds of dilemmas are involved in cooperation between foundations and grassroots SOs in China?
To answer this question, I formulated the following hypothesis based on a study by Shieh (2017, 1787):

> The overarching dilemma between foundations and grassroots SOs is that they criticize each other, which means that foundations complain they cannot find capable grassroots SOs to make grants, whereas grassroots SOs complain that foundations prefer to carry out projects by themselves rather than fund grassroots SOs.

Together with the case studies in this chapter and consideration of the criticism between foundations and grassroots SOs, I divided the overarching dilemma as follows:

Dilemma 1: The abilities of grassroots SOs are not robust, for example, with leadership, financial management, and organizational development.

Dilemma 2: Grassroots SOs lack funding resources, and grants from domestic foundations are too small to cover the cost of projects that need a lot of work.

Dilemma 3: Current project requests are different from grassroots SOs' goals.

Dilemma 4: Chinese foundations think grassroots SOs get used to overseas funds and cannot get along with Chinese foundations.

Dilemma 5: Foundations' requirements of "short-period, safety, immediate efficiency" are different from the development and strategy of grassroots SOs.

Dilemma 6: Which one is professional? Foundations' staff or grassroots SOs' staff? They all think that they are more professional than each other.

5.4 Discussion

Prior to 2004, there were no interactions between SOs and government-dominated foundations in China; however, this situation changed gradually and was especially stimulated by the 2008 earthquake. The 2008 earthquake inspired Chinese foundations to recognize the role of grassroots SOs and then to prompt foundations to start funding grassroots SOs, which marked the beginning of the interactions between SOs and government-dominated foundations. However, the interactions did not go as smoothly as expected, not only because of foundations and grassroots SOs' divergent developmental pathways but also because of their different values and expectations.

The reality is that very few grant-making foundations exist in China, and few of those make grants to grassroots SOs. Some grant-making foundations have never included grassroots SOs in their funding scheme. Some grant-making foundations spend only a small percentage of their funding to support grassroots SOs, and those selected are normally influential or excellent ones. As a result, grassroots SOs that are underdeveloped or have no connection with foundations have little hope of gaining access to funding resources. It can be concluded, therefore, that the funding resources available to grassroots SOs are far from sufficient.

The main complaint from foundations is that they cannot find capable grassroots SOs, whereas grassroots SOs say that they cannot find grant-making foundations that are willing to support them. Thus, foundations have further reduced their grant-making budgets and turned to support projects such as infrastructure construction and the philanthropic ecosystem, or they foster some newly established grassroots SOs because they think the existing grassroots SOs are unprofessional and unqualified to apply for foundations' projects. Meanwhile, SOs that have matured are forced to change their strategies, and their staff may have to turn to other professional endeavors.

The foundations' philosophy is that cooperation with grassroots SOs is only one aspect of an operation, whereas, for grassroots SOs, cooperation with foundations is about survival. Although a grantor faces a lot of pressure when complaints arise or there is poor communication with a grantee, once a foundation is dissatisfied with a grantee, it can usually take certain measures, such as stopping a project or not funding it. However, most grassroots SOs choose to remain silent when they are dissatisfied with foundations for fear of negatively affecting the cooperation between them, as well as other foundations' views of them.

6 Understanding how foundations interact with grassroots SOs from the perspective of foundations

Given that disagreements arise frequently between foundations and grassroots SOs in China and that the number of grant-making foundations is increasing, this chapter explores how interactions between the two develop and lead to cooperation throughout the grant-making process, including selection criteria and the implementation and assessment methodology adopted by Chinese grant-making foundations. Questions addressed here include, how do foundations select and finalize terms with grantees; how do foundations process contracts; and what is the usual amount funded and the timespan of projects? Note that, in several instances, cases were collected from foundations' websites or their open calls and selected as samples.

6.1 Grantee selection before interactions and cooperation

Because many overseas foundations had already made their entry into China, grant-making was not originally a completely new concept in China. However, how Chinese foundations would start grantmaking and to whom they would grant funds were unclear. "Where are the partners?" has become a question that foundations in China frequently ask. Moreover, although there are a large number of social organizations in China that need financial resources, not many of them can meet the funding requirements of Chinese foundations. Thus, during the interviews with foundations, this question was presented:

> Foundation_Q1: How could your foundation look for the grantees or grassroots SOs? For example, recommendation, online application, workshop, visiting grassroots SOs, etc.

Among the sixteen Chinese foundations I interviewed, seven of them were oriented as grant-making foundations, six were mixed foundations with grant-making projects,[26] and the other three were completely operating

---

26 One of them is oriented as both of operating and grantmaking foundation, so I exclude it as a grantmaking foundation but as a mixed foundation in this study.

foundations and were interviewed as references. This section focuses only on the foundations that made grants to grassroots SOs, namely Foundation B, D, E, F, G, I, J, K, L, M, N, O, P.

Regarding the interview question on how foundations seek grantees or grassroots SOs, representatives of all thirteen foundations said they used several approaches to seek partners, including active and passive approaches. Of the respondents whose foundations were oriented as grant-making foundations and those who had grant-making projects, ten of thirteen said that they sought grantees through online applications; four of thirteen said they needed recommendations or recommendation letters from experts; ten of thirteen said they looked for partners actively by themselves; and six of thirteen said they attended or organized various workshops where they could learn more about selecting potential partners.

Additionally, those foundations' application procedures were found to be constantly changing. For example, Foundation G accepted requests for proposals from applicants before 2017, but due to the changing organizational, it adopted a procedure in which applications came from partners or peers or potential partners were sought actively by the foundation's staff. In some cases, a foundation's application procedure and grant-making or not will be determined by the main donor, who is the real decision-maker. Mostly, the selection of projects depends on the logic of the project itself and the foundations' team.

Table 6-1: How the foundations interviewed sought grantees

Foundation	Different ways to find grassroots SOs
A	Not any because it is an operating foundation
B	Through online applications
C	Not any because it is an operating foundation
D	Actively sought potential partners and grassroots SOs for united fundraising
E	Through recommendations by board members or other peers
F	Mixed ways
G	Through requests for proposals from applicants before 2017; since 2018, through partners or peers who actively sought potential partners
H	Not any because it is an operating foundation
I	Through open calls, recommendations, workshops, networks, and actively sought grantees
J	Through open calls; in 2018 actively sought grantees (but not sure how to do so)
K	Through open calls, recommendations, workshops, networks, and actively sought grantees
L	Mostly through grassroots SOs connecting with the foundation directly for united fundraising

Foundation	Different ways to find grassroots SOs
M	Through open calls
N	Through open calls, recommendations, workshops, networks, and actively sought grantees
O	Open calls, recommendations
P	Open calls, recommendations

Additionally, in all foundations interviewed, experts or scholars served as judges during the recommendation period, or during the selection period, or during the evaluation period, or throughout all three phases. Two potential explanations can be offered for this. First, some Chinese foundations that are still exploring how to find partners or grantees believe that experts and scholars can accurately measure professionalism. Second, the involvement of experts and scholars provides perspectives on selected projects that help ensure objectivity and impartiality, as well as reduce the limitations foundations place on grantees. More importantly, the objectivity of the experts depends on how they are selected, the type experts they are, and whether individual or collective experts will play a role in the process.

6.1.1 Seek grantees actively

Even with their complaints of one another, foundations and grassroots SOs started working with each other in various ways. As previously mentioned, how to find capable and suitable partners is both important and difficult to do. In addition, interpretations of what is a capable or suitable partner are still vague; it could be that a potential partner meets a project's requirements, or has a staff that is easy to get along with, or has a professional staff and a perfect institutional setup. Domestic foundations, like foreign foundations, are gradually exploring their own way to look for partners, for example, seeking for partners actively, getting recommendations from experts and peers, requesting proposals, building cooperative networks, and so on. My interviews showed that, rather than a single approach, most of the foundations used a combination of approaches to find partners, which were, to some extent, related to a project' requirements, the development of foundations, funding scale and types, and so on.
Concept paper
A project proposal is a detailed project application submitted by partners to foundations, which is largely an extension and refinement of a project concept book or paper. The project invitation is the beginning of "purchas-

ing," during which "inquiry" and "price comparison" are essential. It helps to guarantee the openness and fairness of selecting partners and proposals.

In reality, when they have a better understanding of grassroots SOs or their leaders, foundations may invite several grassroots SOs to apply for projects. Of course, this is based on trust. Alternatively, when grant-making officials know a group of interested organizations, they may invite these organizations to submit project proposals or concept papers in order to explore the possibility of cooperation in some certain projects.

Chinese foundations have a short history compared with western countries, and the first grant-making foundation did not appear until 2007. Grant-making foundations prioritize actively seeking partners, especially newly founded foundations. The main benefits are twofold. First, because taking the initiative to know others can help reduce risks, contacting grassroots SOs enables foundations to a closer look at them and determine whether their goals are in alignment. Second, foundations' staff members are probably not knowledgeable in certain fields, so contacting grassroots SOs can be a learning process. If a foundation's focus is relatively clear, it will very likely find the right grassroots SOs to work with. However, if that focus is not clear and if the foundation is not sure about how to approach grassroots SO or even whether it wants to cooperate with them, it is difficult to find a satisfactory partner, in which case the foundation may choose to execute the project itself

During my interviews, Foundation I's representative talked about the foundation's approach to searching for partners positively:

> *Foundation I is determined to make grants to support grassroots SOs since its establishment, even without any experience in China besides of few experiences from overseas organizations by that time. But they still started with its way to look for partners initially under the clear organizational orientation as a grant-making foundation to support and cultivate potential individuals and grassroots SOs. Ms. Li, currently as deputy secretary-general, has participated in grassroots SOs' meetings and events as a project officer to look for potential individuals and grassroots SOs.*

6.1.2 Public tendering and a request for proposal

A request for proposal (RFP) is a document that describes a project's requirements in detail and seeks qualified partners with proposed solutions in a certain field. It is issued by foundations online or, to reach more grassroots SOs through other foundations or grassroots SOs, is distributed by email or social media. RFP is one of the most important approaches foundations can take to seek qualified grassroots SOs and to inform the public that the foundations are fair and transparent. Through public tendering, the foundations set out measurable and concrete requirements to ensure reaching their project goals.

Except for one newly established foundation (Foundation E), all the other foundations chose to issue an RFP to collect proposals or concept papers from the public as one of their main approaches to finding potential partners. Foundation E did not publish a public tender for two reasons. One reason was that the foundation was small and newly established and could find enough grantees through the recommendation of experts or founders. The second reason was that the foundation's funding came from several private donors, so there was no specific need to make the selection process transparent to the public. Two other leading grant-making foundations (Foundations K and N), which were well known for supporting newly founded grassroots SOs, had a precise RFP booklet, consisting of an introduction of the project, qualifications for grassroots SOs, selection methods, reviewers' suggestions, Q&As, and an introduction of the foundation itself. It is worth noting that a few special foundations submit open calls to the public.

In May 2019, Narada Foundation posted a collective RFP through WeChat with eight projects from seven different foundations (Bosch China Charity Center, the center that manages all Bosch's charitable activities in China, is also concluded in the list) with the title, "What to do without money? Here is a list of funding projects without restricted fields."[27] This collective RFP was recommended by many of the foundations interviewed. Although that was not the first time such applications occurred simultaneously, it did indicate a fresh situation. Table 6-2 shows that 300,000 RMB per year was the highest amount provided by a foundation in China. The total request for proposals is nevertheless good news for all SOs that are looking for funding resources.

---

27 Narada Foundation, https://mp.weixin.qq.com/s/XTmz74FrOBE1bkLAyFuOuA, accessed June 15, 2019.

Table 6-2: RFPs by Chinese foundations in May 2019

	Project name	From which foundation	Support areas	Amount
1	Ginkgo Plan	Ginkgo Foundation	To individuals, twenty to forty years old, no nationality restrictions, working on public welfare in mainland China, have devoted themselves to the current work for more than two years. At the same time, it is in line with the conditions of "being excellent individuals, being at a proper stage of growth, and playing greater leverage with this funding."	$14,089 per year
2	Ai You "Philanthropy + Partnership"	Ai You Foundation	To nonprofit organizations such as CNI and associations, as well as business registration groups that are restricted to public welfare and whose articles stipulate no dividends; and organization is in a stage of rapid growth and strategic upgrades. Those that meet the following criteria have priority: 1) have a great social impact on a certain field of public welfare; 2) main working area of the organization is unspecified with great demand, the previous practice received good results; and 3) working model of the organization is clear and duplicable.	300,000 RMB per year
3	Ai You "Philanthropy + Maker"	Ai You Foundation	To nonprofit organizations such as CNI and associations, as well as business registration groups that are restricted to public welfare and whose articles stipulate no dividends; and organization is in a stage of rapid growth and strategic upgrades. Those who meet the following criteria have priority: 1) work areas can fill the gaps or be close to public life; 2) innovative working models, or with public welfare attributes; 3) strong public mobilization ability, or continue to be active in the public areas; 4) good public welfare performance.	100,000 RMB per year
4	K2 Action Program	K2 Foundation	Operating social organizations in three major areas: education, environmental protection, and social innovation.	Unspecified
5	China Effective Philanthropy Multiplier	Narada Foundation	High-quality public welfare products that have proved to be effective in solving social problems and can be scaled up.	Unspecified

	Project name	From which foundation	Support areas	Amount
6	Social Enterprise Investment	Yifang Foundation	Applicants: Business registration enterprises. Applicants should comply with relevant national laws and regulations, conduct business activities for more than one year, and have clear social goals and business models. Enterprise operating funds are mainly obtained through commercial activities. Commitment to 100% financial transparency to investors and shareholders.	Unspecified
7	Bosch China Charity Center	Bosch China Charity Center	A. Quality public welfare projects on education and poverty eradication. The funding for a single project does not exceed 1 million RMB, and the project period is approved by the Bosch China Charity Center for a minimum of one year and a maximum of two years. Applicants initiate the application amount and period of funding according to the actual needs of the project, and Bosch China Charity Center finally determines the funding amount. B. Support for public welfare organizations. The small-scale public social welfare organization approved by the Bosch China Charity Center has received funding of no more than 200,000 RMB. The funding period is at least one year and no longer than two years. In the end, the charity center will determine the funding amount and period according to the applicant organization's situation.	Unspecified Note: A. The funding for a single project does not exceed 1 million RMB, and the project period is approved by the Bosch China Charity Center for a minimum of one year and a maximum of two years. B. The small-scale social public welfare organization approved by the Bosch China Charity Center has received funding of no more than 200,000 RMB. The funding period is at least one year and no longer than two years.
8	Chaoren Mother	China Women's Development Foundation	1. The project must be initiated by or led by women. 2. Fileds of working involved in the project should be, for example, education, environmental protection, targeted measures in poverty alleviation, women's health, and sustainable development. Generally, personal assistance projects are not accepted.	Unspecified

Source: Originally from WeChat https://mp.weixin.qq.com/s/XTmz74FrOBE1bkLAyFuOuA, accessed June 15, 2019, and adapted by the author.

6.1.3 Recommendation from peers, colleagues, and experts

Peers, colleagues, and experts often recommend to foundations that they have connections with or know certain SOs that are seeking financial resources to apply toward projects. In the interviews, representatives from Foundations K and N said they liked to accept recommendations from other foundations, peers, colleagues, or experts. And some foundations, such as Foundation I, were open to introducing their grantees to other foundations or, after a project was completed, add their grantees to one or multiple WeChat groups where open calls or application information are shared with partners.

The JinCao Peer Project, a well-known grant-making project that focuses on environmental organizations in a growth phase, considers recommendations as mandatory. This project, which started in December 2012, was jointly initiated by the SEE Foundation and the Global Greengrants Fund and was later supported by other Chinese foundations. One interesting point is that this project provides each selected SO 300,000 RMB of unrestricted funds for three years, which catches the attention of many because three-year projects are rare in China. Additionally, this project provides a mentoring group of peers referred to as the JinCao project that consists of entrepreneurs and experienced professionals in public welfare. The application for joining JinCao peers notes, JinCao Peers Project implements the Real Name Recommendation System, and the applicants must be nominated by the recommenders.

Recommendations from peers, colleagues, and experts are commonly used to connect foundations and grassroots SOs. Because they can learn more about recommended organizations and trust them more, some foundations are particularly inclined to use this approach.

6.1.4 Connecting through workshops, networks, and competition via TV and online platforms

Partners can be found through workshops, networks of foundations and grassroots SOs, and competitions on television and online platforms. The representative of the K2 Foundation indicated the value of competition, as follows:

By means of competition, it will create a competitive environment for social organizations. At the same time, it will provide a large amount of manage-

ment fees, professional mentors, high-quality networks, and multi-learning resources to strongly support the organization's professional ability.[28]

During the interviews, some influential foundations pointed out that one of the most important tasks for foundations was building up the infrastructure of the entire philanthropic sector, not providing funds for grassroots SOs. They believed, what grassroots SOs need most is not funds, but knowledge about how to improve their abilities in fundraising skills and organizational development. How to change the ecosystem of the philanthropy sector has been a long-running topic among grant-making foundations, a topic promoted by the Narada Foundation. For example, the words "to change the ecosystem of the philanthropy sector" and "incite public welfare resources" are very often mentioned by foundations labeled as grant-making foundations.

Empirical research by Lai (2017, 58–59) showed that the Narada Foundation has played an important role in building domestic philanthropic infrastructure as a supporting platform for grassroots SOs. The China Effective Philanthropy Multiplier program established by the Narada Foundation exemplifies how to increase the influence of foundations' decision-making and help them find suitable grantees efficiently.

The database of Chinese nonprofit organizations was jointly sponsored by the Narada Foundation, the NGO2.0 project, and the School of Philanthropy at Sun Yat-sen University. This database, which was the first one to cover charitable organizations in mainland China, served as a platform in philanthropic infrastructure. Moreover, this database provides information that is relevant to research institutions and that can improve the quality of research, including targeted samples for large-scale quantitative research.

In the interviews, the most impressive thing was that foundations were more interested in whether they received positive reviews than in informing people about their foundations, which is one reason many foundations constantly adjusted their strategies to increase their social impact. Some foundations wanted to cooperate with grassroots SOs in order to increase their civic impact, rather than enable effective SOs to take the lead in project planning. This hesitancy was due to the uncertainty of risks during project implementation, which was why many of the foundations were not willing to support grassroots SOs directly.

---

28 See http://www.xianfeng.org/index.php/Home/Support/support_introduce/pid/2 5/fid/25.html, accessed October 15, 2019.

6.1.5 Findings and problems

Foundations' continuous innovations and timely adjustments of their approaches to selection of grantees have greatly improved the grant-making process, and some foundations have even standardized grantee selection. However, foundations' selection processes have received many negative evaluations. The interviews unveiled three problems: foundations' positioning, length of the section process, and a high degree of competition.

Given the selection stage, the positioning of most foundations is very important, namely to cooperate or not to cooperate, and how to cooperate. An often-mentioned example is the You Cheng Foundation, which has been cited as an unclear positioning of being a grant-making foundation or an operating foundation. Lack of clarity about its positioning has led to confusion about its funding areas and the timespan of its projects. Although the You Cheng Foundation has always insisted on a grant-making approach, it has designed and implemented, on its own, a large number of projects, and thus has worked similar to an operating foundation. Hence, its own operating projects and funds have exceeded grants made to grassroots SOs (Woqi Foundation 2018).

Similar issues of unclear positioning persisted in the interviews I conducted, for example, with Foundations G and J. The former's decision, which was made by its top leader, shifted the foundation's focus, which adopted a completely new concept of funding from Western philanthropy as Foundation G's new strategy[29]. Even project officials did not quite understand what the foundation would do in the future, that is, whether it would support grassroots SOs or not. On the other hand, funds for the projects shown in its financial reports were mostly direct donations to schools for poverty alleviation or education-related projects, and grassroots SOs did not need to be involved.

In an article, Xu (2009) noted that some grassroots SOs complained that the Chinese Red Cross Foundation paid much more attention to constructing hardware facilities and promoting its reputation than on project activities, which is not the strength of grassroots SOs. In the end, because of pressure from the media and other publicity, the grassroots SOs decided

---

29 I also asked two other people who work with foundations at that time about the term, and they said they didn't know or understand it. This article doesn't mention the term mentioned by Foundation G because it is easy to recognize Foundation G.

to stop cooperating with the Chinese Red Cross Foundation, even after this organizations' application was approved by the Chinese Red Cross Foundation.

A similar case happened to a nationwide PFF, Foundation P. The one-year project provided by Foundation P had taken more than a year to call for proposals and the first and final selections. The final selection process was similar to the defense of a doctoral study, according to two applicants, SO 4 and SO 10 (one doctoral graduate and one doctoral candidate representing SO 10 were assigned to defend their dissertations during the final selection). The selection committee criticized both SO 4 and SO 10 for their lack of professionalism in describing what a professional organization and project are; thus both organizations' applications were not approved in the end. Also, from the first selection to the final selection, each shortlisted applicant was required to make a public service video to promote Foundation P's project slogan, which is exactly what grassroots SOs are not good at. Besides, when announcing the finalists, media participation and speeches from leaders of national government departments have also been used.

Foundation P's tendering project contained five significant features: corporate funding, government guidance, expert participation, media promotion, and then hosted by the foundation. This case showed that the selection process followed prior to cooperation (which took about one year to complete) can be complicated.

However, the selection phase is not always a problem for foundations, especially large-scale foundations, because they have enough funding to cover their overall budget; and some large or long-standing grassroots SOs can prepare for a small budget. However, the process is not a small investment for grassroots SOs, and organizations with only three to five people, it is a significant loss if they do not succeed in the end.

A long-term selection phase is no exception. Foundation G invited a third party to evaluate its entire application process, and the result showed that the process was too long because it took around three to six months of telephone communication from the very beginning to the final decision to make a grant and start a project. For example, the length of a detailed due diligence report was equivalent to an academic paper. From the perspective of Foundation G's project official, it is unrealistic for grantees to wait such a long time for a one-year project because a regular project's timespan is one year. However, he was only able to fulfill the role of a project officer in accordance with the rules of the foundation but had no role in decision-making.

Low Percentage of Funding Application Approved

Foundations cannot accept every request, and the percentage of applications approved is an indicator of the competition for funding among foundations, though it is not the only one. However, a low percentage of funding applications might affect some applicants' decisions about whether to apply.

Below are cases from three foundations concerning the percentage of funding applications approved.

> *Case_1:* "The 2nd ME Welfare Innovation Funding Plan was launched in September 2016, totally receiving 400 public welfare project applications. After strict review, 21 beneficiary organizations were selected. The total funding was over 10.5 million yuan" (China Foundation for Poverty Alleviation Annual Report 2016, 15; adapted by the author).
>
> *Case_2:* "By December of 2017, a total of 50 research project applications were received, of which 45 were rejected. The percentage of funding application approved is 10%" (*Source: from* 2017 Annual Report of Yifang Foundation; adapted by the author).
>
> *Case_3:* "From June 17th to June 19th, 2016, the final selection review meeting of the sixth 'Creating a Green Home' project from SEE Foundation was held in Wuhan. A total of 165 environmental public welfare entrepreneurship teams have submitted their applications. After the project team's compliance review and interview, 51 teams entered the final selection. After the fierce thought collision in the final selection, 43 teams were selected into the sixth 'Creating a Green Home' project. The percentage of funding applications approved is accounting for 26%." (*Source:* from SEE Foundation 2016, http://www.see.org. cn/clj/newsdetail.aspx?id=1642, accessed November 10, 2019; adapted by the author)

The percentage of funding applications approved for the ME Welfare Innovation Funding Plan launched by the China Foundation for Poverty Alleviation organization was only 5.25 percent, the percentage of applications approved for the Yifang Foundation was 10 percent, and the percentage of applications approved for the "Creating a Green Home" project launched by the SEE Foundation was 26 percent. The Yifang Foundation listed various reasons for the low number of approved applications (*Yi Fang Foundation Annual Report 2017,* 06). Fourteen percent of proposals fell outside the Yifang Foundation's fields of workings. Thirty percent of proposals focused on implementing activities, which fell outside the Yifang Foundation's interests. And the remaining 62 percent of proposals were not approved because of their weak social impact, as they focused on nonurgent or repeated fields or impractical and unprofessional skills. The Yifang Foundation also noted that 38 percent of applicants submitted proposals even though they knew that the projects they were applying for were not eligible for grants.

Seeking suitable partners is the first step that foundations can take to start interactions with grassroots SOs. Through the experiences and lessons learned in past years, foundations have found their own ways to start cooperation, and they are still exploring ways to do so. In the context of individual foundations, the relationship between a foundation and its partners will change according to the dynamic development of foundations and grassroots SOs. In particular, individualized differences are the main driving force between foundations and grassroots SOs. Similarly, the competition is very intense for grassroots SOs during project applications. This also means that many grassroots SOs do not receive resources if domestic foundations' resources are limited.

6.2 *Concerning the application guidelines*

In the partner–grantee searching process, the second concern is whether a foundation provides guidelines for applications and documents that explain the application process and its requirement. For parties to work efficiently, it is important that grassroots SOs fully understand the application procedure. Clear guidelines help grassroots SOs determine whether they can meet the criteria, which saves time and energy for both foundations and grassroots SOs. Thus, the following question was formulated:

> *Foundation_Q2: Does the foundation have the guidelines for applications or documents that explain the application process and its requirements?*

Nine of thirteen foundations interviewed said that they had guidelines or documents explaining in detail applications' procedures and requirements. When the interviewees from foundations were asked whether they had such guidelines, they usually said they kept a formal set of those documents in case they wind up making grants to others. One guideline on the RFP from Foundation B, which was located in a provincial area, was as thick as a book, with more than two hundred pages, including how to fill in various forms and applications. They were positioning themselves as fair and transparent organizations with demanding requirements for their grant-making projects and grantees, mainly due to pressure from donors, the public, and the media.

The experience of a newly established foundation, Foundation E, was an exception. Its representative said it did not have application guidelines or documents because it was established in 2016 with a small annual budget and is still exploring grant-giving and would like to select some grantees under the recommendation of other foundations or peers. Once it finds projects that match its general fields, for example, primary education in rural areas of China, Foundation E will consider offering financial support. Instead of talking about what the foundation would like to become or support in the long-term, they want to consider what grantees need and then make efforts in that direction. Compared with large-scale foundations, this small foundation sounds as though it will be more flexible and rooted in grassroots SOs.

As revealed in the interviews, most foundations formulated guidelines that helped applicants understand the application process and requirements. I provided one special example from the SEE Foundation to explain what is included in the guidelines, namely Free Flying Wings (FFWs). Because SEE provided a lot of data and conducted a lot of research, the guidelines indicated that more than 100 wetlands were in urgent need of protection and that twenty-four species of rare and endangered water birds were prioritized for protection targets.

Project official's role

> *Foundation_Q3: Does the foundation have a professional staff to help applicants during the application process?*

A project official's role is very important throughout a project's lifespan, and also, to an even greater extent, for grassroots SOs, because the official may be their only connection with foundations. Foundations believe that project officials have two main functions: to ensure the completion of approved projects and to ensure that grassroots SOs spend the funds granted only on worthwhile projects. Therefore, project officials spend many days on fieldwork and writing various reports, such as preliminary investigative reports, due diligence reports, and field research reports. A representative from Foundation G noted that "writing [a] field research report is equal to writing an academic thesis, which even takes one or two months or even longer by project officials." A project officer's main role is to help foundations and grassroots SOs communicate with each other.

An analysis of the process foundations follows reveals the ongoing progress in the professionalization of Chinese foundations. Because of grassroots SOs' complaints that project officials are unprofessional, foundations have attempted to improve the officials' abilities. On the other hand, Chinese foundations believe their staff is making more progress toward professionalism than grassroots SOs are making. For example, a recent study by Woqi Foundation (2018) mentioned the "learning by doing" approach proposed by the SEE Foundation and the Guangzhou Harmony Foundation.

> In terms of the choice of funding objects, we [SEE Foundation and Guangzhou Harmony Foundation] have different sensitivities and perceptions than others. Our experience is to constantly acquaint with the interesting areas, and finally, staffs' cognition and professionalism from our foundation exceed the grantees on specific topics or fields. (142)

The study by Woqi Foundation (2018) also included the following comments by Mrs. Miaoting Li, from the Guangzhou Harmony Foundation, on how to improve project official's grantmaking-abilities.

> Project officials who do not have the experience of grantmaking are suggested to work in grantees' organization for a while, so as to gain a grantees' perspective.
>
> Project officials are encouraged to learn through learning platforms and training opportunities provided by the foundation.
> Through learning by doing, newcomers can learn from their predecessors or experienced personal. (85)

The pressure on project officials comes from many stakeholders, including grantees and experts, board members, executive directors, and donors. In an interview, one representative who had previously worked for foreign and domestic foundations explained the struggle of being a profficerficial in a Chinese grant-making foundation. The foundation she worked for at the time of the interview was one of the few such foundations in China, and its leaders encouraged her to work with grantees independently, for example, with international grant-making foundations. Although she had accumulated experience in grant-making approaches from her work in a foreign foundation, she still encountered many difficulties during the design and grantee selection phases. In addition to understanding applicants' rationale for their projects, she had to consider questions that the strategy committee, secretariat, and experts might ask during the defense stage, which forced her to consider all the factors of each project that might affect the success of the project.

Also, in cases where project officials understand problems that board members do not understand, the board members might impose ideas that will not allow the official to defend a project, even when the official did a lot of work during the preselection process. In some cases, project officials think that committee members and experts do not understand a specific field but that those committee members and experts have more opportunities to express their opinions and comments. Project officials may eventually lose the prospect of convincing experts about a project's professional viability and the value of funding it. Particularly when decision-makers are experts from the business sector, their language and expectations may be different from those of nonprofit sectors about the outcome of projects.

Project officials also face challenges in communicating with grassroots SOs, as mentioned during the 2013 and 2015 of China Foundation Rankings. In some cases, one project officer is responsible for dozens of grantees, for example, in Foundation D. SOs that receive grants are located throughout the country, so the cost of communication is very high, particularly if they do a preliminary investigation and due diligence for each program. The representative from Foundation D said, "Whenever we start a new project, due diligence is the most time-consuming and tiring phase." A similar case can be found in China Charities Aid Foundation for Children (Woqi Foundation 2018, 194), as well as Foundations G and N in the interviews. Some grantees' project staff work in remote mountainous villages and do not even use QQ,[30] which means they spend a lot of time and energy on communication.

In some organizations, personnel changes are very high. For example, after project officials spend a great deal of time and energy to achieve mutual understanding, the grantee's contact person may suddenly leave and a new staff person comes on board, in which case, the work involved in communicating needs to start again. The frequent turnover of foundation project officials is equally troublesome for grassroots SOs. In the interviews, Foundation G said that one time his foundation could not find the right contact person after its project officer left but that the grantee organization did not report the matter for a long time. This meant both parties had to spend extra time to restart communication.

---

30 QQ is an instant messaging software service and web portal developed by the Chinese tech company Tencent that was used for work in Chinese before WeChat.

6.3 How to finalize cooperation

The previous chapter described several approaches that foundations and grassroots SOs use to find a good match for one another. In this section, I explain how Chinese foundations select and then cooperate with grassroots SOs and how their cooperation is finalized.

To determine the stakeholders who make the decision to finalize cooperation and how they do so, I formulated this question:

> *Foundation_Q4: Who finally decides which application to accept? Please describe (such as the management of the foundation).*

In the interviews, most foundations' representatives said that, depending on the amount funded to a project, the final decisions are made by department leaders, the secretary-general, or the board of directors. My observation is that all foundations have a rigorous process for approving and evaluating projects that are related to the increased supervision of social media and complaints from grassroots SOs. Two case studies are provided to illustrate how two influential Chinese grant-making foundations finalize the process of cooperation, namely the Narada Foundation and One Foundation.

Narada Foundation Case Study: To explain who are involved in the finalization of the cooperation process, I start with Narada Foundation's analysis of its project approval process[31]:

> *Step 1: Approval through emails*
> *After the comments from the project review team in the project department, and communicating with applicants, "Project Approval Report" (together with "Project Proposal") will be submitted to Yu Cheng [Vice Chair of the Board] for approval through email, which should be copied to Zhouhong [Secretary-General] who can make comments. After approval by Yu Cheng, she will forward it to the project department again. The project department will report to Yongguang Xu [Chair of the Board], who will make the final approval.*
> *Step 2 : Written approval*
> *After the approval by Yongguang Xu, the project department will inform Yu Cheng, Zhouhong Liu and financial staff, print the Project Approval Report*

---

31 Narada Foundation website, http://www.naradafoundation.org/content/1137, accessed September 15 2019.

out, which will be signed by Yu Cheng and Zhouhong Liu and saved as a file.

The third step: sign the funding agreement

After approval, the project department will draft the funding agreement and report it to Yongguang Xu which needs to be signed and stamped. Then the funding agreement will be posted to the applicant to be signed and sealed and filed.

One Foundation Case Study:

After Narada Foundation's project approval process, One Foundation, as one of the most influential PFF in China, is adopted to understand who has the right to finalize the cooperation with its recipients during the grantmaking.

Table 6-3: Authority of approval based on the amount of grant from One Foundation

Approver	The authority of the approved grant amount
Project manager	The approved budget is less than/equal to 10,000 RMB.
Team leader	The approved budget is over 10,000 RMB and less than/equal to 100,000 RMB.
Branch secretary-general	The approved budget is over 100,000 RMB and less than/equal to 500,000 RMB.
Secretary-general	The approved budget is over 500,000 RMB.

Source: (One Foundation 2017, 9) and adapted by the author.

Two documents, from Narada Foundation and One Foundations, are used to specify different project officials' authority in order to examine and approve projects based on an approved budget. In One Foundation, the minimum amount was less than 10,000 RMB (around $1,461) on July 1, 2019, which could be approved by the project leader. Generally, only a secretary-general has the authority to approve projects, except for a few foundations that allow project officials or deputy secretary generals to approve projects. What's more, all the work of foundations, regardless of their size, needs the approval of the secretary-general.

As shown earlier, project officers directly participate in calling for proposals, preliminary investigations, and due diligence, during which process they contact applicants. The interviews revealed that, in most foundations, project officers actually had no chance to present projects in person but did so in long, time-consuming reports to decision-makers. Foundation I, located in Guangzhou, was an exception. Its project officers, who knew and better understood the foundation's partners, played an important role in interactions between the foundation and its grantees.

Project leaders' power to examine and approve projects

The Narada Foundation's Jingxing Plan has been one of the most outstanding grant-making projects awarded to grassroots SOs in China. Thus, its process and standard are provided to help analyze how it seeks its grantees. The Narada Foundation's project officers have four main focus areas: Product, People, Operation, Finance (PPOF), based on the nonprofit organizational life cycle (Woqi Foundation 2018, 110–114).

How to select partners: Three phases must be completed, namely organization scanning, preliminary investigation, and due diligence. Organization scanning means to examine projects and products, preliminary investigation means to examine the entire team and its leadership, due diligence means that project officers should go to the project sites and examine multiple factors, paying special attention the project's potential for overall development, for development of its leaders and team, and development in terms of innovation and governance.

Table 6-4: A study on how the Narada Foundation's Jingxing Plan selects its grantees

Periods	Organizations' screening process	Preliminary investigation	Due diligence
Investigation phase	— Products/projects/tasks — Basic indicators of the organization's size	— Leadership — Organization breakthrough Critical period — Ready for change	— Products/projects/work effectiveness and potential expansion — Leaders and team growth potential — Prepare for change and governance
Main tasks	— Accept applications — Conduct an initial review	Communicate application content and leadership with leaders	— Project site investigation — Project team and main partners investigation
Information sources	— Application documents — Organization website — Evaluation reports	— Leaders — External experts — Key funders	— Target groups/objects — Team members (including former staff) — Funders (main partners) — Expert peers

Periods	Organizations' screen-ing process	Preliminary investi-gation	Due diligence
Notes	Peripheral inspections to avoid high expecta-tions	— Introduce the position and ra-tionale of the Jingxing Plan — Explain that if ap-plicants enter the period of due dili-gence, they will be asked chal-lenging questions and about re-quirements.	Cross investigation from as many perspectives as possi-ble

Source: Liu's study (2017, 077). Adapted by the author.

> *After completing due diligence on one grassroots SO, there will be two results — the project officer personally thinks [about] whether to fund or not, the foundation decides whether to fund or not, the former involves personal val-ues, preferences, judgment, and the latter involves the foundation's funding standards and decision-making mechanisms.* (Liu 2017, 079)

In conclusion, foundations' leadership and experts have the right to make decisions about whom they will cooperate. Due diligence and site visits are conducted by project officials, after which a foundation's expert teams or leadership will decide which projects to fund.

6.4 Grant-making management and control

Based on the complaints already mentioned, we can assume that many conflicts arise during the process of cooperation. Hence, this section ex-plains how foundations process grants with grassroots SOs, including pay-ment, management, and evaluation. Regarding how to control and man-age the execution of projects in unexpected situations, the interviewees were asked the following questions:

> *Foundation_Q5: After the approval of applications, what main elements are written in the contract?*
> *Foundation_Q6: What is the average amount funded and what is the aver-age lifespan of a project?*
> *Foundation_Q7: How is the grant transferred to grassroots SOs (e.g., how of-ten)?*

A contract made between foundations and their grantees is a legally binding document, recognizing and governing the rights and duties of the two parties, and is legally enforceable because it meets the requirements and approval of the law. It contains a list of standard terms and conditions, typically specifying grant amounts, starting and closing dates, reporting practices and payments, and planned project activities and goals. A contract can be terminated at any time before the original termination date if there is a breach of the terms and conditions set forth in the contract.

In the interviews, foundation representatives noted that all parties to projects signed formal contracts, although, in questions about the format of the contracts, they answered the questions in general terms, because a contract is, after all, a relatively fixed format. A representative from Foundation D said that they rarely withdrew their funding, even when grantees did not implement a project's activities in accordance with the signed contract. Instead, they tried their best to help the grantees find solutions. Thus, a contract can be construed as a document that facilitates the completion of a project by both parties, but does not strictly show a certain deterrent. In other words, the contract is only a superficial form and has not become a way to restrict cooperation or promote cooperation.

6.4.1 Average amount of funds and duration of the project.

Generally, but not exclusively, the timespan of grants that Chinese foundations award for projects is one year. As a leading and influential grant-making foundation, Foundation N is among the few foundations that make three-year grants, with maximum grants of 300,000 RMB per year. Foundations D and G normally make one-year grants ranging from 5, 000 RMB to 50, 000 RMB. However, regardless of a grant's lifespan, the contract is signed annually. When I asked why the contract is always signed every year, the representatives said this is just the rule of foundations. One is that no foundation has a long-term grant-making strategy at present, and the other reason is that the foundation has no plan to continuously support the same grassroots SOs.

To expand foundations' influence and to avoid spreading funding too thinly, foundations' strategy is to award short-term grants and small grants to grassroots SOs. The downside is that it is difficult to understand the future impact of short-term and small projects and difficult to further develop them.

6.4.2 Mostly multiple installments.

After a project is approved according to its requirements and execution plans, the foundation may pay the grant in one or more installments, whether the project's lifespan is one or more years. (Note that a one-time provision is rare.) When there are, for example, three installments, one is generally paid before the start of the project, the second one in the middle of the project, and the third one after the project is completed, generally with the first installment higher (e.g., 40%, 30%, and 30%, respectively).

Three reasons can be given for why foundations provide multiple installments. One is to control the financial situation of the grant and thereby carefully monitor the overall progress of a project's activities in order to comply with financial management regulations. The second reason may be that the project is still in a period of exploration, and the foundation wants to monitor the project's short-term effects. The third reason relates to the foundations' distrust of grassroots SOs. That is, even though most grants are one-year grants, they may require long and detailed interim and financial reports that will take a long time for grassroots SOs to prepare. Moreover, some foundations require grantees to submit all bills, as complained by partly grantees in the 2013 and 2015 China Foundation Rankings. This issue is particularly a problem for many grassroots SOs' projects that are located in communities and even remote rural areas where invoices are not available. In addition, project activities often change due to the occurrence of special events at the project site or other unexpected factors, and there may be a delay in completing the project. Such intensive financial monitoring can be challenging in certain situations.

During one annual forum organized by CFF, one grassroots SO, the Gesanghua Education Foundation (Gesanghua) in Qinghai province, applied for a grant amounting to 1000,000 RMB from another foundation. The granting foundation contracted to make three grants to Gesanghua and requested that Gesanghua split the purchase of the equipment it needed into three purchases. Gesanghua complained that said this approach was very unprofessional and impractical, as the distance from the office location to the place where they should purchase the equipment was more than 2000 km, a total journey of more than 6000 km. The speaker from Gesanghua provided this case of multiple installments with the hoped to find an effective communication with foundations.[32]

---

32 http://mag.shechuang.org/magazine/179.html accessed on September 20, 2020.

6.5 Project monitoring and evaluation by foundations

As shown in an earlier study (Deng 2001, 82), a very common problem is that many people question the nature of nonprofit organizations in China. A few people think that nonprofit organizations, including foundations and other SOs, are for-profit in reality. This question has greatly affected the development of foundations, such as with personnel recruitment and fundraising from the public. The reasons for this question are manifold. One of the most important reasons is that China does not have a mechanism to assess the lack of profitability of nonprofit organizations.

Accordingly, a foundation's project evaluation process is not only a necessary tool for assessing projects but also is a powerful defense of the foundation in the face of external challenges to specialization grants. Foundations need to be able to report to their donors, shareholders, or the public evidence of the achievements and outcomes of projects, which is generally to "emphasize grassroots SOs sustainable development and use more nuanced and long-term indicators to assess performance" (Kang 2019, 507). On these grounds, in the interviews, the following question was formulated:

> Foundation_Q8: Do you evaluate your grassroots SOs' projects? In what way? How often?

All foundations except for Foundation J evaluated their grant-making projects. Foundation J's representative said that, although doing so was still under consideration, they did not evaluate individual projects. Results from the interview showed that two key factors were considered during the foundations' evaluation process: financial reports and project activity reports. Activity reports refer to progress reports and the final report. All respondents from foundations prioritized two factors when monitoring a project: "whether the grantee submits [s] the progress report in the due time" and "whether the grantee prove[s] that they spent all of the money and submit [a] financial report."

What's more, evaluations have different purposes: for example, to access whether a project was completed as planned, to know what other impacts the project made, to understand a project's challenges and problems, to examine whether cooperation will continue (which may not apply to one-year grants). The most important objectives are to access whether a project was completed as planned and to determine the strength and quality of a project.

Representatives of Foundations E and J said they did not evaluate some projects because of their complexity. For instance, Foundation J provided grants to individuals for scientific research in public welfare. After the grantees finished their studies or research, most of them changed their jobs at social organizations or foundations to jobs at universities. The representative took it as a failure and planned to evaluate this scholarship project. However, the difficulty is how to make a reasonable and effective assessment. With no experience evaluating funding of individual projects, Foundation J's simplest approach would be to determine whether the grantees completed their research.

By all means, some foundations with rich grant-making experiences provide comprehensive details in their evaluations. China Foundation for Poverty Alleviation (CFPA) is a good case in point:

> *In the progress of the project, CFPA requires project managers to communicate at least once with each grantee every month. In addition, each grantee is required to have a staff in each project site to write work logs and submit monthly project briefs. In addition, CFPA also invites [a] third-party to participate in the monitoring and evaluation, and monitoring records are required every month. CFPA conducts analysis and feedback based on monitoring reports and monthly feedback forms submitted by grantee[s]. Finally, CFPA summarizes the comprehensive issues that arise in each project and how the problems need to be addressed. From CFPA's perspective, grantees' self-monitoring and self-assessment abilities are still weak, especially the assessment of social impact, which are also abilities that grantees should learn from them. CFPA hopes that grantees can transform the abilities of evaluation and monitoring into improving their organizational capacities* (Woqi Foundation 2018, 175).

The evaluation described above is very detailed and intensive, providing monthly communication, daily work logs, and monthly project briefs, as well as social impact, which has always been a factor to be reckoned with in foundation-led assessments. Such an evaluation takes a lot of time and effort. It requires knowing more than whether a project was completed and may be seen as an additional burden on grantees.

6.6 Sustainability of cooperation

> Without the shadow of the future, cooperation becomes impossible to sustain.

> (Axelrod 1984, 182)

After cooperation begins between foundations and grassroots SOs, they need to consider how to sustain it. To enhance the chances for doing so, foundations and grassroots SOs need to interact frequently over time. Otherwise, it will be hard for foundations to ascertain the development of their grantees' projects. Thus, the following interview question was formulated:

Foundation_Q9: After the implementation of projects, do you still connect with the grantees? In what way?

As I mentioned earlier, the majority of projects are funded for one year. However, when foundations recognize the capabilities of grassroots SOs or projects that have been executed, the two parties usually try to keep in touch to further enhance the exchange in the information. Very often, foundations' project officials will consider inviting accredited grassroots SOs to apply for another new grant from other foundations with the grant-making application. In that way, a project officer can play a critical intermediary role. The negative effect of frequent staff turnover is also one of the factors that interrupt the connection between them.

Because foundations are immersed in their donors' values and practices, including business-related ones, foundations tend to select grassroots SOs and projects that produce highly visible outcomes in a short period. As result, they do not encourage long-term developmental projects or projects that cannot produce visible outcomes, which greatly affects the.

Sustainability of a project affects both foundations and grassroots SOs. In the interviews, Foundations B, I, and M explained that their grant-making projects usually lasted only one year because they were easier to sustain than longer projects. Foundations D, E, J, and L had no intention of funding long-term projects. Foundation F still made two-year and three-year grants to grassroots SOs at the time of the interviews. Foundation K originally had three-year grants, but changed its organizational strategy and had stopped making three-year grants by the time of the interviews.

Another strategy for sustainability is to recommend grantees to large foundations. The representative from Foundation I said that, after supporting one grantee, they introduced the grantee to Foundation N for multi-year grants. The representative also said that his foundation introduced their grantees to the Ai You Foundation for large multiyear grants. The advantage of this recommendation is about trust. For example, it is easy to get the trust of the Narada Foundation as it is under the recommendation of the Harmony Foundation. However, one disadvantage is that some outstanding grassroots SOs take limited financial resources away from other Chinese foundations. One grassroots organization could be a grantee of several Chinese foundations, while other grassroots SOs never get involved in the funding game.

One representative from Foundations G provided a wonderful illustration of this situation: "It happens that some well-known SOs are supported by one foundation this year, and same SOs are supported by another grant-making foundation next year." What's more, Foundation K also provided a similar case. It means that some grant-making foundations in China take turns making grants to several well-known grassroots SOs, while other grassroots SOs are excluded from finding sufficient funds.

6.7 Discussion

Here I review and discuss cooperation between foundations and grantees according to the three stages of cooperation: initial, middle, and final.

In the initial stage, foundations subjectively select funding objects and their grantees through documents and prescribed procedures. Their expectations for potential funded grassroots SOs are included as three points: (1) Selection of grantee organizations is based on foundations' preferences and whether the grantee organization is in line with the foundations' strategies and values; the final selection is made mostly by experts, bosses, and boards. The role of project officials is more to ensure error-free project implementation and due diligence. (2) In the selection of grantees, the establishment of the trust is critical to deciding whether to start cooperation. (3) To ensure fairness and transparency in the selection process, most foundations choose to select grantees through public bidding and expert review procedures.

In the middle stage, during the process of cooperation, a foundation's funding work gradually forms a standardized working model, as follows: (1) The foundation builds a set of procedural methods and procedures for project operation, supervision, and evaluation; (2) to ensure the effective use of public welfare funds and help grantees, the foundation retrains grantees through various programs, such as finance, project management, and even requiring the growth path and scale of grantees; (3) due to the trust and requirements of the foundation, most projects have low funds and short lifespan; and (4) the project officer mainly completes due diligence procedurally during the execution of the project. During this period, I found that many factors affected cooperation between the two parties. For example, project implementation was still based mainly on the foundations' error-free perspective, and the project officials' work was mainly due diligence and reporting.

In the final stage, after the completion of the first round of cooperation, there was no continuous follow-up cooperation.

Overall, Chinese foundations are in a transition that ranges from changing their strategy toward grantmaking and how they operate, to how they improve the skills of project officials, to how they select grantees. The positive side is that Chinese foundations are starting to recognize and reflect on their problems and then adjust them as needed, for example, refining the selection process and guidelines. However, on the negative side, it is difficult for its partners, e.g. grantees, clearly understand the foundation's changing positioning. In this transitional phase, the foundations prefer to fund excellent SOs and make them better rather than provide timely funds to help SOs that are less robust but are in urgent need of funding.

Foundation funds are unevenly distributed to grassroots SOs. The Narada Foundation and the K2 Foundation are examples. That is, the Narada Foundation clearly states that it funds excellent SOs, and the K2 Foundation explicitly proposes to support SO "unicorns." Also, foundations tend to alternately support well-known social organizations. In other words, many foundations have made numerous grants to only a few well-known SOs.

Foundations lack the funding resources needed to make grants to grassroots SOs. For foundations, especially PFFs, how to find a stable funding source that can be used for grant-making projects is always a huge challenge, including some large foundations such as the China Foundation for Poverty Alleviation (Guo and Wang 2018, 179). Although some foundations, especially PFFs, take advantage of the government's mechanism for fundraising and administration, they are restricted by the government's mechanism for decision-making and grantmaking.

Foundations are influencing and reshaping their grantees through workshops and training. From the practice of due diligence, to face-to-face project reviews and defenses, to evaluation and other training exercises, Chinese foundations influence grassroots SOs in various and versatile ways. In the case of weak and unprofessional SOs, the foundations' philosophy is to turn away from them toward new social organizations and cultivate them and develop them into responsible foundations.

7 Understanding cooperation from the perspective of grassroots SOs

To describe the status of cooperation from the perspective of grantees, this section explores how grassroots SOs cope with various foundations as their primary potential donors in China and how they judge that cooperation.

Previous studies (e.g. Chan et al. 2005; Deng 2013; Spires et al. 2014) showed that survival is the biggest challenge for Chinese grassroots SOs. To verify whether Chinese foundations are highly important financial resource providers for grassroots SOs, my first interview question to grassroots SOs was as follows:

Grassroots SOs_Q1: Is your organization granted by domestic foundations? Are domestic grants very important to your organizations?

A total of thirteen grassroots SOs were interviewed. All of them gave a positive answer to the question, which meant that domestic grants were very important to all of them, whether now or in the future. All representatives had applied for grants from domestic foundations, and nine of them received the grants, although most were only small grants for one-year projects. For example, SO 10 had an organizational budget totaling only 2 million RMB with only 20,000 RMB from one Chinese foundation. Instead, most of the funding for another SO (SO 2) came from leading domestic grant-making foundations, such as the Narada Foundation, the Ai You Foundation, the Guangzhou Harmony Foundation, and so on. Abundant domestic resources were very important for SO 2's development over the years. Also, SO 12 was approved for a five-year grant by a domestic foundation focusing on environmental protection. Therefore, the interview samples showed diverse funding sources and included SOs from eight provinces in China.

Table 7-1: Profile of social organizations interviewed

No.	Location	Interviewee	Legal Status	Registration Status	Applied or not	Successful or not
1	Yunnan	Founder & execu-tive director	Yes	CNIs	Yes	No
2	Yunnan	Executive director	Yes	CNIs	Yes	Yes
3	Yunnan	Executive director	Yes	CNIs	Yes	No
4	Henan	Founder & execu-tive director	Yes	Social asso-ciations	Yes	Yes
5	Gansu	Project staff	Yes	CNIs	Yes	Yes
6	Beijing	Deputy secretary-general	Yes	Social asso-ciations	Yes	No
7	Hainan	Project manager	Yes	Social asso-ciations	Yes	Yes
8	Shaanxi	Founder & execu-tive director	Yes	Social asso-ciations	Yes	Yes
9	Beijing	Founder & execu-tive director	Yes	CNIs	Yes	Yes
10	Yunnan	Founder and deputy director	Yes	CNIs	Yes	Yes
11	Shaanxi	Founder & execu-tive director	Yes	CNIs	Yes	Yes
12	Anhui	Founder & execu-tive director	Yes	CNIs	Yes	Yes
13	Sichuan	Project officer	Yes	Social asso-ciations	Yes	Yes

Grassroots SOs, what I interviewed are legally registered as CNIs or Social associations。 SO 13 is registered as Social associations founded in 2007, which still has a strongly political connection with the local women's federation. All of the other interviewed SOs are independently operated and managed, even though their founders might have more or less political connection with the government.

Most of the interviewees were founders and executive directors at organizations, as a distinction was found between top leaders and general project staff members or even project officers during the interviews. The interviews showed that only the top leaders, such as founders and executive directors, cared about the survival of their organizations and were normally motivated to seek funding resources. The project staff member for SO 5 said that she was not clear about the organization's funding; she also said that fundraising is normally the leaders' responsibility in her organization.

7. 1 How to seek potential foundations by grassroots SOs

As discussed, foundations' initiative to find potential grantees, seek appropriate partners, and select grantees are the core elements of their grant-making approach in the beginning. The same is true for grassroots SOs; they must find appropriate foundations that are willing to make grants and learn how to create a targeted application. In the interviews, I formulated the corresponding question as follows:

Grassroots SOs_Q2: How does your organization find foundations?

In the interviews, a total of thirteen representatives, mostly founders or executive directors, shared their attempts and experiences on how to seek the funding needed for survival. All representatives said that open calls were still the most effective way for them to seek and start connecting with Chinese foundations. Even if they knew people from foundations that they met, say, during workshops or had worked within their field, they still did not see any possibility of future support from domestic foundations because most of them are operating foundations and do not make grants to other organizations, with the exception of several leading grant-making-orientated foundations.

Regardless, foundations are still regarded as privileged organizations due to their fundraising advantage, which, may make them the best partners for grassroots SOs. SOs realize that the total number of Chinese grant-making foundations is increasing, and those foundations are exactly the ones providing funding to grassroots SOs. Representatives from SO 2, SO 7, SO 9, and SO 12 thought that their organizations could get easy access to grant-making foundations. Two project staff members from SO 5 and SO 13 had no experience in fundraising. However, the remaining seven funding seekers, SO 1, SO 3, SO 4, SO 6, SO 8, SO 10, SO 11, were disappointed after preliminary attempts. Three SOs, SO 1, SO 3 (this organization didn't successfully apply for any domestic projects), SO 10, had no funds from Chinese foundations, but had overseas funding or grants from domestic organizations, though not from foundations.

Four SOs (SO 2, SO 7, SO 9, and SO 12) were supported through more than three grants. Nine other organizations received different amounts of funds, ranging from zero by SO 6 until the end of 2018 (zero means that they have no fund from foundations but they still co-organize events or activities with some foundations or are in the process of applying for grants), 20,000 RMB (SO 10, accounting for 1.3% of the total annual expenditure in 2017) to 150,000 RMB (accounting for less 30% of the total annual expenditure in 2017).

Competition through TV/online vote collection: A representative from SO 8 received a grant of 30,000 RMB from a domestic foundation through a TV show, which could be a competitive environment for grassroots SOs in which they could build a good reputation and provide excellent advertisements for their foundations. A representative from SO 9 participated in ME Funding for Philanthropy Innovation's selection process (see the case study in section 6.8) but failed in the end, because other players' online votes surpassed those of her organization.

Interestingly, not all of the grassroots SOs interviewed said were interested in applying for grants from Chinese grant-making foundations, even though they knew they needed those foundations' financial resources. Their reasons were diverse; for example, they thought the selection process took too much time or the grant was too small. A representative from SO 4 agreed and said it took about two years to get approval for an 8,000 RMB grant from one foundation. A representative from SO 8 said it was "looking for a needle in a haystack" to describe the odds against finding financial resources in China.

Some SOs did not apply for grants from domestic foundations due to differences in fields of workings and approaches. One representative from an experienced grassroots SO (SO 6) mentioned the concept of marketization of the third sector that was popular in domestic foundations. The marketization of the third sector means that non-profit organizations adopt the values and methods of the market to make grants and operate the projects. She said her organization was an influential SO working in developmental fields and on complicated social problems, which took a long time, and that the visible effects were hard to see during the process. However, the concept of marketization the third secto has led more and more Chinese foundations to work on short-term projects with visible results, for example, building a house or library in remote areas or distributing "Love Packages" directly to a targeted population[33]. As relatively mature grassroots SOs holding different ideas about Chinese foundations, SO 6 could not find appropriate Chinese foundations to cooperate.

---

33 Love Package, a project of China Foundation for Poverty Alleviation since 2009, was launched to improve the comprehensive development and living conditions of rural pupils in poverty-stricken areas by organizing donations of care packages. It has given children loving care and helped bring about their childhood dreams.

A similar situation happened to another mature grassroots organization (SO 10) and a newly founded grassroots organization (SO 3) on a local level. Even with different ideas about Chinese domestic foundations, three of them (i.e. SO 3, SO 6, SO 10) had made efforts to apply for grants in order to acquire the funds they needed to survive. One of them (SO 10) applied successfully for a grant in a specific field after long-term cooperation with a Chinese foundation, but the grant was only 50,000 RMB for one year. The representative said that the grant did not enable them to afford one staff member's salary who implemented the project from this Chinese foundation, after deducting the project costs, like office expenses and traveling to project sites.

An analysis of the preceding interviews indicated that grassroots SOs regarded Chinese foundations were similar to government officials for the selection of grantees. Although research on this topic is scarce, Kang (2019) clearly described the process of selection similar to the perspective of grassroots SOs:

> *In project selection, generally, foundations closely follow in [the] government's footsteps in avoiding certain themes, such as the promotion of social citizenship, empowerment of specific minority groups and political advocacy; when a SO representative made this statement in a focus group, the other participants all concurred and expressed their disappointment in foundations' attitude: "We think the foundation managements are more open-minded, but ultimately, they are similar to government officials in lacking imagination. They prefer services over advocacy activities, focus on mainstream themes, and see work in controversial areas as a threat to societal harmony." (Kang 2019, 508)*

7.2 Foundation project official's role during project application, implementation, and evaluation

Foundations' project officials normally are the only or most important connection between foundations and their grantees and can influence and reflect their relationship. To capture their roles from the perspective of grassroots SOs, the following questions were formulated:

> *Grassroots SOs_Q3: At the beginning of an application, do you understand the application process and requirements?*
> *Grassroots SOs_Q4: During the application and implementation phases is there professional staff from foundations to supervise when necessary?*

Grassroots SOs had different experiences and comments about foundations' application processes and how they implemented projects. The majority of grassroots SOs' representatives said that they understood the application process and requirements and that foundations' staff were available during the application phase. For example, when a foundation understood an applicant or was very interested in a proposal, its project official would likely contact the applicant and seek more details or request more options. The representative from SO 2, which had received grants from several Chinese foundations, said that the Guangzhou Harmony Foundation was an ideal grantor in China, as its project officials were very supportive and respectful during the project application, monitoring, and implementation phases. Whether good communication exists between those seeking grants and a foundation largely depends on its project officials. When the application was submitted for the Guangzhou Harmony Foundation's project, the proposal was revised several times, and many professional suggestions were made by the foundation's project officials.

More representatives just waited after submitting the project application in accordance with foundations' application procedures, and did not think that project officials could play a very important role in the project application stage. Some representatives of grassroots SOs even believe that project officials did not understand the professionalism of grassroots SOs' projects, and sometimes even criticized the applicants very unprofessional. In addition, representatives of grassroots SOs believed that the project proposal was more important than the project officer when it came to whether the project could be successfully applied.

7.3 Grant amount and period of grants

The amount and length of grants are important factors in regard to cooperation between foundations and grassroots SOs. Thus, for the interviews, this question was formulated:

> *Grassroots SOs_Q5: If SOs are/were granted successfully by domestic foundations, how long and how much are/were granted for the project?*

The lifespan of a Chinese foundation's project is generally one year. This creates a strong sense of urgency on both sides, causing them to focus only on the effects of short-term projects, rather than on the development and impact that the project or the grassroots organization can make. (As noted earlier, when a grant is for more than one year, foundations require that contracts be signed annually.)

The interviews showed that three of the thirteen grassroots SOs that applied for multiyear grants successfully received grants for more than two-year projects from Chinese foundations. Moreover, three of them agreed that, once they gained the trust of Chinese foundations through cooperation, it was easy to get access to other foundations and then find more opportunities for long-term projects or new grants.

In the interviews, it was found that grants ranged from several hundred RMB to 20,000 RMB, which are generally considered to be small grants. For example, SO 10 had a budget of 2 million RMB, but received only 20,000 RMB from a Chinese foundation. SO 11's project was the only one to receive 150, 000 RMB from a Chinese foundation. SO 13 normally had grants for less than 100,000 RMB for projects in different years. Two well-known SOs (SO 2 and SO 12) were approved for much larger grants from leading domestic grant-making foundations, such as the Narada Foundation, the Ai You Foundation, the Guangzhou Harmony Foundation, and so on. An exception was provided by the representative from one local SO that had been approved to receive 300,000 RMB through competition on a television show (SO 8). The granting foundation, a company foundation, allocated the grant in a lump sum immediately after the show. Later, the foundation changed the use of the funds according to SO 8's specific needs and applications of the funds. The negative side of this grant was that the administrative expenses and staff salary were excluded.

Expenses related to management are frequently mentioned by representatives from grassroots SOs. Although Chinese foundations currently provide funds for such expenses, for example, for administrative and personnel expenses, the number of grassroots SOs foundations among them is still very small. Grassroots SOs, even those with only two or three staff members, cannot survive with one or two projects because the grants are generally too small. As noted previously, it is even more difficult to make contact with a foundation that will provide administrative and personnel funding.

So what is the impact on grassroots SOs without these funds? A grassroots representative (SO 8) said that very few Chinese foundations were willing to provide staff and administrative funding for their projects. Finally, after a long time of communication, one foundation agreed to provide 1,200 RMB per month as part of the staff's salaries, and another foundation agreed to provide another 1,000 RMB per month for the salaries. There were two full-time staff members at her organization, each receiving

1,500 RMB (the rest was paid by funds from another foundation) according to the minimum wage for that area. The representative indicated that they could not hire more staff because they could not afford the cost of doing so.

SO 8's representative had worked in that grassroots organization since the 1990s, so she had cooperated with foreign foundations in the past when most grassroots organizations were still supported by foreign organizations. She had noticed a difference between domestic and foreign foundations during that time. For example, she said that she appreciated that foreign foundations were very professional in designing projects without too many interventions, which improved capacity building and allowed the staff to implement projects freely. Moreover, she pointed out that the development and growth of grassroots organizations were inseparable from the funding they received from foreign foundations. Although it has been fifteen years since her organization's cooperation with a foreign foundation, when being asked about the development of grassroots SOs, she pointed out that her organization's brochure was designed and printed under the funding support of that foreign foundation, and that the design is still being used.

A representative from SO 7 had rich experiences when applying for domestic and overseas foundations. However, compared with overseas foundations, the grants from Chinese foundations were much smaller, but they were more likely because overseas foundations were sensitive to the government's perspective on certain types of projects, especially environmental protection projects. Concerning the lifespan and amount of domestic grants, the representative from SO 7 said,

> *While improving the professionalism of my organization, we can get more financial resources instead of doing a lot of small-grant projects as we do now, because small projects cost a lot of manpower and energy (compared to large projects). If a project can have more financial resources in the future, instead of spending too much time on the application and reports of the small grants project, our project staff can be getting more professional and in-depth in the projects.*

Although SO 7 had cooperated with different domestic and foreign foundations, the organization constantly made great efforts to seek and apply for grants from domestic foundations. Whenever they learned about open calls from Chinese foundations, they made attempts to submit applications and kept contacting the foundations for possibilities. They see overseas funding as being uncertain, and then they find domestic foundations more acceptable.

7.4 Project evaluation and further cooperation

Grassroots SOs see project evaluations as important assessments for continuing recognition from and cooperation with foundations. Rather than being just additional work, an effective project evaluation allows grantees the opportunity to show what they have achieved and their sustainably. Thus, for the interviews, this question was formulated:

> *Grassroots SOs_Q6: During the project implementation, do foundations evaluate the project? How often? In what way?*

The interviews showed that foundations viewed project evaluations as necessary procedures; the evaluations were based on reports, such as quarterly reports and semiannual and annual reports, which included all planned activities. Of course, for projects receiving a large amount of funding and for multiyear projects, some foundations used the evaluations of external expert teams.

In general, along with the development and progress of foundations, project evaluations have become standardized tools for both parties. However, project evaluations have not played a pivotal role in furthering cooperation because the lifespan of most projects in China is one year. Even though several foundations offer two- or three-year projects, it is rare to find grassroots SOs applying for multiyear projects or reapplying to the same foundation.

Therefore, to better understand the issue of cooperation, the following question was formulated:

> *Grassroots SOs_Q7: After the project, does your organization connect with foundations? In what way?*

Representatives for some grantees said that they kept contact with grantors after a project was completed. The frequency of contacts depended on various factors. For example, when grantors recognized the good work of grantee organizations, the former were often happy to help the grantees by informing them about other granting foundations. Also, personal relationships within the two parties were very important in terms of future connections and cooperation. On the contrary, some representatives from grassroots SOs said that they did not maintain connections with their funders after projects were over, whether the cooperation had been smooth or not. Overall, future connections proved to be random or unstable.

According to the cooperation theory discussed earlier, enlarging the "shadow of the future" has become necessary for foundations and grassroots SOs, because cooperation can be stable only if the players think the future is as important as the present. Caring about the future can influence the ongoing cooperation and altruism expressed among different organizations.

In addition, foundations' independence is very important to their grant-making and decision-making processes, as well as to their future cooperation with grassroots SOs. This includes independence in their style of governance and management and the ability of their primary founders, or main donors, or top leaders to make decisions on which projects are selected and how they are implemented.

A study by Wiepking (2010) showed that donors who give money to organizations have specific incentives and that different people have different perceptions and attitudes about the money they donate, such as to gain a certain social status. Donors' attitudes and social values play important roles in how grants are selected and how much they are funded, and they also influence the development of foundations.

The current problem in China is that entrepreneurs donate money not because they want to do philanthropic work or solve specific social problems, but because entrepreneurs often see their donations as a form of self-importance, as noted in the interviews by the representative of a supporting platform. He said, "the wealthy Chinese in the past showed off their tastes with wine and golf. Now the rich get together and ask in the first sentence, 'do you have a philanthropic foundation', or boast that 'I went to the Himalayas to pick up trash'. Thus, the foundation has become a symbol of the rich people's identity and social status. Those rich don't care about the up and down of the whole society nor know how to operate and manage a philanthropic foundation." (interviewed on April 19, 2019.) In connection with the wealthy Chinese attitudes on grantmaking, Zi (2015) pointed out that, the wealthy Chinese are more than happy to make visible and immediate donations, rather than supporting long-term projects with the invisible effect but with long-term significance. Under such circumstances, the conditions for the emergence of philanthropists in China are not yet available.

7.5 Are programs mainly planned by foundations or grassroots SOs?

Grassroots SOs think that foundations design and dominate all of a project's processes, while foundations do not fully appreciate or trust the professionalism of grassroots SOs, in part, because they are not the ones that complete feasibility studies. All representatives from grassroots SOs indicated that they completely accepted could understand foundations' strict demands during project selections and evaluations as long as the foundations awarded them grants. After all, survival is still the most important thing for grassroots SOs. It means that grassroots SOs compromise with foundations.

In the JinCao Peer Project, mentioned above, a grassroots SOs representative (SO 9) who had applied for the grant successfully, said that they had experienced a disagreement with their mentors. That is, during the application process, SO 9 had understood that they would be supervised by specific mentors and then could make a change after three years. The representative from SO 9 said that their project aimed to change people by raising awareness at the community level, so the effects were difficult to see in a short period and thus there were no immediate certainties. However, the representative from SO 9 complained that the mentors emphasize expansion, scaling up, and reproducibility. That was to say, the mentors encouraged SO 9 to enlarge the organization through employing more staff and implement the project with visible effect in a short period.

This disagreement created difficulty for SO 9. Even though, the representative said her organizations were satisfied with the grant largely because the grant provided unrestricted funds, which was and remains rare for grassroots SOs in China. Grassroots SOs urgently need unrestricted grants that allow them, for example, to support staff, rather than grants that focus on external activities. Without such funds, they may lack the staff they need to operate, build their capacity, and survive.

However, as a grassroots SO working on development issues with limited skilled staff and budget, the representative from SO 9 hoped that foundations would not continue to push SOs on how to go forward or make changes or impose excessive or unrealistic expectations and interventions on SOs so that SOs could explore and stabilize themselves.

During my observations and interviews, I heard more than once that foundations' staff liken their relationship with their grantees to relationships in general. In a recent study, Woqi Foundation (2018) wrote that Song Wu used the terms "marriage," "bidding system," "having a relationship," and "invitation" to compare different funding strategies (143). This analogy has been disapproved by most of the interviewed grassroots SOs while they expressed the foundation never put grassroots SOs on an equal relationship during the interaction.

The Xin Ping Foundation adopted the invitation system, which is like a relationship. Its staff first learned as much as possible about the grassroots SOs in the areas in which it worked and then selected SOs that they considered being excellent. Then they took the initiative to contact and extend an invitation to the grassroots SOs in order to conduct a "trial marriage" through small grants or short-term cooperation, with the goal of better understanding and getting along well with them. However, from the perspective of some representatives (e.g., SO 3 and SO 10), the relationship between the foundations and grassroots SOs in China is unequal, rather than being a marriage or relationship. A more precise explanation is that a large number of grassroots SOs are vying for very limited resources provided by foundations. Those grassroots SOs that meet foundations' requirements are selected, and those that do not meet foundations' requirements will face severe survival problems.

7.6 Discussion

For grassroots social SOs, funding from domestic foundations produces hope and challenges. Here I review and discuss cooperation between foundations and grantees according to the three phases of cooperation: initial, middle, and final.

In the initial stage, grassroots SOs' expectations in their relationship with potential foundations are that (1) grassroots SOs hope to cater to a foundation's preferences, but they are not sure about the foundation's preferences, or even which foundation might make grants to them; (2) the approval process and communication process are long and complicated—some applicants need to spend more than half a year or even longer to apply and maintain communication; and (3) most interviewed grassroots SOs considered themselves to be among many other applicants and that the chance of a successful application was small.

In the middle stage, in the process of cooperation, grassroots SOs believe that (1) in the project design, the foundation is too dominant and the foundation intervenes too much, such as in the design of the project and the participation of experts and even mentors—some project designs and mentors' opinions are in line with the development path of grassroots SOs, and some are not; (2) the project grant is small and the lifespan is short—

sometimes the administrative and staff costs of a project are too strict, which is not conducive to the development of grassroots SOs; (3) the project execution process is complicated and lengthy, requiring documents, financial approvals, project reports, weekly journals, and so on; and (4) project evaluation of a foundation increases the workload, and the evaluation is mainly from the perspective of the foundation, not from the perspective of the grantee.

In the final stage, the main feature of the late cooperation period is that cooperation is a one-time event with no future cooperation. Grassroots SOs have to change their granters from one foundation to another continuously.

In short, grassroots SOs need help and resources, especially funding resources, from Chinese foundations, but without mandatory and inappropriate stipulations. Grassroots SOs also want to develop and build their capacities in their own ways. Therefore, it is an open question of whether foundation-led projects are suitable for grassroots SOs' operations and growth. Grant-making foundations that respect their grantees' mode of development are the most welcomed foundations by interviewed grassroots SOs. For example, Foundation I considered grantees as strategic partners and stressed equality, respect, and mutual growth and had in place sound principals for grant-making officer training.

Although grassroots SOs have access to limited resources, they do not have effective monitoring and evaluation mechanisms on their projects and organizational development. Secondly, they work under a dual management system that emphasizes government supervision and management, which is ineffective for the growth of grassroots SOs. Moreover, grassroots SOs obtain resources from the public and then take on corresponding social responsibilities, although public supervision of grassroots SOs has been lacking. While acknowledging that grassroots SOs had achieved good development in the past, this progress has not been recognized foundations, government and the public.

8. Analysis of the changing views

The preceding analysis of foundations and grassroots SOs shows that, during their interactions, both sides have very different expectations and interpretations of each other. To present the cooperative relationship between foundations and grassroots SOs more fully, in this chapter, I first summarize and categorize the cooperation between the two and compare their differences in overall logic on three interactive stages of cooperation: the initial stage, the middle stage, and the final stage. Then I adopt specific cases to illustrate two factors that affect the entire cooperation stage, trust and resource interdependency. Unlike in the previous chapters, here I explore the impact of these two factors on the interactive relationship from the perspectives of the two parties. Finally, I do a comprehensive collation of the interviews with third-party stakeholders, such as scholars and experts who have experience working with grassroots SOs or have served as judges for foundations, grassroots SOs, and government-sponsored projects, and analyze the views and opinions that have contributed to current modes of cooperation. Also taken into account are a few interviews with overseas foundations that have cooperated with grassroots SOs in China for a long time, due to their good reputation with Chinese SOs, as shown in the 2013 and 2015 China Foundation Rankings.

8.1 Interactive categories between foundations and grassroots SOs

Table 8-1 lists a set of categories according to the words used most frequently during interviews in which foundations' respondents described their strategy (e.g. joint fundraising proposed by Foundation B) and the classification of their foundations' projects (e.g., special funds mentioned by Foundation M). I postulated a total of six categories that applied to any concrete type of interaction discussed in this dissertation. On this basis, I summarized the characteristics of each category and then analyzed the interviewed foundations one by one and placed them in suitable categories. In addition, I specifically listed representative and well-known foundations in each category, which was also a cooperation strategy often mentioned by these foundations on different occasions.

Table 8-1: Interactive categories between foundations and grassroots SOs

No	Categories	Representative foundation	Interviewed foundations
1	Special funds (zhuan xiang ji jin, 专项基金)	China Social Welfare Foundation	Foundation L, M, O, P
2	Joint fundraising (lian he quan mu, 联合劝募)	Shanghai United Foundation	Foundation B, D
3	High-engagement grantmaking	You Cheng Foundation	Foundation F
4	Making grants to projects	Amity Foundation	Foundation B, E, G, K
5	Making grants to organizations	Narada Foundation	Foundation I, K, N
6	Making Grants to individuals	Ginkgo Foundation	Foundation J

Category 1: Special funds (zhuan xiang ji jin, 专项基金) refers to a fund established by a donor that is in line with the foundation's purpose. The donor specifies the direction and scope of use of the fund, and the initial capital is not less than the prescribed amount. Different foundations have different requirements for special funds, such as the initial capital and its management; this is very common in Chinese foundations (e.g., the China Social Welfare Foundation and the China Soong Ching Ling Foundation).

Category 2: Joint fundraising (lian he quan mu, 联合劝募) refers to a public welfare organization that raises funds in a unified manner in the market and then allocates the funds to grassroots SOs in accordance with certain rules. This approach aims to integrate social resources, build a joint fundraising platform for non-governmental public welfare organizations, and provide support for public welfare promotion, resource mobilization, capacity building, and so on. Shanghai United Foundation is well known for joint fundraising.

Category 3: High-engagement grantmaking emphasizes more intense participation in the development of grassroots SOs and offers platforms for advocacy, capacity building, and other resources apart from financial support. This approach usually provides considerable technical assistance and support, thereby also contributing to the capacity building of grantees in relevant communities. In China, the You Cheng Social Entrepreneur Foundation, the first one to implement high-engagement grantmaking, did so in two ways: (1) by providing resource allocation and financial support and cooperating with other SOs to implement projects led by the foundation and (2) by guiding and subsidizing other SOs to independently implement projects that conform to its philosophy.

Category 4: Making grants to projects involves directing financial help toward tasks and other support related to projects' issues rather than grantees' organizational development. The main focus is on whether a project task is completed by the requirements of the foundation. Most grant-making projects in Chinese foundations are regarded as funded projects. With grants to projects, the foundation and the grantee have a relatively short-term cooperative relationship based on the lifespan of the project.

Category 5: Making grants to organizations refers to providing a variety of financial and non-financial support to a developing grantee organization (e.g., strategic consulting, expansion of social resource networks, the introduction of concepts) that address the needs of the organizations. Compared with funded projects, the foundation and the grantee have a relatively long-term cooperative relationship. It is still very rare in China, with the Narada Foundation being the representative one.

Category 6: Making grants to individuals, as the category implies, relates to those foundations that make grants to persons. The influential foundation here is the Ginkgo Foundation, which subsidizes young people to help them break through bottlenecks to their personal growth and become leaders in the field of public welfare. These grants focus on grantees with the potential to become leaders or founders of grassroots SOs, as well as scholars, media professionals, activists, and grassroots SOs.

Table 8-2: Changing views of foundations and grassroots SOs

Interactive phrases	Questions	Foundations	Other SOs
Before cooperation	1. How to look for each other?	A combination of ways, e.g., open calls, recommendations, workshops, networks, and actively sought grantees	An open call is still the main way, occasionally recommendations.
	2. Application process: 2a. Use clear guidelines or documents that explain the application process and its requirements	Procedure and documentation	Lengthy and unclear
	2b. Use professional project staff's assistance?	Yes	Yes, but not so helpful
	3. Who finally decides which application to accept?	Experts, main donors, board members	

Interactive phrases	Questions	Foundations	Other SOs
During cooperation	4. Professional project officer	Yes	No
	5. Contract, e.g., main elements	Just paperwork, unimportant	
	6. Average grant amount and lifespan	From several to three years, mostly one year, small grant usually	Too short for grassroots SOs; small grant usually
	7. Grant transfer (e.g., how often)	Usually two or three installments	Usually two or three installments
	8. Evaluation: In what way? How often?	Mostly yes	Yes, taking too much time and energy but having no effect on organizational development
After the cooperation	9. Further connection or not? In what way?	Some	Little
	10. Resource dependence	No	Yes

Although foundations select grassroots SOs via different approaches, from the initial stage of cooperation, grassroots SOs have only one effective way to do so. Moreover, only a few foundations make grants to grassroots SOs, so the probability that both parties will meet is very small. The foundation is trying to establish a procedural and documented selection method, but it is a lengthy and unclear selection process for grassroots SOs, and a foundation's project officials play a small role in this process.

Then, during their ongoing cooperation, Chinese foundations influence grassroots SOs in various and versatile ways, from the practice of due diligence, to face-to-face project reviews and defenses, to evaluation and other training exercises. In the case of weak and unprofessional SOs, the foundation's philosophy is to turn away from them toward new social organizations and cultivate those organizations and develop them into responsible foundations. Compared with grassroots SOs with insufficient resources, foundations have an advantage when it comes to obtaining funding and providing their staff with learning opportunities. However, foundations' project officials still do not play an important role except for heavy due diligence reports and other procedural tasks. Contracts are also considered to be a kind of documentary work by conventions and do not play a sufficient role in restricting the two parties and improving the cooperative relationship. As for the grant amount and lifespan, installments and project evaluations are carried out following the requirements of foundations, without considering the needs of the grantees, which sometimes is a waste of time and a burden for grantees.

After the completion of cooperation, a foundation has no continuous financial support, and aspires to use limited funds to support other new grassroots SOs so as to acquire new partners and expand its influence. However, without the support of follow-up funds, this approach is not very helpful for grassroots social organizations.

Foundations receive and accept public supervision because of the pressure and requirements of fundraising. Donors mainly set the requirements for companies or private foundations. Donors may also be directly involved in the specific activities of a project, such as a project's approval and evaluation. To a great extent, this reality has caused foundations' management teams and officials to think that communication with grassroots SOs is not the most important factor. Even if they want smooth communication with grantees, foundations just complete projects' required activities, which does not greatly affect a foundation's survival.

Too much interference from foundations is another complaint made by grantees. From the perspective of grassroots SOs, Chinese foundations interfere too much during project implementation, including dealings with financial mechanisms and project management. Foundations organize many training sessions focused on financial management and reporting, and different foundations have different requirements for how financial reporting is done, even how to paste receipts. These kinds of situations have improved due to the increasing cooperation among parties, which has led to foundations better understanding the financial difficulties of grassroots SOs.

Generally speaking, such foundations are trying to play a leadership role that will enable them to manage all grantees. The purpose of the cooperation is not to support the development of grassroots SOs, but to fund them based on the needs of foundations. Some more mature grassroots SOs realize that the leading role foundations play is too strong and believe that foundations are not "supporting" grassroots SOs but making grassroots SOs "work" for them. These problems are not the intention of foundations. Foundations want to help grassroots SOs through making grants; however, sometimes foundations do not understand projects, as well as grassroots SOs, do, and sometimes project officials lack an adequate amount of professionalism. That said, foundations believe their requirements and mentoring are helping grassroots SOs, whereas grassroots SOs may disagree with this perspective. At times, some of the foundations' practices are not only detrimental to the development of grassroots SOs but also may mislead or hinder the growth of grassroots SOs. Therefore, a grant-making foundation's professionalism is critical to its grant-making approach, otherwise, this grant-making cooperation may affect the relationship between foundations and grassroots SOs.

8.2 How trust affects cooperation

Although I noted in the theoretical framework (Section 3.4.1) that the basis for cooperation is not trust but the durability of the relationship, in practice the foundations still consider trust as a problem or even the main problem when they are interacting and cooperating with grassroots SOs or considering whether to do so. It is an assumption that trust is not the most important factor because foundations can take various measures to control the implementation of projects. Therefore, I formulated the following hypothesis:

Foundations don't like to make grants to grassroots SOs in China because trust is a problem.

All representatives from foundations said that trust was one of the biggest obstacles to deciding which grassroots SOs to fund. There are two ways on how trust affected the interactions between foundations and grassroots SOs, including when foundations make grants to grassroots SOs and whether foundations think grassroots SOs have enough capacity to carry out projects. One is that some foundations do not trust all grassroots SOs, i.e financial management and professionality, so these foundations have been resisting to fund any grassroots SOs. The second is that foundations' officials trust someone in the grassroots SOs, so it will be easier to cooperate and make grants. Moreover, if the foundations do not understand the grassroots SOs at all, how to trust the applicant becomes a big problem, which could affect the foundations' decision of whether to approve the project.

Even though, the representatives from grassroots SOs stated that they could understand foundations' distrust from the foundation's perspective. For example, a representative from a grassroots SO (SO 8) said that she understood that PFFs require transparency and strict evaluations. However, she said that one national foundation always changed its project officials, which meant that her organization had to earn the trust of the new project officials. Moreover, it is possible to suddenly lose contact with a foundation due to the frequent staff turnover of foundations. Therefore, trust is a still problem when foundations make grants to grassroots SOs.

This section provides examples of successful and unsuccessful cases on how trust affected the interactions between foundations and grassroots SOs, including when foundation makes grants to grassroots SOs and how to maintain and sustain the cooperation.

8.2.1 Trust can also be the key to promoting cooperation

The following quotation relates to the cooperation between Shaanxi Women's Theoretical Marriage and Family Research Group (hereafter Shaanxi Women's Group) and the Narada Foundation during the Wenchuan earthquake.

> *Immediately after the earthquake occurred in Sichuan on May 12, 2008, Xiaoxian Gao (the main founder of Shaanxi Women's Group) contacted Yongguang Xu, Secretary-General of the Narada Foundation, about applying funding for emergency relief. Yongguang Xu told her to "take action" over the phone. Soon, ten Shaanxi SOs started to work as a relief group before the funding had even arrived.*
>
> *Soon after, on June 19, 2008, upon arriving at Zundao township in Mianzhu county of Sichuan Province, Xiaoxian Gao, Yongguang Xu and other colleagues [sic], realized that the grant of 50,000 yuan was not enough to cover the villagers' temporary housing. Unexpectedly, Yongguang Xu decided that, "we can do this." In no time, Shaanxi Women's Group had completed a project proposal to apply for 50 temporary houses for the villagers. Later, Xiaoxian Gao recalled that, "I submitted the project proposal on June 22nd, and. the next day, it was accepted and approved." [sic]*
>
> *Moved by the fast response, Xiaoxian Gao sent a text message to Yongguang Xu: "In the past more than ten years working in grassroots SO, I have never met a foundation who can respond to their applications as quickly as Narada Foundation." Yongguang Xu responded to her that "it's all about trust." Additionally, Xiaoxian Gao believes the quick response is also based on the common cultural background, which can reduce procedures for applying for funding in emergencies, compared to the application to international organizations* (Liu, 2009).

It can be concluded that here trust-based cooperation was quite efficient due to flexibility in the mobilization of funds. In addition, common cultural backgrounds and trust between organizations and people contributed to this successful cooperation. Certainly, Gao and Xu have worked, respectively, as pioneers in foundations and grassroots SOs in China since the 1980s. Also, Shaanxi Women's Group has worked since the 1980s as one of the earliest grassroots SOs in China.

8.2.2 Distrust between foundations and grassroots SOs in China

More and more grant-making foundations will award grants to grassroots SOs in China, but the crisis of trust has gradually spread in the foundation sector because of the incapacities of grassroots SOs caused by a shortage of appropriate resources.

As mentioned earlier, a crisis of trust between foundations and grassroots SOs has greatly affected foundations' decisions when determining which partners they will work with. Therefore, foundations need to find the most trusted grassroots SOs. Likewise, grassroots SOs need to have the trust of foundations. This situation means the role of individuals is very important, especially in grassroots SOs, because at times foundations decide to work with a grassroots SO mainly because they trust someone in that organization.

The general perception that grassroots SOs have a low level of development and limited organizational capabilities has persisted since grassroots SOs first appeared in China in the 1980s, even when society as a whole and scholars recognize their achievements. People, therefore, are not sure about the abilities or motivation of these organizations. In the interviews, I heard this idea more than once, from both foundations and grassroots SOs. In general, the role of grassroots SOs is seen as one in which they take charge of advocacy work and low-level professional work, even in the view of trusting foundations already seeking to cooperate with them.

Most Chinese academic studies show that Chinese grassroots SOs are restricted to this role based on their internal and external development. Internally, they are seen as weak from the time of their appearance to the time they begin developing their capabilities, including a deficiency in organizational capacity, a shortage of high-skilled personnel, an unsound management system, and an inadequate capacity to mobilize. Externally, they have not proved themselves to the public and the government, in terms of the public's lack of awareness of their activities and the government's caution due to the lack of transparent systems and monitoring mechanisms. The government does not prefer to select new SOs, but prefers to choose those they already know or have good relationships with.

Overall, these barriers make it hard for grassroots SOs to acquire resources or funding from the government. In light of this limited funding, grassroots SOs put their hopes in domestic foundations as their most important and practical sources of funding.

In an article, Liu (2009) mentioned that grassroots SOs normally use international foundations "as a natural frame of reference" when discussing Chinese private foundations, especially referring to those grassroots SOs that have cooperated with international foundations for almost twenty years. Grassroots SOs have a greater comfort level cooperating with international organizations than with Chinese foundations, while, according to the representative from Foundation N, Chinese foundations complain that they prefer not to support "old grassroots SOs" because they are unprofessional and seldom make great achievements. To a certain extent, domestic foundations do not recognize grassroots SOs that were previously funded by foreign NGOs. Instead, they cultivate grassroots SOs that they consider to be professional and that meet the requirements for funding applications.

In some cases, the trust may be the single, overriding indicator for whether a foundation will cooperate with a grassroots SO. For example, foundations are not likely to trust grassroots SOs when they continue to have financial problems. Also, foundations may generalize specific cases such as this, adding to their lack of trust.

Accordingly, I argue that trust is a problem for enduring cooperative relationships between foundations and grassroots SOs. Therefore, I formulated the following hypothesis:

> *Trust is a problem for maintaining and sustaining a cooperative relationship between foundations and grassroots SOs.*

It was interesting to see that, as a result of their distrust, especially during the early stages of cooperation, all the foundations interviewed went to great effort to select qualified grantees. However, it is a known fact that, after the first run of cooperation, there is little ongoing cooperation between foundations and their grantees, even if they trust each other. When representatives of foundations were questioned about whether they would extend a contract or continue cooperation after the first round of successful cooperation, they indicated that long-term funding was not the foundations' strategy even though they recognized their partners' capabilities, which meant that they already trusted each other. For example, the foundations (Foundation D, G, I) might say that they didn't have a budget or plan at the time, or they (Foundation D, G, I, K, N) might recommend to their trusted grantees other foundations that were in a position to support them. Therefore, trust is not the core problem in sustaining cooperative relationships between foundations and grassroots SOs; instead, the problem lies in the foundations' grant-making strategies that do not favor long-term cooperation with grantees. There are still no Chinese grant-making foundations that emphasize long-term cooperation with grassroots SOs and the development of grassroots SOs. Rather, Chinese foundations hope to leverage more resources from other funding entities such as small grants from the government.

8.3 How resource interdependence affects cooperation

This section explores how foundations and grassroots SOs survive and manage issues such as organizational structure; a professional staff; whether they control their resources or other organizations control them; the kinds of resources foundations need from grassroots SOs, and vice versa; and whether they can help each other achieve organizational goals and how to do so. Also covered is whether foundations' dependence on grassroots SOs is lower than grassroots SOs' dependence on foundations, which would create asymmetric dependence that in turn leads to inequality between foundations and grassroots SOs.

For this research, my study draws on the arguments of Lai (2017) and Xu (2010) on the contradictory relationships between Chinese foundations and grassroots SOs during the grant-making process and explains what kinds of resources they can provide each other and what they need from each other. Accordingly, two interview questions to foundations were formulated as follows:

> *Foundation_Q10: Do you think cooperation between foundations and grassroots SOs helps to achieve foundations' goals? In what way?*
>
> *Foundation_Q11: Do you think foundations need resources from grassroots SOs? Please describe.*

All foundations' representatives said they did not need resources from their grantees. Instead, they hoped that the grantees would implement projects without expectations or scandals, and their main concern was definitely the grantees' financial situation. However, it can be said that foundations need grassroots SOs to raise funds through their activities or through stories that help people identify with them. But these are just icing on the cake, not the key points for survival.

The views from grassroots SOs also need to be taken into consideration. So the following question is analyzed here in advance. During the interview, it was formulated and presented to grassroots SOs:

> *Grassroots SOs_Q8: What kinds of resources does your organization need from domestic foundations? Please describe.*

The answers I got from this question confirmed the research mentioned earlier, which means that what grassroots SOs need most from foundations is still financial resources. Insufficient resources are a typical aspect of the life of grassroots SOs. One might argue that it is unreasonable for grassroots SOs to require financial resources from foundations, as foundations also generally lack funding resources, especially unrestricted funds.

In reality, one of the main conflicts between them is administrative expenses, which can be seen from 2013 of China Foundation Ranking, in which 25 percent of the dissatisfaction related to administrative expenses, as described here:

> *In the process of communication with the XX Foundation, they accused us of excessive administrative costs, high cost of trainers, etc., so that we must strictly control administrative costs, but it is really difficult for those of us who need to rely on human intellectual support to do things. The foundation also suggested us to learn from another newly [formed] organization which has only three people and can control administrative costs. At this point, we have too much disagreement with the foundation, which finally led to the failure of cooperation.*
>
> *There are differences in administrative expenses, and the foundation doesn't understand and respect the actual situation of grassroots SOs on this. (31–32).*

Based on the different responses of foundations and grassroots SOs on resources, the biggest difference is that what foundations focus on is their provision of funding and technical support, capacity building, and so on; whereas, in addition to the funding support, what grassroots SOs want is independence.

Unequal relationship between resource providers and resource receivers: One case study calling for a stop to "ME Funding for Philanthropy Innovation" project
ME Funding for Philanthropy Innovation, a collaborative project that started in 2015, was implemented by China Foundation for Poverty Alleviation under the funding support of China Minsheng Banking Corp., Ltd. In response to the trends of the time and the need for innovation and en-

trepreneurship in the public welfare sector, as well as its advantages, China Minsheng Banking Corp., Ltd. launched the project on its twentieth anniversary, with the purpose of undertaking corporate social responsibility, creating a unique social responsibility brand, and solving social problems. Through funding organizations and projects with developmental and social impact potential, this project aims at encouraging more institutions to discover and solve social problems. The selection process is referred to as the Expert Review and Public Review. During this review, forty organizations are selected for a second round, and then each of the top twenty selected can receive funding support of 500,000 yuan, with a total amount of 10 million yuan. At the same time, to encourage more organizations to participate and to help organizations better develop and build stronger social influence, the plan will provide 20,000 yuan of ME innovative public welfare development funds to each of the remaining twenty organizations.

However, on January 5, 2018, when the project had been implemented for three consecutive years, more than ten grassroots SOs, including Friends of Nature, proposed an initiative to stop ranking funding projects by canvassing. According to the initiative, ME Funding for Philanthropy Innovation used public voting numbers as an important evaluation indicator that directly affected the final selection of organizations to fund. The initiative also pointed out that this process caused public voting to bear weight on public welfare projects in that the number of votes was regarded as an important evaluation indicator that directly affected the project's funding from China Minsheng Banking Corp. Ltd. Within ten days, forty-four projects received a total of nearly 2.5 million votes through WeChat canvassing. Under such an impressive number of votes, a survey of nearly six hundred participants in a single day showed that 60 percent of respondents expressed their dislike of ME's voting activities. From 2015 to 2018, the project's selection process has become a tug-of-war that

a) pushes public welfare practitioners to make limited efforts to cope with the vote by canvassing;
b) makes the public welfare industry a platform for competing media resources and capital among organizations; and
c) forces those nonprofit organizations that should serve disadvantaged groups and the public's interest to become a medium for serving the corporate brand and the public relations of China Minsheng Banking Corp., Ltd.[34]

---

34 China Philanthropy Times, http://www.gongyisixiang.org/nc/zhuanlan/master/?t
    x_newsfrontedit_pi2%5Bnewsid%5D=7286&tx_newsfrontedit_pi2%5Bname%5

Three appeals of the open letter are as follows:

a) The resource provider stops any attempt to determine the ranking of funding projects by canvassing.

b) The resource provider shall promote the development of public welfare in a way that promotes cooperation and sharing.

c) To establish an equality and respect relationship between the resource provider and resource recipients, and to listen to grassroots SOs' voice during the project implementation.

The appeals have also claimed that the vote places foundations and non-profit organizations in an unequal relationship, while both of them should respect each other. Overnight, nonprofit organizations that should have cooperated have become competitors due to the voting process, including obtaining the greatest number of votes possible and competing for scarce resources for communication, rather than sharing them. Large-scale organizations monopolize resource channels via more media resources. No one seems to cares about the effect this contention will have on the development of the public welfare sector.

This unequal relationship is by no means an isolated example for grass-roots SOs. One similar situation occurred during my fieldwork, as presented in the previous section where I talked about Foundation P (see section 6.1.5). After the Foundation P's project tendering was over, I interviewed two applicants, SO 4 and SO 10. Both of them complained that Foundation P was dogmatic and criticized them during the selection. For example, the representative from SO 4, who has worked in his village for more than 30 years, was criticized by one of the experts from the selection committee that "the project you are applying for is not something you should do" during the final defense. SO 10's response indicated that this selection process had made SO 10 unwilling to face or speak with the media. Although many members of the staff had doctorate degrees in agriculture, they had little to no experience on camera or with the media, and it was hard for them to cooperate with the media with confidence.

In addition to being asked to record a promotional video for Foundation P, one of the experts from the selection committee asked the representative from SO 10 a controversial question during the final defense, which the representative regarded as unprofessional. In this instance, the crux of the problem was that, to protect the local environment, the government

---

D=&tx_newsfrontedit_pi2%5Baction%5D=detail&tx_newsfrontedit_pi2%5Bcontroller%5D=News&cHash=2fffdf80c2b597a889f4d447be7cf09a, accessed October 1, 2019.

prohibited the cultivation of garlic, a product of high economic value that needed a lot of water and fertilizer. SO 10's project proposed, therefore, to plant crops such as rice and broad beans (traditional crops in the area) that would enable a reduction in the use of fertilizers and pesticides. However, the expert mainly considered the economic value of the crops, and strongly recommended that SO 10 looks for an alternative cash crop. The representative's opinion was that it took a certain amount of investigation and experimentation to choose a rational cultivation method, and also local farmers were not familiar with some of the crops suggested by the experts. In the end, the two sides did not agree on the issue, but it was clear that the experts were not satisfied with SO 10's answer. The final result was that, without knowing exactly why, SO 10 received only the minimum funding of 20,000 RMB, half of what other applicants in the final selection process received.

Obviously, a professional representative from SO 10 and an experienced representative from SO 4 did not have any advantage in this case. The amount of the project was attractive enough for grassroots SOs if approved by Foundation P, which was exactly what grassroots SOs needed at the time. So the applicants had to endure this unequal attitude.

Experts and foundations still instruct and select elite grantees from a dominant position, instead of respecting what grassroots SOs are doing in their own way. However, under the pressure of funding shortages, grassroots SOs are changing their working methods in a way that is more acceptable to funders.

8.4 Views from experts and supporting network/platform

The following tables help to clarify the interviewees' backgrounds, roles, and experiences in the third sector. In addition, to protect the anonymity of interviewees, the names of institutions and universities are not included in the following analysis.

Table 8-3: Profile of interviewed experts

Interviewee	Roles in the foundation or/and grassroots SOs	Years of experience in foundation and/or grassroots SOs	Age
Expert_X	An influential practitioner working in academics, founded and still managing one grassroots SO, frequently taking part in foundations and grassroots SOs' monitoring and evaluation as an expert for the local government department	15-20	56+
Expert_L	Working in academics, focusing on foundations and grassroots SOs' development over ten years	10-20	35-45
Expert_D	One of the leading researchers in the third sector and SOs and NPOs in academics; frequently taking part in foundations' grantmaking selection, monitoring, and evaluation as an expert for the government	20+	56+
Expert_N	Working in academics; has worked in an international NGO for 7 years; founded a grassroots SOs.	10-20	35-45
Expert_K	Working in academics; frequently taking part in foundations' grantmaking selection, monitoring, and evaluation as an expert for the local government department	15-20	56+

Table 8-4: Profile of interviewed supporting platform/network

Interviewee	Purpose of interviewed platform/ network	Years of experience in foundation and/or grassroots SOs	Age
Network_Z	Grant-making foundations alliance	15-20	56+
Network_C	Providing comprehensive information about the foundations	15-20	56+
Network_L	Organizing workshops for Chinese foundations	15-20	35-45
Network_H	Philanthropy Research Institute	20+	56+

Table 8-5: Profile of interviewed overseas foundations

Interviewee	Roles	Experiences in China	Age
Overseas _ Y	Being in charge of China projects in an American foundation	15-20	35-45
Overseas_F	Consultant in an American foundation	15-20	56+
Overseas _ M	Being in charge of China projects in a German foundation	15-20	56+

As indicated in the preceding tables, all the experts and practitioners interviewed had more than ten years of experience with Chinese foundations and/or grassroots SOs. Some interviewees with particularly rich experiences even witnessed the development of Chinese foundations and grassroots SOs or participated in the formulation of foundation– and grassroots SOs–related policies, such as Network_H and Expert_D. One German and one Chinese interviewee, working in German and American foundations, respectively, had worked with a Chinese program for fifteen to twenty years and had accumulated rich experiences in the process of communicating and working with Chinese foundations and grassroots SOs. Their views were valuable for studying the development of Chinese foundations and their cooperation with grassroots SOs.

When investigating the cooperative status between foundations and grassroots SOs, I found that experts and practitioners gave a positive view of the overall development of foundations, but a negative comment on the cooperation between foundations and grassroots SOs. On the one hand, the above interviewees recognized that in recent years foundations had developed very quickly in quantity and scale. Expert_D, an influential expert who had studied the field of the third sector for many years, said,

> *If we discuss foundations' development under China's social environment, especially with the limited staff and funds, it is not easy for China's foundations to develop to the present stage.*

Another positive comment was provided by interviewee Expert_K, who often participated in the foundations' strategy formulation and project selection:

> *From the rapid growth of foundations, it can be seen that many people are beginning to realize the importance and necessity of foundations. Foundations should be regarded as an important supporting force for the whole public welfare. The public is aware of their impact on society from increasing numbers and scale. In addition, the participation of entrepreneurs has played a positive impact on promoting public welfare as a whole. With the growing number and scale, foundations' working fields have been broadened, from disaster relief in the past to many working fields at present.*

On the other hand, while acknowledging that foundations have made considerable achievements in terms of development, the interviewees in the field of foundation research and practice also discovered various problems in that development that impedes their being the driving force behind social welfare. Among the interviewees, Expert_X and Expert_K pointed out that, in recent years, the major achievements have been done with the support of foreign organizations. For example, Expert_X said,

> *In fact, the Chinese foundation has been doing its own projects and rarely supporting other organizations. On the whole, the foundation is still playing on its own, and it has not changed to be more open with the growth of its number and wealth. It should have played a very large leverage role, but the role it can play in the current development is still very limited. Chinese foundation has been criticized a lot by the public and other SOs. In recent years, it is still foreign foundations that can really promote and help the development of grassroots SOs.*

In this regard, Overseas_Y and Overseas_M from an American foundation and a German foundation, respectively, were interviewed. Both have worked in China for more than ten years. On the one hand, early overseas foundations played a big role in promoting the development of SOs in China; on the other hand, the operations of some grant-making foundations in China have always been influenced by those overseas foundations.

In addition to the different perspectives of foundations and social organizations on cooperation noted in chapter 6 and chapter 7, here I analyze interviewees' views according to three factors: the independence of foundations, the dominance of projects, and projects' lifespan and the amount granted, which often cause disputes between foundations and grantees.

8.4.1 Independence of foundations

Whether a foundation is independent or not is related to the positioning of the foundation and even to the choice of the foundation's partners. The uncertainty of a foundation's positioning also has a great impact on whether and how to fund it.

Regarding whether foundations are independent, all interviewees alleged that Chinese foundations were not independent. Instead, they said that government agencies or government officials did the main decision-making for PFFs and that donors or enterprises did the main decision-making for NPFFs. For example, in an interview, Network_L said,

> *Within the Chinese system, China's foundations have basically never considered the issue of independence from the beginning. They either listen to the government or donors. With the mobilization of the government, such as the Belt and Road Initiative and Poverty Alleviation, the government calls on all social forces to do these things. When all social organizations do [the]*

same things, whether the organizations are independent is not originally important for Chinese foundations. There is no need to consider whether the foundation is independent.

Corporate and public donors generally play a decisive role in whether to make grants to other SOs, even in the selection of partners. Based on their experience, the foundations' view is that they are beholden only to the government, or to donors (or both), or companies. These entities affect whether and to which partners foundations will make grants, which of course is affected by their position on supporting other SOs. Expert_X, who had a similar view, said,

Many of Chinese foundations are corporate foundations, or many foundations have a large funding proportion from companies, which seriously affects the independence of foundations. When many corporate foundations are established, the boss becomes the main executive of the foundation not for solving certain social problems, but mainly to achieve the goals of the company. Therefore, the implementation of the project should be short, safe and rapid. The people who can make decisions for foundations do not have sufficient thinking and experience about how to operate charities and foundations, while the steering committee and project officials have no right in decision-making.

Then, what kind of influence will a non-independent foundation have on a foundation and its partners? Expert_D noted,

Currently, most of the domestic foundations are NPFF, behind which are companies or bosses. These foundations have relatively high-performance requirements. In the future, if the professionalization of foundations is improved, they will become more independent, and then the secretariat has more voice in decision-making. In addition, it is more challenging for a project officer in a grant-making foundation than an operational foundation. You must be responsible for both the entrepreneur and the grantees. Many foundations donate only a small part of the funding. Many foundations turn to be grant-making foundations for different reasons, for example, some are market-driven, some are changed under the promotion of individuals, like Yongguang Xu. The mission of Chinese foundations is not strong, and the decision-makers treat the foundation as their own private property. The foundation does not [have to] be so focused on the mission to raise funds. It works on AIDs today, and then changes environmental protection tomorrow, or concentrates on working left-behind child the day after tomorrow.

Likewise, another expert Expert_K commented the dependence of Chinese foundations is closely related to the development of the political and social environment,

> *Chinese foundations have big problems in the development, which are closely related to the social, cultural and historical background during foundations' survival and growth. What kind of problems China has, and there are similar problems with foundations. For example, if the country is not democratic, then the governance of foundations is not democratic. In recent years, many foundations have begun to do part of the grant-making work, which is a big social change compared to operation foundations. Some foundations have a long history and strong mission, e.g., the Red Cross has been focusing on disaster relief with the help of the government. However, small foundations have no long-term goals or restrict their development goals to something specified by the government, lacking research on professional management and social problems. This is why many small foundations do things for a while and do nothing for a while, and then become zombie foundations.*

The above interviews show that, even if a foundation was always independent, this fact did not affect its survival. However, a non-independent foundation will have various developmental problems, especially in working fields and the certainty of a grant-making strategy. I propose that the proliferation of NPFFs after 2004 did not bring about a fundamental change in the governance of foundations.

8.4.2 The dominance of the project

Whether a project is led by foundations or grassroots SOs is also a controversial issue. A big gap exists between foundations' understanding of professionalism and the status quo mentality of social organizations; thus their expectations are different. For example, Expert_X said,

> *The institutional development direction of the Narada Foundation and the design of their projects seem to be very good, focusing on SOs' capacity building and personnel training as two cores to grassroots SOs' development. This foundation's design of projects conformed to the development path of grassroots SOs, so it was given high expectations, but it slowly deviated from the original track in the process of implementing the project. For example, once they see a certain social problem or a problem with a grassroots SOs, it will arouse the foundation's staffs' desire to control its partners and then destroy the entire grant-making strategy of the foundation. . . . A considerable num-*

ber of foundations in China have a strong desire to control, which is related to the origin and growth of the foundation.

Expert_K explained the foundations' desire to control the project because their personnel were unprofessional and didn't understand social problems. He said,

> *Many foundations' project staff, even secretary-generaleral or deputy secretary-general, are young people. Although they graduate from prestigious universities, live and study in China, they have no experience in working in SOs and lack social problem thinking and research. Coupled with the misunderstanding of the marketing-driven philanthropy in recent years, these young people are even more unclear about how to do foundations.*

In addition, Expert_L also offered a long-term observation of why young project officials tend to control projects:

> *Many foundation project officials have just graduated from college. Once they graduate, they are in charge of important funding resources. They will have an illusion that money is their own, and they will have an arrogant attitude in their work and hope to control the whole project, and they will not understand social problems and grassroots SOs' problems. Conflicts will easily arise during cooperation.*

Who leads a project and which side is more professional? Foundations consider themselves more professional than grantees and design projects in great detail, thinking that the grantees' jobs are limited to executing projects accordingly. However, grantees think that the project designs do not take into account the actual problems and difficulties that they face. In this regard, Expert_X claimed,

> *From the perspective of the working area distribution of foundations and grassroots SOs, foundations and experts in places such as Beijing and Shanghai cannot see the value of local grassroots SOs. Grassroots SOs can't be measured only by funding resources nor by organization scale and social impact. I understand that the foundation is not easy, but because [of] some grassroots SOs that I have worked in for many years, sometimes I need to contact foundations when applying for projects. But it's hard to tolerate their arrogant attitude when talking with people from the foundation. Anything new has a process of nurturing, and so does [sic] grassroots social organizations. This does not mean that you have to start new things according to the standards of the foundation. But the staff of the foundation equated themselves with the attitude of the capitalists behind them, and acted with an arrogant atti-*

tude. They didn't do things from a professional perspective. Instead, they complained that the grassroots SOs were not qualified, and then they operated projects by themselves. Foundations with corporate backgrounds have entrepreneurial goals and attitudes, and foundations with official backgrounds have official backgrounds and attitudes.

Michelle Busgen, who once worked for the Heinrich Böll Foundation and the Misereor Foundation in their Beijing offices, was able to observe the development of China's philanthropic foundations and grassroots SOs for more than ten years. He did a study in which he evaluated Chinese donors, and noted the following:

It takes a long time to become a real baker through training. However, foundations' project officers often start to be in charge of grant-making projects as soon as they take office, and they may never have experience in grantmaking. A senior in the public welfare sector was also surprised to find that a university student who has just graduated has become the secretary-general of the two foundations, is responsible for a huge amount of grant (Liu 2014).

A similar situation concerning project officials' professionalism and experiences came up in my interviews. The representative from one supporting platform organization (Network_L) was dedicated to promoting cooperation between Chinese foundations and grassroots SOs. He remarked that "the current grantmaking process in China is that a group of project officials born in the 1990s is making grants to a group of [grassroots SOs] applicants born in the 1960s." His remarks implied an awkward situation for grassroots SOs. As previously discussed, newly recruited project officials frequently do a significant amount of fieldwork and reporting and play a vital role in linking foundations with grassroots SOs; however, the most experienced staff member, or the founder, or the director are the ones most qualified to conduct fundraising for Chinese grassroots SOs.

Another similar situation happened to another representative interviewed (Expert_N) who had worked in a well-known international organization for many years. At the time of the interview, she was conducting academic research while also working as one of the founders and a project officer for a grassroots SO in Beijing. As someone with rich experiences both academically and in practice, she said that she often felt it was awkward to attend events organized by foundations. She knew that foundations can pay competitive salaries to attract graduates from excellent universities, who then usually start their careers in the foundation sector. Even if they have no experience, because they are working for providers of funding resources, some of these people may come across as arrogant. Also, Expert_N had a personal reason for not attending activities promoted by foundations; that is, she felt that she was always the oldest participant (age 38). Regardless, what led her to think this way was her sense of professionalism, her role as a foundations' project officer, and her work with underdeveloped grassroots SOs.

It is worth reiterating that one of the biggest challenges for grassroots SOs is the shortage of professional staff because of low wages and limited career development. Lack of professional talent exists in the entire third sector in China, and much more so for grassroots SOs in their early stage of development. Hence, SOs' founders or primary leaders must carry the burden of caring for the survival of the organization. A common situation is that, before creating grassroots SOs and working to solve social problems, these founders or top leaders had already found and understood social problems during past working experiences.

So, is there a problem with the capacity of grassroots SOs? The answer is yes. Expert_K, who often participated in the selection and evaluation of two grant-making foundations in China, said,

> *From the perspective of ability, grassroots SOs have many problems, and the same with the foundations. When participating in the selection of foundation projects, some experts have a very arrogant attitude. Regardless of whether the applicants can be successful, they first criticize the applicant from top to toe. There is no equality at all. Moreover, with limited grants, some experts or entrepreneurs require applicants to solve all problems of the project site. This is simply impossible. The foundation should be appropriately tolerant of others when dealing with grassroots SOs.*

Another factor influencing a project being led by a foundation rather than the recipient is that the foundation hopes the positive impact of the project will directly benefit the foundation, rather than the recipient organization or target group. For example, in an interview, Overseas_M, a German project officer who used to work in making grants to grassroots SOs and foundations in China, said,

> *There is a big cultural difference between the foundations in China and Germany. For example, a well-known Chinese foundation funded a small grassroots SO to do a project. The public will pay attention to this well-known foundation, being attracted by its fame, and will not pay attention to what the small grassroots SO does. We have a totally different view. We hope the grantees put our name behind the project, because the most important thing*

is the target group of the project, as well as the people that the project needs to help.

Similarly, a project officer, Overseas_Y, who was still working in an overseas foundation at the time of the interview also mentioned their views on partners:

Our grant amount is very small, so we hope to give priority to the needs of the grantee organizations both in the application and in the later project implementation process. If the project can promote grantees' organizational development, we feel very gratified. It is also our hope to help grantees survive.

At the same time, she had also worked in a grant-making foundation for several months in China, provided this example of a "ready-made" project, as a typical case where a project was designed by a foundation instead of grantees:

Chinese foundation's project officials are also very conflicting and difficult when designing the project. First, they need to convince the council to approve the project, so it takes one to two years to investigate the related basic information across the country. They have to be very cautious and formularize this project, and finally it turns to be a "ready-made" project when it comes to grantees. There is no space for grantees to play, nor is it conducive to the development of grantees' organizational capabilities. It's like hiring someone to do an activity or activities, but this activity is presented as a project. Some projects are called "labor contractor" (bao gong tou) projects. When the foundation initiated the project application, all the activities and details that the project should include were specified in detail, and it was called "based on scientific investigation, expert guidance, and social organization's participation." Even though the project was well planned in the early stage, it could not be successful in the later stage of implementation. The lack of long-term goals' activities is controversial, so grantees should ask clearly before working on a project. Instead, there are around 30 grants in the X foundation (one American foundation that the representative is still working for), so it is impossible to follow-up the details with every project. It doesn't mean which one is better. However, after I stopped working for that Chinese foundation, I felt that the freedom and creativity for grantees would be very small if the foundation follows up all details.

In the meantime, my working in foreign foundations makes me feel that a grant of 2,000 US dollars is very small, which is also the building of trust. For domestic foundations, however, a few thousand dollars is not a small amount of money. In many cases, the problem needs to be analyzed very clearly and the workload is large during the initial stage. However, domestic foundations are not very professional on certain issues and have no confidence that the grantee can do a good job, the pressure and requirement of the project will be transferred to the grantee, which in turn make their grantees discomfort.

In general, experts and overseas observers have the impression that, while funding grassroots SOs, some domestic-funded foundations try to play a leading role, that is, bring all funded organizations into their own unified management and establish their own industry-leading position. Correspondingly, Expert_K, who often participates in project evaluation, mentioned that he heard complaints from many grassroots SOs during the evaluation:

Some grantees prefer to use the term "joint cooperation" rather than funding to describe the interactive relationship with foundations. The grant from the foundation is not only pitiful and does not help a lot with the development of grantees, but it must also implement the project in accordance with the requirements of the foundation, and even follow the development strategy required by the foundations. Therefore, the term "joint cooperation" is more in line with the expectations of foundations and does not affect the independence of grantees. And then both can respect each other.

8.4.3 Grant lifespan and amount

Obvious features of cooperation are short project lifespans and the small amount of funds awarded, factors that cause unstable cooperation. Expert_K, who often participates in project approvals and evolution, noted these two features and what he had observed:

The amount of funding from the foundation is small, because the foundations have limited funding resources. This is the main reason. At the same time, many grassroots SOs that applied for are also small-sized. The foundation believes that the capabilities of these institutions are limited. The project lifespan is short because many grant-making foundations have no guarantees and uncertainties in raising funds.

Moreover, Network_C expressed a similar view—that foundations, especially those working on grantmaking, generally have a lack of funding:

There are still very few very large-scale foundations in China, and most foundations themselves are still facing the pressure of survival, let alone making grants to others. There is still no such kind of big-size foundation, which is similar to foreign family foundations that have sufficient financial resources themselves. Therefore, even if some foundations can fund projects, they start with short-term and small-amount projects. In addition, I think that domestic grassroots SOs have indeed the problem of insufficient capacity and have not yet grown up. Therefore, most foundations are either unwilling to make grants or just fund projects with a short-term with a small amount. Additionally, it matters a question of trust between them.

When asked why there are no big-size foundations or big family foundations in China, Network_L, who regularly organized foundation meetings in China and had close communication with nearly all grant-making foundations in China, also stated the difficulties of the foundations:

China does not have a particularly large-size foundation, nor is it because entrepreneurs do not want to make the foundation bigger, but it is caused by various reasons such as taxes. Take Fujian Cao Dewang Foundation as an example, if he donates the equity, he has to pay a lot of taxes. It is difficult to implement good policies, and the local government personnel does not consider the development of foundations and grassroots SOs into their performance achievements. So, they are unwilling to take risks, and they have no motivation to mobilize and encourage the establishment of SOs. Therefore, many foundations are called perceptual charity, or one-off charity, when they do projects, because the foundation has no way to think about its long-time goal and strategy.

Another factor is that the boss, e.g. main donor or founder of a foundation, does not care about the length of the foundation's projects, who just take the foundation as a symbol of social status. This can be seen in Network_L's words:

In the past, the rich discussed wine and golf while getting together, but now it's different. Now the rich will ask directly, do you have a foundation and what does your foundation do? The way to meet and say hello has become "to protect a leopard today," "I just went to the Himalayas to pick up rubbish" and such words, to show their social status their height of posh.

When talking about the project lifespan and grant amount, two interviewees, one from the United States and one from Europe, had completely different views. Different from Chinese foundations, one German foundation prefers to select long-term cooperation because their understanding of social problems could not be solved in a short time. For example, Overseas_M said,

Our project focuses on development issues and capacity building. When we received the project application, if the applicant thought that this problem could be solved in one year, we thought it was impractical and we were unwilling to support such organizations. On the contrary, we would rather support some two-year and three-year projects. After the project is completed, we would generally have the second and third rounds of support. From the perspective of the Chinese foundation, it will criticize that our project is inefficient and costs so much money. In our opinion, however, this project is worthwhile as long as it has been working on planned activities and is gradually improving. We believe that it is not feasible to quickly solve social problems. The problems of social development and organizational development cannot be solved all in a short period according to our research. Therefore, many of the grantees we have worked with are five years or even longer than ten years.

In conclusion, from the perspectives of the above interviewees, scholars and practitioners engaged in foundations and grassroots SOs have a positive evaluation of the development of foundations, along with voices of doubt and criticism on their cooperation with grassroots SOs. Undoubtedly, both foundations and grassroots SOs need a process of growth on their own. The expectations of foundations are obviously different from those of grassroots SOs. Foundations are influenced by various intervening factors, such as foundation governance and limited funding resources, which causes problems in the development process.

9 Conclusion and Discussion

Here, I first summarize this study's findings from the perspective of foundations' historical development and the in-depth interviews. Then I explain how the findings and previous research relate to the focus of my research in regards to the interaction between foundations and grassroots SOs in China, which is followed by a discussion of its limitations. Finally, I offer suggestions related to future cooperation between Chinese foundations and grassroots SOs.

9.1 Findings

This study examined the historical development of philanthropic foundations in China from the founding of the People's Republic of China in 1949 until 2017, with a focus on the different actors from the very beginning, to the appearance of PFFs, to the success of NPFFs. The overall historical development of philanthropic foundations shows that they played an important role in social changes, whether as a supplement to public affairs or as an independent sector focused on social welfare and benefits. Under the great influence of the political environment and policies, Chinese philanthropic foundations have had a succession of good and bad experiences; for instance, each change in policies and political circumstances affects the number of foundations. The findings indicate that foundations are increasingly government-like (Kang 2019, 509) because of the long-lasting working models and mechanisms in China.

This study's statistical analysis shows that, from 2008 to 2017, philanthropic foundations experienced a rapid growth pattern and funding scale and a rapid increase in resources and fields of workings, especially the growth of NPFFs after the promulgation of RMF-2004. Given that government priorities are still structuring the field of Chinese foundations in key and consequential ways through registration and governance, NPFFs still work similarly to PFFs within a "government-organized philanthropic ecosystem," such as the fields of working, operating approaches, and so on. The vast majority of Chinese foundations are still operating foundations, but with several kinds of grant-making activities.

In chapter 5, I explained that cooperation started in 2008 because of the gradual withdrawal of overseas funds and the mutual needs of both parties. The key financial resources reside with foundations in the third sector, while grassroots SOs need funding for their survival. However, rather than smooth cooperation, they are caught in a dilemma and encounter problems. Among the few grant-making foundations in China, some large grant-making foundations do not want to support grassroots SOs because they think grassroots SOs are too weak, while grassroots SOs are reluctant to apply for grants from foundations for various reasons, such as the amount of funding is too low, the process is too complicated, and foundations interfere too much. So cooperation starts, but the process is full of twists and turns.

In chapter 6, I investigated how and why foundations interact and cooperate with grassroots SOs from the perspective of Chinese foundations, based on the cooperation and resource interdependency theories. This includes how to look for and select grantees, how to monitor projects during cooperative interactions, and how to evaluate and maintain the project in the end. The foundations interviewed for the study showed their cooperation through supporting high-performing and highly efficient grassroots SOs. In the views of these foundations, funding is known as a very important source for grassroots SOs but not the most important one that foundations should provide to grassroots SOs, while foundations think infrastructure construction is very important to grassroots SOs.

In chapter 7, I tested similar research questions, i.e. how to start with and process the cooperation, and monitor and evaluate the projects, with grassroots SOs and gained additional comments from experienced scholars and experts. From the perspective of grantees and experts, grant-making foundations provide not only funding but also professional knowledge and technical and human resource support, though these supports sometimes interrupt recipients' development; and grassroots SOs see domestic foundations as the best prospects for providing crucial and long-term funding, though some grassroots SOs prefer to have greater autonomy than is generally afforded.

In chapter 8, I summarized and categorized the cooperation between the two and compare their differences in overall logic on three interactive stages of cooperation: the initial, the middle, and the final stage. Then, from the perspective of both parties, the purpose of this chapter was to provide a comprehensive analysis to highlight the impact of two factors, trust and resource interdependency, and the views of third-party stakeholders. It included scholars and experts who have experience working with grassroots SOs or have served as judges for foundations, grassroots SOs, and government-sponsored projects, as well as representatives from overseas foundations. The interpretation contributed to further understand the expectations of foundations are obviously different from those of grassroots SOs.

Based on the preceding observations, Chinese foundations play an important role in promoting social change and solving social problems, but their cooperation with grassroots SOs is not robust. It can be regarded as "unsustainable cooperation" without the shadow of the future according to the cooperation theory. Chinese foundations' grant-making logic does not overlap with the needs of grassroots SOs, because they do not fully understand each other's difficulties and because their focus and path of development are not the same, resulting in less interaction.

9.2 Review of research questions and their connection to previous research

9.2.1 Two main research questions

This section goes back to two research questions mentioned at the beginning of the article, together with the hypothesis in the article.

9.2.1.1 Research question 1: How do Chinese foundations interact with other grassroots SOs?

Chinese foundations interact with grassroots SOs in six different ways, namely special funds, joint fundraising, high-engagement grantmaking, making grants to projects, making grants to organizations and making grants to individuals. These interactions with other social organizations are now common. Among the different needs for interactions, the greatest one is funding for grassroots SOs, especially in light of their struggle for survival (response to hypotheses H2-a and H2-d). Foundations can achieve their missions and extend organizational influence through grantmaking to grassroots SOs (response to H2-b).

As a matter of fact, grantmaking still is not the main operating mode of Chinese foundations for two reasons. First, there were only a few Chinese grant-making foundations at the end of 2018 with a total of 17 grant-making foundations. The sample of grassroots SOs included in this study shows that no more than fifteen foundations make grants to grassroots SOs regularly. Among the grant-making foundations in China, at times, they do not include grassroots SOs their funding strategy, or only part of their grants are made to grassroots SOs. Second, grant-making processes are still in a trial phase, although it is a popular topic for many foundations, whether they are grant-making foundations or operating foundations. However, some foundations have only started such discussions, so the future is filled with uncertainty.

In my samples, only three foundations made grants to grassroots SOs regularly, while the others made grants occasionally or had been doing so for only one or two years.

Among the few grant-making foundations, interactive mechanisms are being established and improved gradually, while effective communication and dialogue between foundations and grassroots SOs are still lacked. Rather, trust is still a problem when foundations make grants to grassroots SOs (response to H1-b), although it is not regarded as a problem for maintaining and sustaining a cooperative relationship (response to H1-c). Moreover, the dilemma between foundations and grassroots SOs exists throughout the entire cooperation process, such as their different logic about an application, project implementation, monitoring, and evaluation (response to H1-d).

Through excessive interference (e.g., a high degree of engagement, adjunct mentors, construction of philanthropic infrastructures, etc.), Chinese foundations try to shape grassroots SOs' course of direction. This interference includes the consistency of working areas, such as education, poverty alleviation, environment protection, child health care, child welfare, and so on. In my sampling, I did not find evidence that foundations and grassroots SOs compete for overseas funding or domestic private and public funding (response to H1-a). Instead, Chinese foundations encourage grassroots SOs to diversify their funding sources.

9.2.1.2 Research question 2: Why do they act the way they do?

From the perspective of mechanisms, the development of Chinese foundations is highly influenced by how earlier PFFs operated and by current political restrictions and organizational governance. Due to the restrictive regulatory framework in China, both foundations and grassroots SOs have difficulty sustaining their philanthropic efforts and have struggled to develop since their appearance. The concepts of independence, autonomy, and cooperative participation necessary for civil society are far from inspiring and far from being the consensus in China. At the same time, in an authoritarian government, it is difficult for foundations and grassroots SOs to mature as an independent third sector. On the other hand, organizational governance still influences foundations' dependence and strategies, even the grantees they should select.

From an operational perspective, based on comments from all interviewed scholars and experts' comments, professionalism is still a big challenge for Chinese grant-making foundations because the grant-making process is still in a trial stage in China. Grassroots SOs are not involved in foundations' funding mechanisms in China. Foundations face external pressure on their policy and fundraising measures and internal pressure on their organizational transformations, short-term and small-scale projects, and how a single founder or decision-maker influences their funding strategy, all of which add to their shortcomings.

From the perspective of culture, the unequal relationship between foundations and grassroots SOs requires human concern; that is, foundations' dependence on grassroots SOs is lower than grassroots SOs' dependence on foundations, which creates asymmetrical dependence (response to H2-c). Trust is an inconstant factor relegated mainly to foundations' dominance in deciding whether and which grantees to fund. Project officials, as the direct connection between foundations and their grantees, should play an important role in grantmaking, which could introduce more empathy during project implementation and monitoring.

9.2.2 Connections to previous research

A recent study pointed out that domestic foundations are more willing to cultivate grassroots SOs' "competitiveness" through grantees selection, which to some extent is a donor-dominant process (Kang 2019, 504). In other words, projects by Chinese foundations are mostly foundation-dominated projects from the perspective of their grantees. Kimball and Kopell (2011,37-38) noted that problems were raised by foundation-designed projects to the grantees. They demonstrated that the more foundations dominate the way grantees solve social problems, the more they constrain grantees' expertise and innovative abilities, and doing so contributes to the foundation's bureaucracy (Kimball and Kopell 2011, 38).

Lai (2017) noted that being organizations that provide funds to other nonprofit organizations, foundations are seen as having strong institutional advantages (29). Previous studies (see Kang 2019) and practices have confirmed the appearance of two trends: grassroots SOs need funding resources for survival and domestic foundations and the government is becoming their major donors (499). So, the question is, does the fact that international foundations and organizations gradually withdrew funding from Chinese grassroots SOs mean that domestic foundations have replaced that funding as a way to support grassroots SOs in China? According to Spires, Tao, and Chan (2014), "the reality is that the typical NGO operates at a very small scale and with extremely few resources" (90) despite the blossoming of a support system for these grass-roots groups (this information was based on Spires and colleagues' 263 samples of face-to-face interviews with grassroots SOs' and non-registered grassroots organizations' leaders).

Grassroots SOs are hardly able to raise funds and acquire donations in China, and overseas funding is currently almost unavailable. Hence, the Chinese government and foundations are expected to reshape how funding is conducted in China. In recent years, the Chinese government has provided the main financial support to Chinese grassroots SOs, particularly through the government's purchase-of-services contracting procedure.

Recent studies have supported this idea. Lai (2017, 9–11) and Kang (2019, 501–511) noted that the Chinese government and foundations have different approaches to working with and influencing grassroots SOs, through their different focus on funding, selection, evaluation criteria, and scaling strategies. More worrisome is that government funding will affect the independence and autonomy of grassroots SOs. More important, Chinese foundations are particularly regarded as an alternative and more attractive funding source than the government.

In view of the above, Chinese foundations continue to be the primary source of funding for grassroots foundations, functioning as an engine to drive the development of the third sector.

9.2.3 Connection to theories

The conditions for cooperation are pointed out in chapter 5; specifically, the 2008 Wenchuan earthquake enabled foundations to realize that cooperation based on reciprocation was available. Accordingly, cooperation was triggered. Similar to the live-and-let-live system in Cooperation theory, foundation practitioners noted that cooperation with grassroots SOs was "only if you [grassroots SOs] live well, can [the foundation] I live better."

In my analysis of field research in chapters 6, 7, and 8, I found that cooperation takes place only within a small group, and I also realized that the conditions for cooperation are based largely on those organizations with the ability to be recognized. Only a few foundations have unlimited funding resources, and those foundations' understanding is that the capacity of most grassroots SOs is relatively low, both of which make it hard for the two to cooperate with each other. In this regard, it is questioned whether foundations are funding the "grass-top SOs," which means a few of the best-perceived grassroots SOs, instead of "grassroots SOs" in general. From the perspective of Cooperation theory, if cooperation is done by scattered individuals, cooperation cannot be established because they do not have enough chances to meet each other. I also found that well-known grassroots SOs continue to cooperate with foundations one after another through recommendations or encounters, but that it is difficult for new grassroots SOs to meet foundations' personnel. In addition, their cooperative behavior is not clear, such as a foundation's positioning and grant-making strategy, and the two parties cannot adapt to each other's logic. Instead, foundations are reshaping and changing organizational growth and working approaches through grantmaking, such as the use of business key performance indicators, foundation-designed projects, mentors' participation, and high-engagement grant-making approaches. In short, cooperation between the two entities is unstable. Two parties will cooperate because of continuous interactions with each other, but the cooperation between a foundation and its grantee is not continuous but a one-off experience. This kind of one-off cooperation is very short-term, mostly one year or even several months.

Even though conditions for cooperation are available, the parties' interactive environment cannot help the stability and sustainability of cooperation. Their cooperation occurs only in small groups, and future interaction is not taken into consideration by one party [the foundation]. One more important point is that, before a foundation will begin cooperation, trust is needed, but trust is not related to subsequent cooperation under the premise of the foundation's strategy and limited funding resources. Therefore, I propose that foundations need the courage to trust grassroots SOs and take risks.

From the perspective of resource interdependence, foundations are an important funding resource for grassroots SOs, whereas most Chinese foundations operate their own projects and few foundations provide funding to support grassroots SOs. Foundations' funding is a very important survival source for grassroots SOs, not the other way around. Unsymmetrical dependence is the pattern manifested in the relationship between foundations and grassroots SOs in China. In this case, the foundations' work approach has been to try to use unequal resources to reshape and change foundations, and then change from a "partnership" relationship to a leader relationship between superiors and their subordinates. Therefore, I propose that a foundation's care for humanity and the professionalism of project officers are very important for the beginning and maintenance of cooperation under unequal resources.

9.3 *Limitations*

There are four limitations in this study. First, the scarcity of data is a substantial limitation. In this study, I used official data and data from highly esteemed and reliable organizations. However, data provided by departments or organizations can change over time; for example, the total number of Chinese foundations can change from year to year.

Second, data on grant-making projects, grant amounts, periods covered, and so on are particularly limited. Both foundations and grassroots SOs were reluctant to discuss the money they funded in any detail, most notably when the amount was low.

Third, this study focused only on registered grassroots SOs, excluding unregistered grassroots organizations, business-registered social groups, or organizations that were generally seen as NGOs in previous research.

The fourth limitation of this study is the limited number of samples included. Before their selection, a balance of samplings (e.g., PPFs and PFFs, local and national level) were taken into consideration in order to represent the width and breadth of experiences. Several foundations selected were reluctant to be interviewed, some of which were highly representative foundations. A long-term project of this kind with a larger sampling is needed, but it will require significant energy and ability.

In addition, a few concerns about the samples need to be addressed. First, both foundations and grassroots SOs tried to avoid making negative comments or talking directly about problems, but preferred to give answers that the others agreed with. Second, if participants made negative comments about their own organizations, they would not allow me to record them, which made it difficult to convey their views properly.

9.4 Suggestions for the future

The number of NPFFs will continue to rise along with the economic growth and social development in China, which will bring more possibilities for grant-making foundations and grant-making activities in China. Several controversial issues regarding the grant-making process need to be addressed, such as the definition of grant-making foundations, the difference between foundations and other social organizations.

Under current political restrictions and limited financial resources, scaling up will be different for foundations and grassroots SOs. Unlike PFFs, business-affiliated foundations are regarded as the essential engines for the development of China's grant-making foundations because they have more freedom to decide whether to award grants to grassroots SOs working in areas that do not show visible results in the short term. However, this approach flies in the face of what grassroots SOs need. Entrepreneurs believe that "the fact that grassroots SOs keep the same scale for more than ten years is completely intolerable" (Lai 2017, 97), while from grassroots SOs' perspective, it is very difficult to survive under the harsh political and economic environment in China. Therefore, civil society can only grow by urging the government to decentralize and open up public affairs.

Concerning interactions between foundations and grassroots SOs, foundations' grant-making logic and their relationship with grassroots SOs must improve, even though the conflicts between the two parties are caused by multiple and complex factors. Whether the parties will be able to consider each other's perspective will have a great impact on their future cooperation.

Bibliography

Anheier, H. K. (2001). Foundations in Europe: a comparative perspective. Civil Society Working Paper series (18). Centre for civil society, London school of economics and Political Science, London, UK.

Anheier, H. K. (2005). Nonprofit organizations: Theory, management, policy. London, UK: Routledge.

Anheier, H. K., & Toepler, S., eds. (1999). Private Funds, Public Purpose: Philanthropic Foundations in International Perspective. New York: Kluwer Academic/ Plenum Publishers.

Anheier, H. K., & Daly, S., eds. (2007). The politics of foundations: A comparative analysis. New York, NY: Routledge.

Anheier, H. K., Forster, S., Mangold, J., & Striebing, C. (2018). Foundations in Germany: A portrait. American Behavioral Scientist, 62(12), 1639–1669.

Axelrod, R. (1984), The Evolution of Cooperation, New York: Basic Books.

Axelrod, R. & Hamilton W. D. (1981), The Evolution of Cooperation. Science 211, 1390-1396.

Axelrod, R. (2000). On Six Advances in Cooperation Theory, Analyse & Kritik, (22), 130-151.

Bartley, T. (2007). How Foundations Shape Social Movements: The Construction of an Organizational Field and the Rise of Forest Certification. Social Problems, 54(3), 229-255.

Bentley, J. G. (2003). The Role of International Support for Civil Society Organizations in China. Harvard Asia Quarterly, 7(1), 11-20.

Bradshaw, P. (2009). A contingency approach to nonprofit governance. Nonprofit Management & Leadership, 20(1), pp. 61–81.

Chan, K. M. (2010). Commentary on Hsu: Graduated control and NGO responses: Civil society as institutional logic. Journal of Civil Society, 6(3), 301-306.

Chan, K. M., Qiu, H., & Zhu, J. (2005). Chinese NGOs strive to survive. Leiden, The Netherlands: Brill, 131-159. In Y. Bian, K. Chan, & T. Cheung, eds., Social transformations in Chinese societies.

Chan, K. M. & Lai, W. (2018), Foundations in China: From Statist to Corporatist, American Behavioral Scientist, pp. 1-19.

Chan, K. M., Qiu, H., & Zhu, J. (2005). Chinese NGOs strive to survive. In Y. Bian, K. Chan, & T. Cheung, eds., Social transformations in Chinese societies. Leiden, The Netherlands: Brill, 131–159.

Cheng, G. and Han, H. (2018). The development of Chinese foundations (1981-2017). In Yang, T. (ed.). Annual report on China's philanthropy development. Social sciences academic press (China), 106-131.

China foundation center (2012). The development of Chinese foundations: an independent research report 2012. Social sciences academic press (China).

China foundation center (2013). The development of Chinese foundations: an independent research report 2013. Social sciences academic press (China).

China foundation center (2014). The development of Chinese foundations: an independent research report 2014. Social sciences academic press (China).

China foundation center (2015). The development of Chinese foundations: an independent research report 2015. Social sciences academic press (China).

Cooper, C. M. (2006). "This Is Our Way In": The Civil Society of Environ- mental NGOs in South-West China. Government and Opposition 41, (1), 109-36.

Deng, G. (2001). Non-Profit Organization Evaluation, Social Sciences Academic Press (Originally in Chinese: 邓国胜. 非营利组织评估. 北京:社会科学文献出版社, 2001 年).

Deng, G. (2003). Public-welfare project evaluation- Case-study on Project Happiness, Social Sciences Academic Press (Originally in Chinese: 邓国胜. 公益项目评估——以"幸福工程"为案例. 北京:社会科学文献出版社, 2003 年).

Deng G.et al. (2007). NGOs Evaluation: Theory, Methods & Indicator System. Beijing University Publishing House (Originally in Chinese: 邓国胜等. 民间组织评估体系：理论、方法与指标体系. 北京大学出版社, 2007 年).

Deng, G. (2013). The Decline of Foreign Aid and the Dilemma of the Chinese Grassroots NGOs. Religions & Christianity in Today's China, Vol. III, 2013, (1), 24-31.

Deng, G. (2015). The influence of elite philanthropy on NGO development in China. Asian Studies Review, 39(4), 554–570.

Deng, G. & Tao, Z. (2017). The development of Chinese foundations: an independent research report 2017, Social sciences academic press (China).

Dickson, B. J. (2000). Cooptation and corporatism in China: The logic of party adaptation. Political Science Quarterly, (115), 517-540.

DiMaggio, P., & Powell, W. W. (1983). The iron cage revisited: Institutional isomorphism and collective rationality in organizational fields. American Sociological Review, 48(2), 147– 160.

Estes, R. J. (1998). Emerging Chinese foundations: The role of private philanthropy in the new China. Regional Development Studies, 4, 165–180.

Feng, C. (2017). The NGO law in China and its impact on overseas funded NGOs [online]. Cosmopolitan Civil Societies: An Interdisciplinary Journal, 9(3), 95-105.

Feng, X. (2015). China's charitable foundations: Development and policy-related issues. The Chinese Economy, 48(2), 130–154.

Froelich, K. (1999). Diversification of revenue strategies: Evolving resource dependence in nonprofit organizations. Nonprofit and Voluntary Sector Quarterly, 28(3), 246–268.

Fulda, A. (2017). The contested role of foreign and domestic foundations in the PRC: Policies, Positions, Paradigms, Power. Journal of the British Association for Chinese Studies. 7, 63-99.

Gazley, B. (2017) The Current State of Interorganizational Collaboration: Lessons for Human Service Research and Management, Human Service Organizations: Management, Leadership & Governance, 41:1, 1-5, DOI: 10.1080/23303131.2015.1095582.

Guo, X. (2015), Research on the Supervision of Non-Governmental Organizations in China by Chinese Government (Doctoral dissertation), Hunnan University. (Originally in Chinese: 郭欣蕾. 我国政府对在华境外非政府组织的监管研究 [D]; 湖南大学; 2015 年)

Han, J. (2016). The Emergence of Social Corporatism in China: Nonprofit Organizations, Private Foundations, and the State. China Review, 16(2), 27–53.

Han, J. (2017). RETRACTED: Policy influence of social organizations in China. Nonprofit and Voluntary Sector Quarterly. Advance, 46(2), NP2–NP19.

Hammack D. C. and Anheier, H. K. (2010). American Foundations: Their Roles and Contributions to Society. In Anheier, H. K. and Hammack, D. C., eds., American Foundations: Roles and Contributions. Washington, DC.: The Brookings Institution, 3-27.

Hasmath, R., & Hsu, J. Y. (2014). Isomorphic Pressures, Epistemic Communities and State–NGO Collaboration in China. The China Quarterly, 220, 936–954.

Hasmath, R., & Hsu, J. Y. J. (2016). NGO governance and management in China. London and New York: Routledge.

Hassid, J. & Jeffreys, E., (2015). Doing good or doing nothing? Celebrity, Media and Philanthropy in China. Third World Quarterly, 36(1), 75-93.

Heurlin, C. (2010). Governing civil society: The political logic of NGO–state relations under dictatorship. VOLUNTAS: International Journal of Voluntary and Nonprofit Organizations, 21, 220–239.

Heurlin, C. (2016) "(Dis)Trusting NGOs in China. In: Hasmath, R., & Hsu, J. Y. J., eds. NGO governance and management in China, London and New York: Routledge, 89-106. In: Hasmath, R., & Hsu, J. Y. J., eds., NGO governance and management in China.

Hildebrandt, T. (2011). The political economy of social organization registration in China. The China Quarterly, 208, 970–989.

Hildebrandt, T. (2013). Social organizations and the authoritarian state in China. New York, NY: Cambridge University Press.

Hsu, C. (2008). "Rehabilitating Charity" in China: The case of Project Hope and the rise of non-profit organizations. Journal of Civil Society, 4, 81-96.

Hu, J. (2010). Legal Research on the Foundation's External Supervision. Legal system and society, (18), 108-109 (Originally in Chinese: 胡婧.基金会外部监督之法律研究.法制与社会;2010 年 18 期: 108-109).

Heydemann, S., & Toepler, S. (2006). Foundations and the challenge of legitimacy in comparative perspective. In K. Prewitt, M. Dogan, S. Heydemann, & S. Toepler (Eds), The legitimacy of philanthropic foundations: United States and European perspectives (pp. 3-26). New York, NY: Russell Sage Foundation.

Jing, Y. (2008). Outsourcing in China: An Exploratory Assessment. Public Administration and Development, 28(2), 119–128.

Jing, Y. & Chen, B. (2012). Is Competitive Contracting Really Competitive? Exploring Government–Nonprofit Collaboration in China. International Public Management Journal.

Jing, Y. & Hu,Y. (2017). From Service Contracting to Collaborative Governance: Evolution of Government–Nonprofit Relations.Public Administration and Development, 37, 191–202.

Johnson, J. M. & Ni, N. (2015). The Impact of Political Connections on Donations to Chinese NGOs. International Public Management Journal, 18 (4), 514–535.

Kang, X. et al. (2011). The development of Chinese foundations: An independent research report in 2011. Social Sciences Academic Press (China).

Kang, X. & Han, H. (2008). Graduated Controls: The State-Society Relationship in Contemporary China. Modern China 34 (1), 36–55.

Kang, X. (1997). Create Hope: A Case-Study of the China Youth Development Foundation. Lijiang Publishing Press & Guangxi Normal University Press (Originally in Chinese: 康晓光,创造希望:中国青少年发展基金会研究. 漓江出版社, 广西师范大学出版社).

Kang, X. (1999). Power shifting: The change of China's power structure during a time of transition. Zhejiang, China: Zhejiang People's Publishing House. (Originally in Chinese: 康晓光, 权力的转移–转型时期中国权力格局的变迁, 浙江人民出版社, 1999 年 10 月).

Kang, Y. (2017). The development of grassroots Chinese NGOs following the Wenchuan earthquake of 2008: Three case studies, four Modi Vivendi. VOLUNTAS: International Journal of Voluntary and Nonprofit Organizations, 28(4), 1648–1672.

Kang. Y. (2019). What Does China's Twin-Pillared NGO Funding Game Entail? Growing Diversity and Increasing Isomorphism. 30(3), 499-515.

Kimball, K. & Kopell, M. (2011). Letting-go. Stanford Social Innovation Review, 6(2), 37-41.

Knutsen, W. L. (2017). Retaining the benefits of government– nonprofit contracting relationship: Opposites attract or clash? VOLUNTAS: International Journal of Voluntary and Nonprofit Organizations, 28(4), 1373–1398.

Lai, W. (2017). The logic of foundation funding: Making grant to grassroots NGOs in China (Doctoral dissertation). The Chinese University of Hong Kong.

Lai, W. & Zhu, J. (2013). Collaboration between Foundations and Grassroots NGOs in China: From the Grantmaking Perspective". In J. G. Zhu, Blue Book of Foundation: Annual Report on China's Foundation Development 2012 (pp. 132–155). Social Sciences Academic Press (China). (Originally in Chinese: 赖伟军, 朱健刚. 基金会与 NGO 合作——资助的视角，载朱健刚（主编），中国公益发展报告 2012 : 132-155. 北京：社会科学文献出版社, 2013).

Lai, W., Zhu, J., Tao, L., & Spires, A. J. (2015). Bounded by the state: Government priorities and the development of private philanthropic foundations in China. The China Quarterly, 224, 1083–1092.

Lefroy, K. and Tsarenko Y. (2014). Dependence and effectiveness in the nonprofit-corporate alliance: The mediating effect of objectives achievement. Journal of Business Research, 67(9), 1959-1966.

Li. T. (2008). Silent partners: American modern charity foundation research. China Society Press (Originally in Chinese: 李韬. 沉默的伙伴：美国现代慈善基金会研究. 中国社会出版, 2008).

Li. T. (2005). Causes for the Flourishing of Philanthropic Foundations in the United States. American Studies Quarterly, 19 (3), 132-146 (Originally in Chinese: 李韬.慈善基金会缘何兴盛于美国. 美国研究, 2005, 19 (3): 132-146).

Liu, H. (2011). On the non-public offering foundation's public welfare supply function: classification, supply mode and optimal decision. China Nonprofit Review, (1), 1-29 (Originally in Chinese: 刘海龙. 论非公募基金会的公益供给功能: 分类, 供给方式与最优决策. 中国非营利评论，2011(1):1-29)

Liu, X. (2017). Seeding change: the Narada foundation approach to venture philanthropy, Social Sciences Academic Press (China) (Originally in Chinese: 刘晓雪. 散财有道——南都公益基金会公益风险投资的理念与实践探索. 社会科学文献出版社, 2017 年).

Liu, Z. ed. (2013). Annual report on China's foundation development (2012). Social Sciences Academic Press (China) (Originally in Chinese: 刘忠祥. 中国基金会发展报告(2012). 社会科学文献出版社, 2013 年).

Liu, Z. ed. (2014). Annual report on China's foundation development (2013). Social Sciences Academic Press (China) (Originally in Chinese: 刘忠祥,马昕. 中国基金会发展报告(2013). 社会科学文献出版社, 2014 年).

Liu, Z. ed. (2015). Annual report on China's foundation development (2014). Social Sciences Academic Press (China) (Originally in Chinese: 刘忠祥,马昕. 中国基金会发展报告(2014). 社会科学文献出版社, 2015 年).

Lu, W. (2012). Foundation evaluation's process, development status and characteristics. Research of Administration of NPOs , 2012 (2), 10-16 (Originally in Chinese: 卢玮静, 基金会评估历程、开展状况与特点. 社团管理研究, 2012(2): 10-16).

Lu, W. et al. (2014). Foundation Evaluation: Theoretical System and Practice, Social Sciences Academic Press (China) (Originally in Chinese: 卢玮静等. 基金会评估:理论体系与实践. 社会科学文献出版社, 2014 年).

Ma, J., Wang, Q., Dong, C., and Li, H. (2017). The research infrastructure of Chinese foundations, a database for Chinese civil society studies. Scientific Data. Vol.4.

Ma, Q. (2002). Defining Chinese Nongovernmental Organizations. VOLUNTAS: International Journal of Voluntary and Nonprofit Organizations 13, no. 2, 113-30.

Ma, Q. (2006). Non-governmental organizations in contemporary China: Paving the way to civil society? New York: Routledge.

Ma Q. (2013). To Change China: The Rockefeller Foundation's Century-long Journey in China, Guangxi Normal University Press (Originally in Chinese: 马秋莎. 改变中国:洛克菲勒基金会在华百年. 广西师范大学出版社, 2013).

Martin, D. G. (2004). Nonprofit Foundations and Grassroots Organizing: Reshaping Urban Governance. The Professional Geographer, 56(3), 394-405.

Milgrom, P.R. (1984). Axelrod's "The Evolution of Cooperation". The RAND Journal of Economics, 15(2), 305–309.

Moody, M. (2008). "Building a Culture": The Construction and Evolution of Venture Philanthropy as a New Organizational Field." Nonprofit and Voluntary Sector Quarterly, 37(2): 324-352.

Morton, K. (2005). The Emergence of NGOs in China and Their Trans- national Linkages. Australian Journal of International Affairs 59, no. 4, 519-32.

Ni, N., and Zhan, X. 2017. Embedded government control and nonprofit revenue growth. Public Administrative Review, 77 (5): 730–742.

Ni, N., Chen, Q., Ding, S., & Wu, Z. (2017). Professionalization and cost efficiency of fundraising in charitable organizations: The case of charitable foundations in China. VOLUNTAS: International Journal of Voluntary and Nonprofit Organizations, 28(2), 773–797.

Nickel, P. M. & Eikenberry, A. M. (2009). A critique of the discourse of marketized philanthropy. American Behavioral Scientist, 52(7), 974–989.

Nie, L., Liu, H., and Cheng, W. (2016). Exploring Factors that Influence Voluntary Disclosure by Chinese Foundations. VOLUNTAS: International Journal of Voluntary and Nonprofit Organizations 27 (5): 2374–2400.

Ou. Z. (2012). Viewing the Absence of the Supervision System of the Foundation from the Perspective of the Abnormal Operation of the Foundation. Legal System and Society. (3), 94-95 (Originally in Chinese: 区展玲. 从基金会运作失范事件看基金会监管体制的缺失[J];法制与社会;2012 年 03 期:94-95).

Qian, C. (2003). American private foundations and U.S.-China relations–on the socialization of international politics (Doctoral dissertation), China Foreign Affairs University. (Originally in Chinese: 钱春元. 美国私人基金会与美中关系-兼论国际政治社会化[D], 外交学院, 2003 年).

Research Group of China Foundation Development Report (2016). Annual Report on China's Foundation Development (2015-2016), Social Sciences Academic Press (China).

Roelofs, J. (1987). Foundations and Social Change Organizations: The Mask of Pluralism. The Insurgent Sociologist, 14(3): 31–71.

Saich, A. (2008). Providing public goods in transitional China. New York: Palgrave Macmillan.

Saidel, J. R. (1991). Resource Interdependence: The Relationship between State Agencies and Nonprofit Organizations. Public Administration Review, Vol. 51, No. 6 (Nov. - Dec., 1991), pp. 543-553.

Salmenkari, T. (2014). Encounters between Chinese NGOs and the State: Distance, Roles and Voice. Issues & Studies, 50(2): 143-177.

Shang, Y. (2003). Analysis of the current situation and system of foundations in China. https://wenku.baidu.com/view/717a975e804d2b160b4ec056.html.

Shen, Y., & Yu, J. (2017). Local government and NGOs in China: Performance-based collaboration. China: An International Journal, 15(2), 177–191.

Shi, G. (2014). A Study on Factors Affecting the Credibility of Charitable Organizations. Chinese Public Administration 2014(5), 95–100.

Shieh, S. & Deng, G. (2011). An emerging civil society: The impact of the 2008 Sichuan earthquake on grass-roots associations in China. The China Journal, 65, 181–194.

Shieh, S. (2017). Same Bed, Different Dreams? The Divergent Pathways of Foundations and Grassroots NGOs in China. VOLUNTAS: International Journal of Voluntary and Nonprofit Organizations, Volume 28. pp.1785-1811.

Song, S. & Hu, B. (2009). On Foundation's Property Rights. (11), 82-84 (Originally in Chinese: 宋胜菊, 胡波. 论公益基金会的产权[J]. 会计之友, 2009 年 11 期: 82-84).

Song, Y. & Fu, L. (2018). Do charitable foundations spend money where people need it most? A spatial analysis of China. ISPRS International Journal of Geo-Information, 7(3), 100–116.

Spires, A. J. (2011a). Contingent Symbiosis and Civil Society in an Authoritarian State: Understanding the Survival of China's Grassroots NGOs. American Journal of Sociology, vol.117, no.1, pp.1-45.

Spires, A. J. (2011b). "Organizational Homophily in International Grantmaking: US-Based Foundations and their Grantees in China." Journal of Civil Society, vol. 7, no. 3, pp. 305-331.

Spires, A. J. & Tao, L. & Chan, K.M. (2014). Societal support for China's grassroots NGOs: Evidence from Yunnan, Guangdong and Beijing. The China Journal, 71, 65–90.

Tai, J. W. (2015). Building civil society in authoritarian China: Importance of leadership connections for establishing effective nongovernmental organizations in a non-democracy. Zug, Switzerland: Springer International Publishing.

Tao. C. et al. (2009). Index System Problems in Foundation Evaluation——Take the Fund-Raising Organizations in Earthquake Relief as Example. Xuehui Journal. Vol. 2: 18-22, 53 (Originally in Chinese: 陶传进, 赵小平、祝贺. 基金会评估中的指标体系问题——以抗震救灾中的募捐组织为例, 学会, 2009 年第 2 期:18-22, 53).

Tao, C. & Liu, Z. (2014). On Foundations. China Society Press (Originally in Chinese: 陶传进, 刘忠祥. 基金会导论.中国社会出版社. 2014 年 4 月).

Teets, J. C. (2013). Let many civil societies bloom: The rise of consultative authoritarianism in China. The China Quarterly, 213, 19–38.

Teet. J.C. & Jagusztyn, M. (2016). The Evolution of a Collaborative Governance Model: Public-Nonprofit Partnerships in China, London and New York: Routledge, 69-88. In: Hasmath, R., & Hsu, J. Y. J., eds., NGO governance and management in China.

Toepler, S. (1999). On the problem of defining foundations in a comparative perspective. Nonprofit Management & Leadership, 10(2), 215-225.

Toepler, S. (2016). Foundations in Germany and the US: Comparative Observations. In: Witkowski, G. & Bauerkämper, A. eds., German Philanthropy in Transatlantic Perspective. Heidelberg/New York: Springer, pp. 23-39.

Toepler, S. (2018). Toward a Comparative Understanding of Foundations. American Behavioral Scientist, 62(13), 1956 –1971.

Tolbert, P. S. & Zucker, L. G. (1983). Institutional Sources of Change in the Formal Structure of Organizations: The Diffusion of Civil Service Reform, 1880-1935. Administrative Science Quarterly, 28(1): 22-39.

Unger, J. (1996). "Bridges": Private business, the Chinese government and the rise of new associations. The China Quarterly, 147, 795–819.

Unger, J. & Chan, A. (2015). State corporatism and business associations in China: A comparison with earlier emerging economies of East Asia. International Journal of Emerging Markets., 10(2), 178–193.

Wakeman, F. (1993). The Civil Society and Public Sphere Debate. Western Reflections on Chinese Political Culture. Modern China, 19(2), 108-138.

Wandi, J. (1992). Acts of Philanthropy Appear in China (Vol. 35). http://search.pro quest.com.ezproxy.gc.cuny.edu/docview/213876737?accountid=7287.

Wang, M. (2007). Development status and policy analysis of NGOs in CHina. China Public Administration Review, (6), 132-149 (Originally in Chinese: 王名. 中国 NGO 的发展现状及其政策分析, 中国公共管理评论, 第六卷:132-149).

Wang, M. & Jia. X. (2003). Foundation Property Rights Structure and Governance. Economic Affairs,(1), 40-45 (Originally in Chinese: 王名, 贾西津.基金会的产权结构与治理 [J] .经济界, 2003（1）:40-45).

Wang, Q. (2016). Co-optation or restriction: the differentiated government control over foundations in China. RICF Working Paper Series. https://papers.ssrn.com/sol3/papers.cfm?abstract_id=2846635. Accessed 3 Oct 2019.

Wang, Q. (2018a). A typological study of the recent development and landscape of foundations in China. Chinese Political Science Review, 3(3), 297–321.

Wang, Q. (2018b). Have foundations become an independent sector in China? Exploring the links between foundations and the state. Asia Pacific Journal of Public Administration, 40(1), 68–73.

Wang, Q. and Yao, Y. (2016). Resource Dependence and Government-NGO Relationship in China. The China Nonprofit Review 8 (2016) 27-51.

Wang, X., Yin, S., Hu, J. (2010). Legal research on Foundations' external supervision. Legal System and Society. (6),108-109 (Originally in Chinese: 王晓雪, 殷实, 胡婧等，基金会外部监督之法律研究[J]；法制与社会；2010 年 6 期：108-109).

Wang, Z. (2014). Development and future of Chinese modern philanthropy. In: Zhu, J. & Lin, M. Philanthropic Studies, Chinese social science press, 157-182 (王振耀. 中国现代慈善事业的发展与前途, 摘自: 朱健刚&林猛, 公益, 中国社会科学出版社, 2014 年第 1 辑).

Wang, M. & Tao. C. (2004) Current Situation and Relative Policy Suggestions about NGO. 2004(1). Chinese Public Administration. pp.70-73. (Originally in Chinese: 王名, 陶传进. 中国民间组织的现状与相关政策建议. 中国行政管理, 2014(1): 70-73).

Wang, X. & Cao, L. (2006). The American Foundation's limits and classification. Xuehui, (2),6-10 (王晓丽&曹庆萍.美国基金会的界定与分类.2006(2): 6-10).

Wang, X. & Zheng, Y. (2004). Tentative Study on Tax Law Regulation on Foundation. Wuhan University Journal (Philosophy & Social Science), (4), 541 (Originally in Chinese: 汪鑫,郑莹. 基金会的税法规制初探. 中国行政管理, 2004: 541).

Wei, Q. (2019). CEO power and nonprofit financial performance: Evidence from Chinese philanthropic foundations. Voluntas: International Journal of Voluntary and Nonprofit Organizations, 1–17.

Wiepking, P. (2010). Giving to particular charitable organizations: Do materialists support local organizations and do democrats donate to animal protection? Social Science Research,39, 1073-1087.

Woqi Foundation (2018). Preliminary Study on the Value of Grantmaking—Review of Case-studies on Grantmaking Foundation. Intellectual Property Publishing House (Originally in Chinese: 沃启公益基金会, 资助的价值初探—资助型基金会案例述评, 知识产权出版社, 2018 年).

Wu, F. (2003). Environmental GONGO Autonomy: Unintended Consequences of State Strategies in China. The Good Society, 12(1): 35-45.

Wu, F. (2017). "An emerging group name 'gongyi': ideational collectivity in China's civil soci- ety." The China Review 17(2), 123–150.

Wu, F. & Chan, K. M. (2012). Graduated Control and Beyond: The Evolving Government-NGO Relations. China Perspective, (3), 9-17.

Xie, B. (2003a). Analysis of the relations between contemporary Chinese public welfare foundations and the government. Academic Journal Graduate School Chinese Academy of Social Sciences. 2003(4), 64-69. (Originally in Chinese: 谢宝富, 当代中国公益基金会与政府的关系分析, 《中国社会科学院研究生院学报》2003(4):64-69).

Xie, B. (2003b). Analysis on Problems of Contemporary Chinese Public Welfare Foundations, 2003(16), pp. 29-33. (Originally in Chinese: 谢宝富, 当代中国公益基金会的若干问题分析, 北京航空航天大学学报(社会科学版).2003(16): 29-33).

Xie, S. (2017), In-depth Explanation of the He Xiangjian Family's 6 billion RMB Charity Plan, China Philanthropist, (8), 28-32 (Originally in Chinese: 谢舒. 详解何享健家族 60 亿慈善计划. 中国慈善家杂志, 2017 年 8 月刊: 28-32).

Xu. G. (2007). The commonweal power of building a harmonious society: Research on the legal system of foundations. Law Press China (Originally in Chinese: 许光. 构建和谐社会的公益力量——基金会法律制度研究. 法律出版社, 2007).

Xu, X. & Ye, M. (2009). Game Analysis on the Internal Corporate Governance of Foundations in China. Journal of Nibo University (Liberal Arts Edition). 22(2),104-108 (Originally in Chinese:徐晞, 叶民强. 我国基金会内部治理问题的博弈分析. 宁波大学学报(人文科学版); 22(2):104-108).

Xu, Y. (2008). Unsymmetrical Dependence: Study on the Relationship between Foundations and Government in China. Journal of Public Management, 33-40. (Originally in Chinese:徐宇珊, 非对称性依赖:中国基金会与政府关系研究, 公共管理学报, 2008: 33-40).

Xu, Y. (2010). On Foundations: the study on the Transformation of Chinese Foundations. China Social Sciences Press (Originally in Chinese: 徐宇珊. 论基金会——中国基金会转型研究. 中国社会出版社. 2010 年 4 月).

Xu, Y. (2012). Reform and Transformation of Public Fundraising Foundations: Dilemma and Innovation. In Yang, T. (Eds). Blue Book of Philanthropy: Annual Report on China's Philanthropy Development 2012.Social Science Social sciences academic press (China), 129-130 (Originally in Chinese: 徐永光, 公募基金会改革转型: 困境与创新.摘自:杨团(主编). 中国慈善发展报告 2012.社会科学文献出版社,129-130).

Xu, Y. (2014). The transformation of public foundations in China. In C. Huang, G. Deng, Z. Wang, and R. L. Edwards, eds., China's Nonprofit Sector: Progress and Challenges. Transaction Publishers, 163-178.

Xu, Y. (2015). Functions of Eight principal forms of Chinese foundations. China National Conditions and Strength, (1), 16-17 (Originally in Chinese: 徐永光. 八种形态基金会的作用及其完善. 中国国情国力, 2015(1): 16-17).

Yang, K. (2015). The Key Factors of Successful Self- organizing Cooperation between Different Social Organizations --Based on the NGOs ' Alliance during the Wenchuan Earthquake Relief in Shannxi Province. Chinese Public Administration. Issue.8, 66-70 (Originally in Chinese: 杨柯. 社会组织间自合作成功的关键因素探讨——以"5·12"汶川地震陕西 NGO 赈灾联盟为例. 中国行政管理, 2015 (8) : 66-70).

Yang, T. (2010). Preliminary analysis of foundation research. Hunan Social Science, (1),53-59 (Originally in Chinese: 杨团, 关于基金会研究的初步解析, 湖南社会科学, 2010(1):53-59).

Yang, T. ed. (2011). Annual Report on China's Philanthropy Development (2011). Social Sciences Academic Press (China).

Yang, T. ed. (2012). Annual Report on China's Philanthropy Development (2012). Social Sciences Academic Press (China).

Yang, T. ed. (2013). Annual Report on China's Philanthropy Development (2013). Social Sciences Academic Press (China).

Yang, T. ed. (2017). Annual Report on China's Philanthropy Development (2017). Social Sciences Academic Press (China).

Yang, T. ed. (2018). Annual Report on China's Philanthropy Development (2018). Social Sciences Academic Press (China).

Yang, T. ed. (2019). Annual Report on China's Philanthropy Development (2019). Social Sciences Academic Press (China).

Yuen, S. (2015). Friend or Foe? The diminishing space of China's civil society. China Perspectives, 2015(3), 51–56.

Yuen, S. (2018). Negotiating service activism in China: The impact of NGOs' institutional embeddedness in the local state. Journal of Contemporary China, 27(111), 406–422.

Zhang, R., Rezaee, Z., and Zhu, J. (2010). Corporate Philanthropic Disaster Response and Ownership Type: Evidence from Chinese Firms' Response to the Sichuan Earthquake. Journal of Business Ethics 91(1), pp. 51–63. http://doi.org/10.1007/s10551-009-0067-3.

Zhang, Y. (2015). Dependent interdependence: The complicated dance of government–nonprofit relations in China. VOLUNTAS: International Journal of Voluntary and Nonprofit Organizations, 26(6), 2395–2423.

Zhou, Q. & Lin. Y. (2014). Inheritance and Reconstruction: The History and Reality of China Charity Development Transformation. Qilu Journal, 239(2), 82-87 (Originally in Chinese: 周秋光 & 林延光. 传承与再造：中国慈善发展转型的历史与现实, 2014 年第 2 期: 82-87).

Zheng, W., Ong, P., Cheng, A., Wong, K. (2016). Contemporary Chinese Philanthropy Literature Review (GCPI Working Paper 3). UCLA Center for Neighborhood Knowledge Global Chinese Philanthropy Initiative.

Zhu J. & Lai, W. (2014). "Incomplete Collaboration": The Strategy for Chinese NGO Alliance：Case Study of NGOs' Joint Action during the Wenchuan Earthquake Relief. Chinese Journal of Sociology, 34(4), 187-209（朱健刚＆赖伟军 (2014). "不完全合作"：NGO 联合行动策略--以汶川地震 NGO 联合救灾为例. 社会，2014(4): 187-209).

Zhu, Z., Tao, C., Liu, C., and Ye, Z. (2015). Foundation analysis: based on case-studies. China Economy Press. (Originally in Chinese: 朱照南等. 基金会分析: 以案例为载体. 中国经济出版社, 2015).

Zi, Z. (1996). The Rockefeller Foundation and China. American Studies, (1), 58-89 (Originally in Chinese: 资中筠. 洛克菲勒基金会与中国. 美国研究, 1996 年第 1 期: 58-89).

Zi, Z. (2003). The way to distribute donations: an analysis of American philanthropic foundation from a Chinese perspective. Shanghai People Publishing House (Originally in Chinese: 资中筠. 散财之道: 美国现代公益基金会述评. 上海人民出版社, 2003 年).

Zi, Z. (2015). The responsibility of wealth and the evolution of capitalism: Revelation of a century's development of American philanthropy. Shanghai Sanlian Publishing House. (Originally in Chinese: 资中筠. 财富的责任与资本主义演变：美国百年公益发展的启示. 上海三联书店, 2015 年).

Zimmer, A. & Freise, M. (2008). Bringing society back in: civil society, social capital and the third sector. Cheltenham: Edward Elgar, 19-42. In: Maloney, W. A.& Deth, J. V., eds., Civil Society and Governance in Europe.

News reports & Annual reports

Anonymous. (2013 & 2015). Evaluation rankings: China Foundation Evaluation Rankings (Originally in Chinese: 评价榜: 中国基金会评价榜. 2013 年&2015 年).

China Foundation for Poverty Alleviation Annual Report 2016.

Bao, M. (2012). 2012 Research Report of Cooperation and Innovation of Chinese Non-Governmental Organizations and Foundations: Strategic Cooperation and Promoting Social Innovation (Originally in Chinese: 包敏. 中国民间公益组织和基金会合作与创新研究--促进战略合作/推动社会创新. 2012 年 5 月).

Du. Z. (2010). Foundations and NGO cooperation: Adult Ceremony is still far from coming. China Philanthropy Times, 2010-08-11. (Originally in Chinese: 杜志莹 .基金会和 NGO 合作："成人礼"远未到来. 公益时报, 2010 年 8 月 11 日).

Fu, T. (2018). Grantmaking shapes healthy development of the non-profit ecosystem-The value of grantmaking foundations (Cases) review. Wo Qi Foundation, http://www.woqifoundation.org.cn/en.php/Home/Report/info/id/12.html, accessed November 1 2019.

Li, Z. (2019). What Kind of Profession Is Grantmaking? China Development Brief, http://www.chinadevelopmentbrief.org.cn/news-20166.html, accessed July 1, 2019.

Liu, H. (2009). The impact of private foundations on domestic NGOs. China Development Brief. Available online at http://www.chinadevelopmentbrief.cn/articles/the-impact-of-private-foundations-on-domestic-ngos/#fn1-206, accessed March 13, 2016.

Liu, H. (2011a). Develop Philanthropy through Debate and Cooperation. China Development Brief. Available online at http://www.chinadevelopmentbrief.cn/articles/develop-together-through-debate-and-cooperation-2/. Accessed March 13, 2019.

Liu, H. (2011b). The Third Path of NGO Development in China – An Interview with Xu Yongguang, Vice Chairman and Secretary General of Narada Foundation. China Development Brief. Available online at http://www.chinadevelopmentbrief.cn/articles/the-third-path-of-ngo-development-in-china-an-interview-with-xu-yongguang-vice-chairman-and-secretary-general-of-narada-foundation/. Accessed March 13, 2019.

Liu, H. (2011c). The Impact of Private Foundations on Domestic NGOs. China Development Brief. Available online at http://www.chinadevelopmentbrief.cn/articles/the-impact-of-private-foundations-on-domestic-ngos/. Accessed March 13, 2019.

Liu, H. (2012). Making grants to "grass top organizations" or the "grassroots organizations"? Social Enterprisers, 49(5), 52.

Liu, T. (2014). Self-cultivation of a grantmaker. China Development Brief. Available online at http://www.chinadevelopmentbrief.org.cn/news-8944.html. Accessed March 13, 2019.

Ma, T., Liu, K. and Jin, Z. (2018). 2017 Report of China Charity Donations. China Charity Alliance (Originally in Chinese: 马天昊, 刘凯茜, 金征. 2017 中国慈善捐赠报告. 中国慈善联合会, 2018 年 9 月).

Ministry of Civil Affairs of China from 2004-2017. Statistical report on the social service development by Ministry of Civil Affairs. Retrieved from http://www.mca.gov.cn/article/sj/tjgb/ , accessed on March 15 2020.

One Foundation (2017). Project Management Mechanism of One Foundation, accessed from One Foundation website, http://www.onefoundation.cn/Uploads/2 01710/59dc62631b74b.pdf, access July 2, 2019.

Shang, Y. (2005). Analysis of the current situation and system of foundations in China. Available online at https://wenku.baidu.com/view/717a975e804d2b160b 4ec056.html, Accessed September 5, 2019.

Social Transition and Foundations in China 2008-2018, compiled by China Foundation Forum, 2018 (Originally in Chinese:社会转型与中国基金会 2008-2018, 中国基金会论坛汇编).

Wang, H. (2018). 2017 National Foundation Annual Report: Over half of public fundraising foundations do not raise fund from the public. China Philanthropy Times. (Originally in Chinese: 2017 全国性基金会年报, 超半数公募基金会公开募捐收入为零. 公益时报, 2018 年 5 月 9 日) http://www.gongyishibao.com/htm l/yaowen/13869.html accessed May 11, 2020.

Xu, H. (2009). Seeking for solutions on the cooperation between foundations and grassroots SOs. China Development Brief, http://www.chinadevelopmentbrief.o rg.cn/news-615.html, accessed November 15, 2019. (Originally in Chinese: 徐辉. 基金会和草根 NGO 合作模式"求解". 中国发展简报, 2009-05-27.).

Xu, Y. (2009). Opening Speech on "Welcome the Era of Cooperation between Foundation and Grassroots NGOs," during the 5/12 Post-Disaster Reconstruction Cooperation Forum in 2009; found on Yongguang Xu's personal website, http://www.xuyongguang.cn/content/304, accessed November 15, 2019.

Yi Fang Foundation Annual Report 2017.

Zhu, J. (2009). NGO Reform will trigger a wave of social organization development. Southern Metropolis Daily, 2019-12-15. (Originally in Chinese: 朱健刚. NGO 变法将引发社会组织发展的浪潮. 南方都市报, 2009-12-15).

Appendix 1: Sampling population

Interviewed Overseas Foundations

No.	Name	Interviewee's role	Interview time	Interview Location
1	Overseas_Y	Project manager	28-04-2019	Guangzhou
2	Overseas_F	Consultant	10-04-2019	Dali
3	Overseas_M	Project manager	18-04-2019	Beijing

Interviewed experienced experts and scholars

No.	Interview time	Interview location
1	15-04-2019	Beijing
2	11-03-2019	Kunming
3	28-03-2019	Shenzhen
4	Many times during 2017-2020	Online or Kunming
5	18-04-2019	Beijing

Interviewed Chinese foundations

No.	Name	Interviewee's role	Interview time	Interview Location
1	A	Secretary General	12-03-2019	Kunming
2	B	Secretary General	13-03-2019	Kunming
3	C	Secretary General	14-03-2019	Kunming
4	D	Project manager	22-03-2019	Hangzhou
5	E	Project manager	22-03-2019	Hangzhou
6	F	Project Manger	23-03-2019	Hangzhou
7	G	Project manager	23-03-2019	Hangzhou
8	H	Secretary General	23-03-2019	Hangzhou
9	I	Secretary General	29-03-2019	Guangzhou
10	J	Secretary General	16-04-2019	Beijing
11	K	Secretary General	17-04-2019	Beijing
12	L	Project Manager	17-04-2019	Beijing
13	M	Department Manager	17-04-2019	Beijing
14	N	Deputy Secretary General	20-04-2019	Beijing
15	O	Project Manager	15-05-2019	Online Interview
16	P	Participating the selection process	20-04-2019	Beijing

Appendix 1: Sampling population

Interviewed grassroots SOs

No.	Interviewee	Interview time	Interview Location
1	Founder & Executive Director	11-03-2019	Kunming
2	Executive Director	12-03-2019	Kunming
3	Executive Director	14-03-2019	Kunming
4	Founder & Executive Director	10-04-2019	Dali
5	Project Staff	11-04-2019	Dali
6	Deputy Secretary General	10-04-2019	Dali
7	Project Manager	11-04-2019	Dali
8	Founder & Executive Director	11-04-2019	Dali
9	Founder & Executive Director	10-04-2019	Dali
10	Two Interviews: Deputy Director and Project officer	20-04-2019	Beijing and Kunming
11	Founder & Executive Director	22-04-2019	Xi'an
12	Founder & Executive Director	20-05-2019	Online
13	Project officer		

Interviewed network/platform

No.	Interviewee	Interview time	
1	Founder and Executive Director	15-04-2019	Beijing
2	Project officer	15-04-2019	Beijing
3	Founder & Secretary General	19-04-2019	Beijing
4	Vice President	19-04-2019	Beijing

Appendix 2: Guide and In-depth Interview Questions to Foundations and grassroots SOs

2.1 Guide to In-depth Interview with Foundations

Firstly, I would like to thank you very much for participating in this interview. My name is Min JI, and currently I am doing my doctorate in the Department of History and Cultural Studies at Free University Berlin, Germany. My research topic is "The Characteristics of Chinese Foundations and their Interaction with grassroots SOs."

I would like to talk about the developing situation of foundations and the interaction with grassroots SOs.

The interview should take around one hour. I will be taping the session because I do not want to miss any of your comments, especially important responses. Although I will be taking some notes during the interview, I ca not write all down fast enough.

The interview should be only used for my research. All your responses will be kept confidential. This means that your interview responses will only be shared with me and my two supervisors. Please kindly remember, you do not have to talk about anything you do not want to and you may end the interview at any time.

If you agree with the interview, please kindly sign your name below.
Interviewee: Date:

2.2 In-depth Interview Questions (to foundations):
1. Could you tell me why you chose to work in these fields? (different topics with different foundations)
2. a) Public foundation: The amount of money spent annually by PFFs on the public benefit activities stipulated in their charter must not be less than 70 percent of the previous year's income. Do you have any problem on this? How do you think about this?
   b) NPFFs annual expenditure on the public benefit activities stipulated in their charter must not be less than 8 percent of the surplus from the previous year. How do you think about this?
3. Does your foundation support or cooperate with grassroots SOs?

4. How could your foundation look for the grantees or grassroots SOs? For example, recommendation, online application, workshop, visiting grassroots SOs, etc.
5. Does the foundation have the guideline on application or documents to explain the application and requirement?
6. Do you have professional staffs to help applicants during the application?
7. Who finally decides which application to accept? Please describe (such as the management of the foundation)
8. After the approval of applications, which main elements are written in the contract?
9. What is the average amount and duration of the project?
10. How the grant is transferred to grassroots SOs? Like how often?
11. Do you evaluate your projects to grassroots SOs? In which way? How often?
12. After the implementation of the projects, do you still connect with them? In which way?
13. Do you think the cooperation between foundations and grassroots SOs help to achieve foundation's goals? In which way?
14. Do you think the foundations need recourses from grassroots SOs? Please describe.
15. Could you please name one or two successful or unsatisfied cases during the cooperation?
    Is there anything more you would like to add?
    I'll be analyzing the information from you. I'll be happy to send you a copy to review at that time, if you are interested.
    Thank you for your time.

2.3 In-depth Interview Questions (to grassroots SOs):
1. Is your organization granted by domestic foundations? Are domestic grants very important to your organizations?
2. a) If "yes" to question 1, please follow Question 3.
   b) If "no" to question 1, Please go to Question 9.
3. How does your organization find foundations?
4. In the beginning of application, do you understand the application process and requirements?
5. During the application and implementation, is there professional staff from foundation to supervise when necessary?
6. If SOs are/were granted successfully by domestic foundations, how long and how much is the project?

7. During the project implementation, do foundations evaluate the project? How often? In which way?
8. After the project, does your organization connect with foundations? In which way?
9. Do you think foundations and grassroots SOs are competitive with each other on overseas funding, domestic private and public funding?
10. Which kinds of resources does your organization need from domestic foundations? Please describe.
11. Could you please name one or two successful or unsatisfied cases during the cooperation or your application to domestic foundations?